THE MAN

WHO COULD

MOVE

CLOUDS

THE MAN
WHO COULD
MOVE
CLOUDS

· A MEMOIR ·

Ingrid Rojas Contreras

DOUBLEDAY   NEW YORK

Jacket images: (center) Sorin Rechitan/EyeEm/Getty Images;
(next two circles) courtesy of the author;
(background) Print Collector/Getty Images
Jacket design by Emily Mahon

LIBRARY OF CONGRESS CATALOGING-IN-PUBLICATION DATA
Names: Rojas Contreras, Ingrid, author.
Title: The man who could move clouds : a memoir /
Ingrid Rojas Contreras.
Description: First edition. | New York : Doubleday, 2022.
Identifiers: LCCN 2021035817 (print) | LCCN 2021035818 (ebook) |
ISBN 9780385546669 (hardcover) | ISBN 9780385546676 (ebook)
Subjects: LCSH: Rojas Contreras, Ingrid. | Rojas Contreras, Ingrid—
Family. | Rojas Contreras, Ingrid—Travel—Colombia. |
Hispanic American authors—Biography. | Colombian Americans—
Biography. | Mothers and daughters—Biography. | Amnesia—
Patients—Biography. | Grandfathers—Colombia—Biography. |
Healers—Colombia—Biography. | Colombia—Biography.
Classification: LCC PS3618.05355 Z46 2022 (print) |
LCC PS3618.05355 (ebook) | DDC 818/.603 [B]—dc23/eng/20211220
LC record available at https://lccn.loc.gov/2021035817
LC ebook record available at https://lccn.loc.gov/2021035818

MANUFACTURED IN THE UNITED STATES OF AMERICA

1 3 5 7 9 10 8 6 4 2

First Edition

To curanderos everywhere.

AUTHOR'S NOTE

This is a memoir of the ghostly—amnesia, hallucination, the historical specter of the past—which celebrates cultural understandings of truth that are, at heart, Colombian. The stories in this memoir are the true lived experience of those who lived it, as told to me. To protect the identity of all subjects, all names—except for a select few—have been changed. Only in one chapter in this memoir has the order of events been changed for narrative effect.

DISINTERMENT

I knew a man, a common farmer, the father of five
    sons,
And in them the fathers of sons, and in them the
    fathers of sons.

—WALT WHITMAN

We don't want to conquer space at all. We want
to expand Earth endlessly. We don't want other
worlds; we want a mirror.

—STANISŁAW LEM

THE SECRETS

They say the accident that left me with temporary amnesia is my inheritance. No house or piece of land or chest of letters, just a few weeks of oblivion.

Mami had temporary amnesia as well, except: where she was eight years old, I was twenty-three. Where she fell down an empty well, I crashed my bicycle into an opening car door. Where she nearly bled to death in Ocaña, Colombia, in darkness, thirty feet below the earth, I got to my feet seemingly unharmed and wandered around Chicago on a sunny winter afternoon. Where she didn't know who she was for eight months, I couldn't remember who I was for eight weeks.

They say the amnesias were a door to gifts we were supposed to have, which Mami's father, Nono, neglected to pass.

Nono was a curandero. His gifts were instructions for talking to the dead, telling the future, healing the ill, and moving the clouds. We were a brown people, mestizo. European men had arrived on the continent and violated Indigenous women, and that was our origin: neither Native nor Spanish, but a wound. We called the gifts *secrets*. In the mountains of Santander, the fathers had passed the secrets to the sons, who passed the secrets to the sons, who passed the secrets to the sons. But none of *his* sons, Nono said, had the testículos required to be a real curandero. Only Mami, strong-willed, unafraid, more of a man than most men in his eyes, whom he liked to call *mi animal de monte,* could have housed the gifts. But Mami was a woman, and such things were forbidden. If a woman came to possess the secrets, it was said that misfortune would soon follow.

Yet, as eight-year-old Mami recovered from her injuries after falling down the well, and as her memories returned, it so happened that, from wherever her mind had gone, she brought back the ability to see ghosts and hear disembodied voices.

The family says Mami was destined for the secrets, and since Nono couldn't teach them to her, the secrets had come directly to her.

Four decades later, when I suffered my accident and lost my memory, the family was thrilled. Tías poured drinks, told one another with an air of festivity: *There it goes again! The snake biting its own tail!*

And then they waited to see how, exactly, the secrets would manifest in me.

This is a story that happens in Spanish, where Mami and the tías call each other *vos,* the archaic "thou," but they use *tú* with me, the informal, tender "you." Theirs is the way of speaking in Ocaña, where our family is from, and where language can sound like a colonial fossil. In Spanish, our stories are slow then fast, and we cackle, constantly.

Mami and I are spooked by the way our lives echo each other's, so we don't often discuss our amnesias. But, increasingly, this is an itch I must scratch. I scrape and scald at its touch, only to want to probe into it again.

The tías ask me to tell them what it was like to live without a memory. I focus on trying to communicate how surreal it was, how cinematic. The tías roll their eyes at me, but they do so while looking at one another, like I am a bad television show they are watching and can safely comment on. *Such a gringa this one, no?* What they really want to know is what I dreamt.

For Mami and for me, during our bouts of amnesia, our waking lives were punctuated by a constant state of confusion—but our dreams were grounding. Mami's dreams were sequential, and in her dreams she was a ghost. In mine, I had no body, and as I say this to the tías out loud, I realize: I, too, believed I was a ghost.

We have a word in Spanish for the walking of the dead— desandar. To un-walk. To walk until the walking is worn thin, to walk until the walking undoes even itself. That ghosts have a particular way of walking is an idea we inherited from the settlers who invaded the continent, but what is intrinsically ours is the sense of porosity, an understanding that we live between the real and unreal, and that often they are one and the same. So, to us, the living go on ghost walks too.

The Indigenous peoples of the state of Santander, where both my parents are from, dreamt of the beasts they were to hunt the following day. At daybreak, they left and looked for their dream sight.

Dreams are important for us too.

Forty-three years apart, during each of our amnesias, Mami and I dreamt of banishment.

Mami was a village ghost. The villagers of the place where she was stuck spoke a language she did not recognize but could nonetheless understand. They worshipped her corpse, unrotting and fragrant, and therefore miraculous.

I haunted a horizon of ocean where sometimes the waves withdrew, abandoning the land, and bared the seafloor. Sometimes the land glitched and the ocean was suddenly replaced, as if it had never gone. The waves shuddered then, coughing up lava and smoke, birthing islands.

When Nono was treating an illness, he asked his dreams to guide him to the herbs he needed, and when he roused from sleep, he hiked until the landscape matched his vision, and there he gathered the medicine. When Mami was a ghost in the dream village where she was stuck, she practiced communicating with the living, and once she recovered her memory and became grounded in her waking life, she knew how to speak to the dead. I observed land being born in my dreams, and, awake, I studied with attention as the self I was becoming created itself.

I wonder if—since my life echoes Mami's, which in turn echoes Nono's—all of us are on the same ghost walk, retracing and undoing one another's lives.

The tías interrupt my thoughts. They've asked a question, but I haven't been listening. They ask again whether my post-amnesia dreams are prognostic in nature. In the long seconds before I answer, they look upon me with fear and hope. They know the secrets to be a blessing, but also a burden. They've witnessed that often an intoxication with power attends the secrets, and that this intoxication can upend lives, bring about alcoholism, depression, self-harm. But in spite of what it may mean, their eyes well with what seems like anticipation, and I read in their gaze a desire for it to be true, for me to be the last recipient of the secrets. I entertain, for the briefest of moments, what it would be like to say yes, to be someone like Mami, to whom all come for help and advice. In the end, I shake my head: I cannot see ghosts like Mami could, I do not hear the dead, and the future is hidden from me as much as it ever was.

The tías nod slowly. They look down. *Bueno.* They pat my hand. I've disappointed them. I had the opportunity to receive the secrets, and somehow I've squandered it. This is the information they've been waiting for, and now that they are in possession of it, they shift their eyes back to Mami, yearning for a different story now, one with death and ghosts and vengeance—but in between looking at me and looking at Mami, they say: *Better anyway to be normal. Live your life. You'll see how quickly you forget, quicker than a witch's fart.*

When I was growing up in Bogotá, Mami kept a fortune-telling business in the attic of our house. At all hours of the day, Mami sat facing her clients, men and women of all stations and class, and told them about their lives. But clients who came looking for her healing, guidance, and advice surprised her with contempt when she introduced herself as a curandera. Supervisors demoted Papi from jobs when they found out what Mami was, excluded them from social gatherings, and men who called themselves friends sexually harassed Mami when they found themselves alone with her. Clients in our own house, after Mami had given them treatment, let their mouths bloat with epithets and refused to pay what they owed. Needing money, Mami allowed their hostility to teach her to call herself a fortune-teller, an occupation that even white, blue-eyed Colombians could take up. This has always been the privilege of being mestizo, to claim proximity to whiteness, even if the cost is a hate directed at half of the self. Mami told herself she was proud of who she was, that she only called herself a fortune-teller for her own safety. In time, though, Mami would drop this last label, too, opting in the end to simply describe herself as someone with an ability to see.

Mami says she lost the gift of seeing ghosts when my sister was born, and the gift of hearing voices when I was born, but in the wake of her decreased power, she retained the ability to foretell the future, as well as the eerie yet modest talent of appearing in two places at once.

Throughout my youth, once or twice a month, Mami's old lovers, close friends, sisters and brothers called to report her visitations. While Mami was at home in Bogotá, her apparition sprang up all over Colombia: knocking on doors in Medellín, shuffling down hallways in Cartagena, tossing strands of black hair in Cúcuta, vanishing into thin air from one moment to the next. Mami celebrated each account. Instead of *apparitions*, she called her doubles *clones*. Mami often asked after her clones—what they had been wearing, what hairstyle they had chosen, where their eyes had seemed to alight.

As soon as Mami hung up, her eyes clouded in a dark and mesmerizing defiance. *I'll tell you what, though,* she'd say, *if someone ever made a real clone of me—I think I would kill her.*

Whenever I've met Mami's old friends and lovers, they look at me like they've seen a ghost, and I, specifically, am that ghost.

I can't get over it, it's like a time machine.

In my presence, Mami's old lovers slip into a past unknown to me. After polite small talk, they seem to forget who I am. They pull out my chair, hold my hand, gaze into my eyes like they are in love with me. Mami's old friends, for their part, gossip about acquaintances I've never met and expect quick-witted commentary I do not have.

They all look from Mami to me, unbelieving, over a meal or a drink. *It's not that the apple didn't fall far from the tree, it's that you had a copying machine,* a childhood friend says to us. Mami shows the whites of her eyes, shakes her head, and recoils, all in one gesture, then says, *Don't even tell me.* I laugh and sip my drink.

At random moments when Mami is visiting me in California and I am going about my day, playing music, dancing, applying lipstick, drinking wine or tea, Mami will throw books at me, pillows, magazines, whatever is near. *Get away from me, you clone!*

It's true that Mami and I have the same thick brows, almond skin, dark, chaotic hair—but I think the gaze of our eyes is different. Where Mami's is hard and imposing, my gaze is gentle, open, and inquisitive. There is also the matter of the moles. Mami and I have the same moles on our bodies. One rests, small and dark, at the upper inner thigh, and the other is hard to see. It sits enshrouded beneath hairs right at the arch of our vulvas. What do these mean, these markings? Mami once called them constellations, maps that proved we belonged to the same place in the sky.

There's another mole we share. It is circular, the diameter of a pencil eraser, dark brown. Except, on our shoulders, it is switched: hers sits on her left shoulder, the same circular fleck as mine on the right. Mami and I, we could stand back to back and demonstrate the symmetry of the dot, how it falls at the same length down and in from the shoulder, how the size corresponds one to the other, how faithfully the color is mirrored.

But because it's on the wrong shoulder on me, I cannot help feeling like a bad copy, like there was a glitch in the machine the moment I was made.

Guerrilla and drug violence drove my family and me from Colombia in 1998, when I was fourteen. This bred a waste of assimilation in my sister and me. Sometimes I imagine: had there been nothing to drive us from our land, had I, in 2007, lost my memory under Mami's roof in Bogotá instead of in Chicago, to which I immigrated alone, I might have received the secrets in the way the tías implied I should. Maybe I would have started to hear and see the dead like Mami, and, in time, appear in two places at once. Mami might have passed me on the landing one day in our house in Bogotá, and after ascending the flight of stairs would be surprised to encounter me again, upright in the middle of her consulting room in the attic, materialized, a column of air.

But we fled. We had to remake our lives. We didn't know at the time that the safety we sought had a cost. We didn't know that this cost would be a gulf—that we would stand before this gulf over and over again and mourn all we'd lost.

Right after my accident, when I picked myself up from the street, new and without a memory, I was overwhelmed by the haunting feeling of having just laid a physical burden down.

Forgetting everything, entirely, was freedom. Amnesia was abundance. The hours lengthened into a certain timelessness, during which a ray of sunlight, never experienced before, was crowned in gold. I forgot myself. On my knees, I followed the ray of light as it cut across my apartment. I stared at the spot where the light met the dark, and in a second I'd rename it: *border, grace.* Everything was new. My daily labor was the act of naming. I raged with a happiness I have not since and will never again feel.

As my memory returned, piece by piece, I grieved. If amnesia was weightlessness, then the opposite was true: every path taken, every word said, every knowledge discovered, every emotion lived—all of it—came back to me with a manifest weight. The narrowing of a life is gravity. Memory is burden. I mourned every ounce of memory returned.

By the end of eight weeks, when I finally relearned all the details of who I was, I lost myself in the wonder of it. I recalled the stories of Nono and Mami, as well as one small moment: Mami holding my hand over a bowl of water, teaching me how to bless it. In my memory of this moment, I am not listening, choosing instead to be captivated by how our hands—if I ignored the tiny detail of my fingers, a hair's breadth longer than hers—looked exactly like twins.

I blessed water each day as I best remembered. Half amnesiac, I gushed to everyone that it was my heritage.

Then, weeks later, like the lagging sound of a film, arriving too late, I recalled that I was supposed to be hiding who I was, that Mami had always demanded it.

My earliest memory is of Mami—her forbidding face towering over my own, making me swear that I would not reveal to others she was a curandera, and her father before her, and his father before him, and his father before him.

Whereas, in the private circles of our family, we freely blessed water and freshly cut flowers, dreamt of the dead, and held close what had been passed down to Nono by his forefathers, out in the world, we remained concealed. She said it was for my protection. *Better stay hidden than be misunderstood; why arm your enemies?* Mami thought we would be outcasts, called superstitious, simple, uneducated, and invite the violence of those who thought themselves better. She had lived it herself.

Under this memory's hold, I saw that what I had construed from Mami's call for secrecy was shame. What I understood was that there was some ineffable wrong to what we were. But as memory returned, though I could recall the shape and weight of this shame, the sting of it was gone. I lost the impulse to hide that I was a brown woman born of a brown woman born of a poor man who said he had the power to move clouds.

When the Europeans took the land that is now Santander with their guns and dogs, bringing disease and war, some tribes fled. The Bari people, whose territory once extended into Santander, retreated to what is now Venezuela, and the U'wa people went higher into the mountains, into the cloud forests, where they took refuge for the next two hundred years.

These are the names of the tribes that lived in the area of Ocaña and which the Spaniards reported to the Crown as extinct: Seytama, Buxarema, Caracica, Borotaré, Beuxitaré, Xinane, Manane, Carquima, Teurama, Cucuriama, Ascuriama, Burgama, Caracaca, Equerama, Chama, Bisarema, Bucurama, Anarama, Carcoma, Tuscuriama, Ceqyerama, Languxama, Saotama, Ocama, Carates, Xergoma, Buroma, Oracica, Buneroma, Bisera, Ercosa, Aytara.

Except there hadn't been an extinction.

The Spaniards captured the men and boys from these tribes and split them up, sending them to far-off gold mines, where they worked alongside other Indigenous people without speaking the same language. The Spanish crown decreed her people lords and masters of any territory they conquered, and, unsupervised, the Spaniards divided the land, treasure, and the Native people among themselves, as if people were things to be portioned out.

It was said that Native people were free, but they owed labor in exchange for "protection" and catechism classes they received. By 1629, in Ocaña, there were 576 Native people trapped in encomiendas. And centuries later, things only changed in name. Spaniards rented the land they'd stolen back to Native families, offering to buy any crops produced, but cheaply, and the money owed for rent always exceeded what the families could make. Native people fell into a perpetual cycle of debt, which, if abandoned, meant their imprisonment. Meanwhile, Franciscan monks ran boarding schools for Native children, and so it was like this that the Spaniards could look around and say that the Indigenous tribes of Ocaña were gone. And throughout those early centuries, the Spanish overtook and raped Native women without repercussion, and the villages became full of mestizos, children who grew to inherit debt from their mothers, and who were rarely recognized by their fathers. Village officials with inquisitorial power threatened these new half-Spanish people with torture if they did not discard their Indigenous traditions, which the Spanish Inquisition catalogued as devil worship and witchcraft, and embrace the Christian church.

I have stood before the old devices at the Palace of the Inquisition in Cartagena, where heretics from all over the country were sent to be burned at the stake. Chains and spikes and shackles. My breasts have ached before the sharpness of large iron pincers that would have been heated over coals, fitted over a woman's breast, and made to bite.

All over Colombia, in the face of this violence, mestizos chose between disappearing, marrying someone who appeared whiter with each consecutive generation—*bettering the race,* as it is still often described—or loving whom they loved and spinning webs of secrecy around themselves to survive. Obscurity became a way of life.

Nono and his forefathers were born in the mountains, a lineage hiding in plain sight. Survival had long bound them to secrecy. What knowledge and traditions they remembered were passed down in hot whispers, in darkened rooms, to well-chosen children, who, long after the burnings ceased, received, along with the old ways, all of the attendant fears of being seen, found out, and set on fire. Over hundreds of years, curanderos kept this well-guarded silence. They added their own stories, too, invented their own prayers and songs, entwined them with Spanish bits of wisdom, sorted the newness of the world into modern sacred hierarchies, and so created a third thing, no longer either Native or Spanish, but a third culture.

I know that, in other parts of Colombia and throughout the continent, women can receive knowledge and become curanderas without being said to release a chain of misfortune. I haven't been able to discover whether the shunning of women from power was a Native or a Spanish inheritance in this part of Colombia.

When I first tell Mami I want to write about all of this, she is furious. She yells at me, afraid I will reveal the secrets, incite people to judge me, ruin my own life. I assure Mami I will run everything by her, write only what she lets me. I beg her to understand: I have to write about what has happened to me, to her, to us, to all of us, no matter what comes of it. She hangs up. I call her repeatedly. After a while, my father picks up, asks me what I've done—my mother says to tell me she will never speak to me again.

Mami and I have fought, but not like this. Usually, we enact little melodramas: Mami yelling, *You're no daughter of mine*, me yelling back, *Fine, better this lamp mother me, better this oven!* We are half fighting, half composing insults we know we will laugh about later. She is temperamental and explosive. I am stubborn and proud. We love and trust each other enough to know that we can show our anger and it won't change our love.

That she won't even yell at me over the phone means I've really upset her, and for the first time in my life, I fear that she means what she's said.

There exist cures against forgetfulness. One involves slipping a mirror beneath a bed pillow. That is what I do after Mami says she will never speak to me again—I bring out Mami's small hand-mirror, which used to lie at her bedside, and I place it beneath my pillow. I keep this mirror hidden most of the time. I don't know if I believe it holds power, but I do believe it is charged with the act of my mother engaging her reflection, charged with the weight of her pillow and her head on top of it, as she herself struggled to remember.

The mirror is edged in looping silver that knits around the small circle of the old reflective glass. On the back, faint roses are repeated across the black enamel. The mirror has fine silverwork on the handle, too, giving the metal a thinned and pliant look, as if it were lace. Now that it's been five years since my memory's returned and my body is heavy with its gravity, my grief over no longer having amnesia has been replaced by a bottomless hunger that only desires more memory, more weight. I want to be entombed in layers and layers of memory, the weight so heavy I cannot move. I hunger for my mother's memories, my grandfather's, his forefathers'. I sleep.

That night, I see Nono in a dream. He appears in white linen, still sixty-three years old, as he was when he died, and I fear he is there to tell me he doesn't want his story told, just as Mami has done; instead, he takes my hand, and immediately we are transported to Bucaramanga, Colombia, to the second house my mother lived in, and Nono is laughing as we run into room after room. He is talking rapidly, unintelligibly. His hands are trembling, and suddenly we are in the back garden and he is pointing down the hill to a glittering river, and I hear him clearly as he says, *This is the scene.*

It feels like the mirror I placed beneath my pillow has clicked something into motion, and I tell Papi the dream, knowing he will convey it to Mami. That week, Mami calls. Without apologizing, she says we must travel together back to Colombia, that it will be good for the book I am working on.

The line is quiet.

Mami is waiting to see if I will make her say sorry. I don't. I listen to her breathe, then ask her what she means.

In addition to my dream, there have been others. Mami and tía Perla and tía Nahía have all dreamt—independently of one another—that Nono wants his remains disinterred. This is a shared dream, and shared dreams are gospel, because unlike dreams you experience on your own, shared dreams have the validity of being peer-reviewed.

In the wake of the dreams, over the phone, we are slower and quieter than usual. Together with the tías, and in pairs, we dissect the dreams, comparing details, analyzing each setting. What we know is that in all the dreams Nono wears white. Though we can't make out what the clothes signify—in one dream his clothes are rags, in another pristine, and in the third they are more made of light than of actual cloth—what we are certain of is the overwhelming message: in all of his daughters' dreams, Nono expressly asked for his body to be exhumed.

We are to unearth Nono's remains.

As soon as it is spoken, we feel bound to the task. We go from imagining what it would mean to planning *how* to dig Nono up.

What do we tell the cemetery?

How much is it going to cost?

What do we do with the corpse?

We don't have answers. Mami tells us it's okay: *This is the way when you follow instructions from dreams.*

Over the next few days, we clear our schedules, bid our lovers goodbye, borrow money, buy airplane tickets, and make hotel reservations. Mami and I will be staying in Colombia for at least three months. Our collective mission is to disinter Nono's remains; my individual mission is to remember. I say to no one, but think to myself, *My hunger is a powerful thing.*

Mami gives us all a familiar last-minute directive: we must dig up Nono secretly.

Until, that is, we discover who or what he is trying to escape.

2

THE MAN WHO COULD

MOVE CLOUDS

N ono was a curandero, but I am sure he would have liked me to use the polite word: *homeopath*. That's what his business card read:

RAFAEL CONTRERAS ALFONSO

HOMEOPATH

CURES YOU OF ALL KINDS OF ILLNESSES:

DIABETES, OBESITY, SINUSITIS, CANCER, AND WITCHCRAFT

LICENSED BY THE SCIENTIFIC CENTER

There is a small black-and-white photograph of Nono just to the left of the text. His hair is messy, his look calculating. One side of his mouth frowns ever so slightly. He wears a suit and a tie.

I always laugh at the last line. I know the story behind it, but still I say, *Mami,* what *Scientific Center?*

Mami and I cannot contain ourselves. *Well,* the *Scientific Center, of course!*

The story is that there is no Scientific Center. Nono put that on his card to trick skeptical clients into believing in his talents. But it is also more than that: Nono was illiterate.

Nono's talents were few, but formidable. He knew how to sign his name, he was good with a hammer, he could do numbers, he knew how to spin a tale.

He could quote from any play or book or prayer even if he heard it just once. Nono accomplished this last feat over and over again in order to become a curandero. He heard the necessary prayers and plant knowledge in isolated and sporadic incidents, and if he did not repeat them immediately and with accuracy he would never be told another secret again.

His memory was prodigious. In it lived not only the secrets, but his favorite stories—which he acquired by having his children (who, with the exception of Mami, went through their childhood thinking their father was literate) read to him out loud.

He liked quoting Shakespeare: *All the world's a stage, and all the men and women merely players . . .*

Mami says the three of us—she, Nono, and I—are alike in this, all addicted to the same things: the captive audience, the well-turned plot, the subtle pulling of the strings.

They say Nono's eldest brother, Luis, had the strongest magic.

But it was Nono who could move clouds.

All the tías and tíos witnessed, but they don't exactly remember.

Mami says he saluted the four directions. He whispered a prayer, held close and guarded between his teeth. Tía Perla doesn't recall Nono saluting the directions at all, but she does remember the way he raised his hand to the sky, palm up, tracing the path he wanted the clouds to take. Nono often moved clouds for farmers who needed rain, and for Mami, who was his favorite.

But it wasn't always like that.

When Mami was born, in fact, he tried to kill her.

Nono and Nona met in 1946 in Ocaña, a small town burrowed into the Eastern Cordillera. There, handmade stucco houses dot the hills, the ground glows wherever enchanted treasure lies buried, brooms are stored upside down to ward off witches, and, when the streets are deserted, at night, the ghosts of a Spaniard and his horse are often heard walking the colonial cobblestones. Just outside of the village, at even higher altitudes in the sierras, tucked into caves, the remains of the Orotones, one of the original peoples of the area, rest. Their bodies lay shrouded for centuries in white cotton, undisturbed. We know the Orotones built roads that spiraled out from an important spiritual center. Even today, Ocaña is a place where the dead live among the living, and people have lifelong relationships with their ghosts.

In 1946, the first time Nono saw her, Nona was twenty-two to Nono's twenty-four. She was laboring up the hill to her house on Cristo Rey, one of the mountains of Ocaña. The whole mountain, many classes below the prosperous valley, was considered its own area, so that at times ocañeros used Cristo Rey to mean the mountain, or at other times the impoverished community living there. Nona was curved over with the weight of two buckets full of water balanced on a yoke across her shoulders. At the steep bend in the road, Nono stepped in front of her and introduced himself. She did not put her buckets down. She saw Nono. Swooping his hat off. Bowing low.

Nono took in the slim, strong muscle of her body, the aggression in her eyes. Basking in her glare, he told her he was an extraordinary man, and one day she'd be the mother of his children. He replaced his hat and turned to go. Nona went from hating him to watching the air sculpt an absence of him. He was already someone to miss. Against her better judgment, she called him back, gave him her name, told him where to find her and when.

Nono came to see her at her house, but not officially. He romanced her through a crack in the outer wall of her patio. One day, Nona's mother, Mamaria, came out to the backyard with a pile of clothes to wash by the large terra-cotta urn brimming with rainwater, and discovered Nona whispering to the wall: *I am still shaking from your kiss.*

On the other side of the patio was Nono, already on the run. Mamaria wanted Nona to marry, but not a shiftless man like Nono, who would only bring her heartbreak.

Covertly, Nona and Nono continued to see each other. They met by the well when Nona was sent to fetch water. He recited poetry he had memorized, and for each poem, she allowed him a kiss. On their wedding day, Nono cut flowers from Nona's yard and presented them to her at the back door of her house. They ran in secret to the church. They made their vows. The pews were empty, and high white candles burned like at a funeral.

Nona gave birth every other year during La Violencia, the civil war that began in 1948 and lasted ten years, stealing three hundred thousand lives.

War was nothing new. Politicians and historians strove to mark the differences, renaming conflict after conflict, but people saw no difference from one war to the next, and even then referred nebulously to the constant state of violence as the Situation. No matter what officials called it—so-called wartime, so-called peacetime— the Situation left behind corpses, disappeared persons, scorched farmland. This was the world they inherited, and the world their own parents and grandparents remembered. From time to time, there were massacres near Ocaña, and burnt fields, which tinged the river red and the skies black. People hid. But as soon as violence migrated, survivors emerged. One way to remember the dead was to bend with joy toward living. Accompanied by singing and hand-cranked record players, survivors drank, danced to the beat of drums, and poured aguardiente onto the ground for the dead.

Nono had a vagabond spirit, like many people during wartime. The trick to survival involved reading people. During La Violencia, one had to know how to answer armed men when they asked if one was liberal or conservative. *Liberal,* Nono said at times. *Conservador,* he said at others.

Acordeoneros, poets, culebreros all traveled the country by foot and by burro to the Magdalena River, on steamboats to the port of Barranquilla, on locomotives to the high cliffs of the coast and as far down south as the trains would go, until they were forced to hack their way into the Amazon with machetes—itinerant men, looking for a glimmer of life. Some women traveled, too, but shorter distances, bearing an oral version of the post called the witches' mail—which didn't involve witches, only fast-walking, indomitable women with great memory. The women toured from town to town, decamping at plazas, delivering missives. Lovers' notes were heard by everyone, as were business transactions, reports about turns of health, classifieds, and general news. When the women got to the end of their messages, they announced where they were going next, and collected a next round of mail in exchange for food, shelter, or payment.

Like these women, Nono earned his way by selling a service, but his was healing and divination. Everyone congregated at the village plazas—curanderos, bands of musicians, the women peddling oral mail, and the culebreros, men who scooped out long snakes from baskets and told old legends and stories as they handled the writhing animals. Peddlers bartered one service for another, and villagers purchased what they wanted with something they had. In this way, wandering from town to town, Nono was gone for four or six months at a time.

Nono had girlfriends. They dotted the Colombian map in a meandering trail, marking his annual journey to the coast and the Amazon, where he visited with other curanderos and local tribes, gathered animals and plants, and traded in knowledge and goods.

Nona tried to cure Nono of his vagabond spirit with her pregnancies. Ten times Nona was pregnant, ten times Nono left.

Each time Nono abandoned her, Nona hid in the outhouse by the lemon trees and locked the wooden door. She laughed hysterically—until she began crying. Until her weeping looped back. Until she was laughing again.

Her growing number of children knelt outside, listening. They tried to laugh with Nona. *What's so funny, Mamá?* It never occurred to them that Nona was crazy with grief.

When Nona emerged from the outhouse, she corralled her children to the kitchen. There was nothing to eat, and she gently instructed Mami to steal the neighbor's cow for the day's milk and asked her son Ángel to sneak into the neighbors' patch to dig up vegetables so she could make them dinner.

Mami thinks Nona hated Nono not because of his infidelities, but because he refused to stay. Whenever he abandoned her, Nona steeled herself against him and swore she would not take him back, but her heart always went soft at the sound of his voice. As soon as she heard it, Nona's anger and grief dissipated. Sick with love, she forgave him everything, happy only that he had returned.

Nono arrived home from his long journeys dressed in dazzling white. He removed his hat, an aguadeño, woven in the state of Caldas from toquilla straw, and sang to Nona—*Mi negra is missing, I mourned her by the sea. Beautiful, mi negra, where can she be?* Nono wore nice linen suits. He was never seen without his hat. When the sun fell, villagers assembled at the plaza. They strolled around the square, saw and greeted one another, forming tight circles around the witches' mail, culebreros, and musicians, and other peddlers who happened to be in town. Each day, Nono and the family put on their best clothes and hiked the thirty minutes down Cristo Rey to the valley, where the village square stood.

At the plaza, Nono tipped his hat and bowed to the women of the town, flashing a wink and a smile. The women colored and giggled: *Oh, that Rafael. Married, but not tied down.* Nona pretended not to see. Nono replaced his hat and offered her his arm, and they circled the plaza together, two or three times.

This hat was the same one that Nono clutched in one hand when he danced to vallenatos and cumbias at the parties that erupted with frequency in Cristo Rey.

For half of Nona's life, Cristo Rey, the undesirable area where she was born, had been known as the Mount of the Noose. It got its name when, in colonial times, the crest was chosen for the extrajudicial killings of heretics. The whole mountain was said to be haunted. Sometimes the unpleasant and unmistakable scent of burning flesh wafted in the air. People were shoved by invisible hands, and tripped on nothing. They heard all sorts of murmurings. When Nona turned eleven, the church heaved a bronze statue of Christ, seven feet tall, up the mountain, and over the

Nono's and Nona's painted portraits, undone by weather.
Cúcuta, 2012

same spot where people had been executed, Christ opened his arms, and the place had been renamed. In Cristo Rey, all it took for a party to start was the waning light and two or three people who could sing. Sometimes neighbors chipped in and hired musicians. The sounds of revelry lured others. Soon there was a crowd, whooping, making music together. Nono swept his hat behind the women who danced, lifting it to the sky, as if trying to catch invisible butterflies. This was the same hat that the tías and tíos would one day burn because they believed it to be cursed.

The year Mami was born, in 1956, just two years before La Violencia came to an end, Nono returned from his annual journey knowing there was a baby. He'd had no idea Nona was pregnant when he left, but after eight months, the spirits revealed Nona was about to give birth, and that this newborn *would end everyone.*

Nono rushed back. As he cut across the Andes by canoe and burro, he convinced himself that the baby was evil and that he was the only person who could save whoever *everyone* was. Once in Ocaña, he got drunk, hiked to their house in Cristo Rey, and chased Nona with a machete.

Nona had given birth a few days before. She ran shrieking through the coffee bushes, around her house, and across the dirt road to her mother's, clutching the baby and clutching her crotch, too, fearing her uterus would fall out of the fresh gash the baby had etched into her. Nona stumbled through great-grandmother Mamaria's door, bolted it, and thrust the baby into her hands. *Hide us, Mamá! Rafael wants to kill us!*

Mamaria told Nona to hide near the well. She helped her out the window in the adobe wall of Mamaria's indoor patio, the same wall with a crack in the corner through which Nono had once romanced her. Mamaria went back inside, and in her bedroom she slipped off the shawl that always seemed to be hanging on her shoulders and wrapped Nona's newborn in it. It was a shawl that had belonged to her mother, and before that to her mother's grandmother. Mamaria whispered a prayer, and threw the baby beneath her bed. The soft bundle slid across the floor, and she heard a small bump as it came to a stop against the wall. When the baby did not coo or cry, Mamaria knew her prayer would work. She was calm when Nono tore down the front door, serene when he bellowed, upended her furniture, entered her bedroom, stripped the sheets, got on all fours and peered under her bed, right in the direction where the baby lay. Seeing nothing, Nono tore out of Mamaria's house, still gripping his machete. Mamaria tarried awhile, then retrieved the baby, who was unharmed. She opened the patio door and called Nona back. After some time, Nona stepped out of the trees. Once they were seated safely inside, Mamaria informed her that her husband had been witched.

I told you that man was a womanizer. Surely he got entangled with a witch, and now look what she's tried to have him do. Surely this baby is what will keep him by your side now.

Nono returned many hours later, confused. He had lost time, he said. He did not know where he had been. Why was there mud on his pants?

In all the years I interrogated Mami on the subject, she never admitted to feeling betrayed. She believed, as did everybody else in the family, that if her father had tried to murder her it was because he'd been possessed.

As a seven-year-old, Mami did like to remind Nono of what he'd nearly done every chance she got. She enjoyed taunting him if he did not give her what she wanted. *Oh, of course, first you try to kill me, now this.*

What Mami wanted was a baby lion. Nono could easily procure one, she reasoned, while on his travels. The animals were Mami's favorite part of Nono's return. He once brought her a lynx tied at the end of a leash, a parrot that could swear, a pair of monkeys in wooden cages, armadillos under his arms, long lizards, an anaconda coiled inside a large woven basket.

The anaconda nobody liked. Nona tried to forbid it from entering the house, but Nono told her the snake was harmless as long as it was fed well and frequently; besides, he was the man of the house, and if nobody wanted it, the anaconda was to be his pet. The anaconda stayed.

Twelve feet long, the anaconda had crackly, oily skin spotted with light-brown circles. It slithered around the house, sweeping dirt, leaving abstract maps. Every seven days, Nono fed the anaconda a chicken or a fluffy white rabbit. After feeding, the snake grew slow and sleepy. Mami could see the little bulk that had been the animal travel through its body.

The snake slept in the daytime, when Nono's clientele—the lovesick, women who wanted to terminate their pregnancies, women who wanted to conceive, people tormented with seizures and venereal disease and fevers, and those who had been possessed—formed a line that wrapped around the living room and out the door, patiently waiting to be seen. In the hot afternoon, Mami's sisters and brothers sat upon the long cushiony body of the snake, far away from its devil-face and coiled, bony tail. They passed the time by scrutinizing the comings and goings of Nono's patients. They loved overhearing what was wrong with each person and observing their faces when they left. Out of earshot of his departing patients, sometimes Nono stooped and whispered short reports to his children: *No cure for that man,* and *That woman will be all better in three days,* and *Poor boy, he is marked for death.*

While they waited for new patients to emerge from Nono's consulting room, the tías and tíos played card games, War especially. They slapped their cards down on the floor, keeping track of the queens and kings, bickering, cheering one another on, forging secret alliances, and exchanging cards when no one was looking—until, that is, the ground moved and the cards on the floor slid past. When they looked down, they saw that the snake—the long, large muscle on which they sat, and which they liked to pretend was furniture—was moving, sweeping them away. They screamed.

They ran, shivering, the feeling of the anaconda moving and alive lingering on their skin. No one could sleep at night. The tías and tíos woke up panting, imagining the slithering snake had made it into their locked rooms. They imagined the snake against their sheets. They feared for their lives. But the next day, they sat again on the snake.

The snake was voracious. When Nono only had one chicken left, and he tired of hunting for the snake, he decided the anaconda had to go. Sharing the same fate as all the other animals Nono brought home, the anaconda was released into the hills of the forest behind their house.

Nono was reckless, but Nona thought he could be changed.

He's going to leave again, Mami warned Nona, each time.

He's not, he will stay, Nona said.

Nona was constantly pregnant, trapping bits of him inside her, growing anchors and responsibilities, but Nono left all the same, decrying her possessiveness. On the road, untethered from anything and anyone, Nono lived with abandon. Then, once he felt lonely and missed the safety and comfort Nona provided by keeping his family and home, he returned. He never once considered the suffering he spun Nona in, or the violence with which he simply took what he wanted when he felt an urge. In seeking joy in his life, he regularly thieved the joy of others, of Nona especially, whom he cast as the one to blame for her own suffering.

Nona thought of leaving him, but she cowered at how people treated divorced women. One divorced woman lived down the road, alone in a hut. No one talked to her. The men referred to her as damaged goods because she wasn't a virgin, and since she had no purity to protect, it was known, she was sometimes assaulted. She showed up at Nono and Nona's door every once in a while, seeking Nono's help to snuff out the life that might be growing in her. Nona bade him to treat her for free, which he did. He patted himself on the back for this deed, deeming himself to be different from the other men in the village, but his life, too, was built on the willful and cruel ignorance of the cost of his own high moods.

Get a gun, Mami begged Nona when Nona confided in her. *Shoot any man who dares to hurt you.* Nona could not find the courage. *What will people say? They'll put me in jail. Then who will take care of you?* Mami hated the man Nono was to her mother, but she loved the father he was to her. She lived in this complicated turmoil.

Mamá is an idiot, Mami confided to Nono upon his return. *She doesn't know how to command respect. Were I her, I would have burned all your clothes and sent you away a long time ago.*

You'd do much worse, my little mountain beast, Nono said. *Oh, why weren't you born a man? All the men I was sent are little women. But you, you I'd love to take hunting and teach.*

Mami knew he meant *teach* as in *teach the secrets to,* and she implored that he bend the rules just for her. She was smarter and fiercer than any man he knew, old or young, and not only did she want to know the secrets, she had an aptitude for magic. Sometimes her dreams foretold when Nono was due back, or she found herself knowing people's past, things that they had never shared, but which she read on them as if in a book. She didn't understand why being born a woman excluded her from a lineage that was obviously hers. Nono shook his head. *This knowledge is not for women. Who knows what disaster will happen? No, better for the line to end with me; then I can see to the consequences myself.*

Nono may have wanted to be the last, but he ran his business with unusual keenness and appetite. When he cured a dentist of a broken heart, and the dentist, grateful for the disappearance of the crushing weight on his chest, gave Nono professional advice, he listened with attention.

Do you know what you need to better your business? the dentist asked. *Atmosphere.*

The dentist described the decorations of his own office to Nono: framed diagrams of teeth, plush leather seats, and the tools of his profession displayed in clear jars or laid out sterilized on steel.

Mami doesn't remember now what the dentist looked like, only that he was tall, and white. Nono only had one table, where a pile of herbs sat, two chairs that faced each other, and an open window, which brought in a parallelogram of light. He presented his tinctures and drafts without fanfare, in regular glasses of water. He was a man who had the power to see; he needed nothing else.

What if, the dentist posed to Nono, *you put up a black curtain and set up an altar in the corner with candles, and beads, and, you know, whatever else can give your patients a sense of "ambience"?*

The dentist told Nono that, with the right atmosphere, there was every chance he could up his fee. Nono had many mouths to feed. He considered the dentist's words. *Do you think that could work?*

The dentist nodded. *I can get you a skull.*

The skull was from the medical school, from an anonymous person who had donated their body to science, and was now unknowingly donating their body to magic. Following the dentist's advice, Nono threw a black cloth on a small table, and put the skull at the center of a hastily built altar. *Who's the skull?* the tíos and tías wanted to know. Nono didn't answer. *Papá, don't you think you probably shouldn't use that skull?* Mami asked. *Mija,* Nono beckoned her in a whisper, *I'm not really using it. It's just there for show. Think of it as a plant in the corner of my office.*

The dentist came back every now and again with thoughts of other decor that might help build atmosphere: *What about voodoo dolls?*

Mami heard them from the floor just outside of Nono's office. Nono had told her about the true provenance of the skull, but had sworn her to secrecy. Now, every time the dentist came around, she made sure to eavesdrop on their conversations.

The atmosphere in my office is what signals to people how powerful and knowledgeable I am as a doctor, the dentist went on. *Don't you think, if you had a string of garlic hanging here in this corner, and then added some voodoo dolls scattered here by the stool, that people would enter your office and say to themselves, Wow, this guy really knows his stuff?*

Strings of garlic had nothing to do with his practice of healing and medicine, but Nono did string up his drying herbs. He made Mami enter and exit the office so she could tell him her impression as he moved the herbs from wall to wall. Mami didn't laugh in his face, but she laughed, she tells me, when she was alone. As showy and superficial as they were, Nono's new trinkets and frills did make people open to higher rates. Nono had never needed anything to do his divinations, but for the sake of his clients and for the sake of ambience, he would walk up to the skull from time to time and ask it the question that had been posed: *Just a moment! This skull belonged to a very powerful curandero. It will give us the answer in one minute.*

The next time the dentist stopped in, he showed off to Nono his business card. *Don Rafael, look—this little paper has my name, occupation, place of business, specialties. I meet someone, hand them my card; next thing I know, I have a new patient, or that person gives my card to someone else, and I have two more patients.*

Nono was impressed by the invention. They spent a whole afternoon, with Nono speaking, the dentist writing. Mami heard them craft what Nono's business card would become, down to the line of the fictional Scientific Center—which, in their opinion, quite elegantly dealt a pre-emptive blow to any skeptic who might dare disbelieve in Nono's abilities. Nono got his cards printed at the same place the dentist used, and at a discounted rate.

In 2012, when I arrive at my parents' apartment in Mexico City to meet Mami before we make our way to Colombia for Nono's disinterment, I assume that none of his possessions survived. In 1984, which was the year I was born, but also the year when Nono's children began to be struck by a series of accidents, strokes of bad luck, and sudden, degenerative disorders, half the family understood these simply to be facts of life; the other half thought of the alluded-to disaster that Nono had warned against if Mami ever came to know the secrets. They imagined a cadre of angry ancestors, all of them curanderos, come to take their revenge for the offense of Mami's illicit knowledge. This makes sense to me. It is easier to explain loss, unimaginable loss, or the threat of it, as an outside force. And so, after Nono passed in June of 1985, the half that blamed Mami concluded that both Nono's personal effects and Mami were bad luck, and the only way to stave off the misery visiting their lives was to cut ties with both. Everything that was Nono's was burned.

I am standing by my suitcase at the entryway of Mami's apartment, tinkering with the airport tags. I don't know how to be. Five years have passed since I've regained my memory, but I still feel uprooted. I often look down at my own two hands with dread, as if they are somebody else's, and from time to time, when I take the measure of my point of view—the limited porthole of what I am able to see, the edges of it fraying at the blind spot—I feel trapped. I regularly think of myself as twofold: the person I was when I had no memory, and the person I became after my memory's return. I oscillate between inhabiting one sense of myself and then the other. My nerves are worn from it. It isn't just the flight: I am permanently exhausted. I let my gaze fall on the golden, blue-flecked, three-foot wingspan of Mami's statue of the goddess Isis, protector of the dead, which sits on her entryway table. I face Mami—the jet black of her hair, the piercing dark brown of her eyes.

Mami closes her hands over my own as if she can read the anguish in my body. She tells me, *A circle has ended and a new one is beginning,* and she leads me into her home.

Walking behind Mami, I settle into the familiar comfort of being her daughter. I like when she takes control in this way. I look at my hand holding hers, then glance at the living-room couch, where I see my father has laid out his ever-growing collection of bootlegged movies, some of which have only just come out in the States.

As we enter Mami's bedroom, Mami bids me to sit on her bed. I smile, grateful I don't have to make any decisions. Our shared experience of amnesia is on my mind all the time now, and I want to ask Mami what she thought about losing her memory, and what she felt in its absence, but I don't have the courage or energy yet to think these questions at the same time as I look at her. Instead, I let my mind empty and try to give myself over to the world before me: Mami kneeling before her closet, opening its doors.

No matter where she lives, the closet is where Mami keeps her secret things. It's an honor to be led there, like getting invited to see the inside of a temple. Hidden among her clothes are amulets, crystals, stones, and probably many things I don't yet know. Mami's right arm disappears in the silk and wool of her hanging garments. She doesn't find what she's looking for, so she pulls out one of her closet drawers and lays it on the floor. It is full of scarves and tiny boxes. She churns the scarves until a red handkerchief emerges, folded in quarters. She lowers next to me and places it on her lap. I am unsure of what she is about to show me, and I hold my breath as she fingers the stiff handkerchief, not touched, it seems, for many years.

She unquarters the cloth, telling me: *This was your grandfather's.*

Lying at the center of the red linen is Nono's business card, yellowed with time.

I gasp and incline my head at different angles, like I am at a museum before a relic I am not allowed to touch. There is text, which I don't yet read, my eyes fixing instead on the small black-and-white photograph of Nono to the left. His eyes are small dashes of black ink. I wonder if, at the moment the photograph was taken, in the 1970s, he knew I'd stare down into his face in 2012, wanting answers. Mami plucks up the card. She beholds it for a second, then extends it to me.

You're giving this to me? I am thankful, but also afraid. *What if he haunts me?*

Mami laughs. *He won't haunt you. You're my daughter. But he might visit you more.*

I smile at her and bring the card to my nose, hoping to catch a whiff of Nono, but all I smell is my mother. Her sweet rose smell, with something vaguely serrated, like sour milk, stirred in.

Rafael Contreras A.

HOMEOPATA

Le cura toda clase de enfermedades:

Diabetes - Obesidad - Sinusitis - Epilepsia - Cáncer y Hechicería

LICENCIADO POR EL CENTRO CIENTIFICO

Boulevar Santander Calle 15 No. 22-87 - Bucaramanga

3

RETURN

Nono and Nona spent their lives circumnavigating the tip of the Eastern Cordillera. They moved back and forth across the Andes, between three small cities that form, when I look at a map, an acute triangle: Ocaña at the northern-most tip, Bucaramanga down and a bit to the right, and Cúcuta to the east. Ocaña is where our bloodline draws back as far as we know, Bucaramanga is where Nono passed away, and Cúcuta is the place where Nona saw the last of her days. Our Bermuda Triangle.

Tía Perla lives in Cúcuta, and in Cúcuta there is an apart-ment with all of our things. We used to vacation there, Mami and Papi, my sister and I. Papi signed the mortgage in 1993, the year snipers shot Pablo Escobar dead on a rooftop in Medellín, and I turned nine. Papi dreamed of retiring there. Month to month, we strained to keep up with the payments. We were always in debt and sometimes in default. Kidnappings were common. Guerril-las used them to fund their war against the government. Each guerrilla front had a cash quota to satisfy, and they abducted the well-to-do, the middle class, and the poor, and beginning in 1994, they were after us. We knew people who'd been released with the ransom, others who were held for a decade, and still others who never returned.

We fled Colombia in 1998. Though we struggled to create a stable life elsewhere, we couldn't bear to part with the apartment in Cúcuta, the bit of earth that belonged to us and to which we belonged. We kept it through the hard years to come, when we migrated from country to country in South America, looking for safety. The last time I set foot in the apartment was in 2002, right before I made my way alone to the United States. Mami and Papi last went to the apartment in 2003, to preserve it for a hoped-for day of homecoming, when Papi finally could hang a hammock on the balcony and put up his feet.

Not once upon a time, but once in a specific time, in a real place, Mami and I return. It is past midnight, and in the shadows I smell dust. We grope for the light switch. It has been so long, we can't remember where it is. Mami palms the spot behind the front door, and I rummage over the entryway wall. Neither of us finds it. Mami heads into the kitchen to hunt for a flashlight she says she left on the counter eleven years ago. I scoff at the improbability. As I wait for her to return, my sight adjusts. I never imagined it would take me ten years to return to Cúcuta, let alone that I would be on an errand to dig up my grandfather's bones.

Rays of moonlight filter in through the sliding glass doors at the back of the apartment. By this bluish light, I start to recognize the familiar silhouettes: the sofa by the balcony, and here, to my right, the dining table and mini bar cabinet tucked just behind. In front of me is the doorway to the kitchen, and to the left, where the moonlight doesn't reach, is the hall that will lead first to my bedroom, then my sister's, then my parents'.

This is hot land year-round and heat draws lines of sweat down my back. A beam of yellow light lurches across the wall. Mami has found the flashlight where she says she left it and, unbelievably, the battery still works. She trains the spotlight over the walls and finds the light switch where neither of us searched: on the wall by the kitchen.

Bright fluorescent light floods the room, and suddenly everything in the apartment is bled of its color. I blink a few times, and it becomes clear I am seeing things as they are: every single thing in the apartment has been wrapped in white fabric.

The dining table wears a gauzy cloth that has been stretched over the tabletop and twisted and fastened around its base. The dining chairs tucked under the table are encased in the same fabric. Through the fibers, I can make out the slatted back of each trapped chair. There are smaller items wound in clear plastic too. I pluck up a plastic-wrapped object glinting at the center of the dining table and turn it in my hands. It fits perfectly in my fist. At a spot where the layers of plastic thin, I see the squared glass edge of a container and, tight against it, rice and salt grains. It's our saltshaker.

That rectangular shape by the window is the sofa, and the fat discs tucked by its corners are the throw pillows. The white squares floating on the walls are paintings, and the treelike shapes in each corner are the floor lamps. Every small item that meets my eye—the table sculpture in the living room, each wineglass hanging on the mini bar, the knickknacks on the entrance table—everything has been singly, painstakingly wrapped in white cloth or plastic film, and placed in its rightful spot. I feel as though I am snorkeling above a bleached coral reef.

Who did this? I ask. *Your father,* says Mami, who walks out of the kitchen wielding a sea-green, wand-shaped wad of plastic wrap. She pushes into it until the winking silver tip of a knife pierces through. She tosses the plastic on the floor and, clutching the knife, marches down the unlit hall.

As soon as she tells me, I remember. When I was in college in Chicago, in that distant past of delayed phone transmissions and echoes, Mami recounted their efforts to preserve our belongings. Papi and Mami were still itinerant then, moving to wherever Papi's company needed. Sometimes they were in South America, other times in the Middle East. They stayed in a country for one year, two at the most. Papi's company provided housing, and with the extra money they continued to pay for the apartment in Cúcuta. They were living in Venezuela when I called from Chicago. Hugo Chávez had just returned to power after a failed coup. The country had plunged into nationwide protests, and Papi and Mami were looking once more for a way to move. I called them using prepaid phone cards that involved dialing an absurd string of numbers before I was connected. Our voices lagged six or eight seconds. Because of the delays, we spoke in monologues. We took turns, reporting updates and news and gossip, struggling to find a smooth rhythm for the things that needed to be said. When we finished speaking, we heard our own voice lag behind, growing hollow, distant, ghostly. Then after a few seconds, as if from nowhere, came a response. It was in this aural landscape that Mami described assisting Papi in laying out the cloth on the floor and turning the furniture over it; pulling, cutting, and sewing until a cover that was faithful to each dip and curve of the object it encased was produced.

Papi has always channeled his anxieties into compulsive behaviors: polishing, cleaning, sanitizing, arranging objects small to large. And back in 2003, when he knew he couldn't stay in Venezuela and couldn't find a job in Colombia, he nurtured the dream of one day coming back to retire in Cúcuta. He treated the apartment the way a conservator would an archeological site. He bought giant rolls of emerald cling film from a man at the airport, and long rolls of gossamer-thin white cloth from a seamstress. He ordered voluminous bales of bubble wrap. He amassed an assortment of scissors and transparent tape, and a small, battery-powered sewing machine that was operated like a gun when the trigger was pressed. Papi's insistence on such precision made of the apartment an untouched, sleeping kingdom.

There's no dust! I say, blinking.

Down the hall from one of the bedrooms comes the sound of plastic ripping, followed by Mami's single cackle. *You think the ghosts came to clean? I hired a cleaning crew!*

I think about how the outlines of each object, fattened with layers of plastic or cloth, provide about as much detail as I can, on my own, recall: all I can remember is this haze of silhouettes. I walk down the unlit hallway to find Mami. Her bedroom door is framed by an aura of light. Inside, beneath a bright ceiling, Mami has

In the apartment. Cúcuta, 2012

stabbed open her mattress along with a bundle of sheets. A great mound of wadded plastic sits in the corner. She is lying on top of one sheet, stripped down to her underwear, already sleeping.

In the daylight, Mami and I wander around the apartment, taking inventory of what we recall. I walk up to the white rectangles that are paintings. The colors of each canvas peek through the infinitesimal holes in the gauze. The one hanging above the entryway table is mostly yellow, and the one over the couch in the living room is blue. We can't summon up either in detail. I marvel at the mini bar. How many hours did Papi spend mummifying the flutes and parabolas of each wineglass and bottle, each plastic cocktail stirrer? My eye is drawn to the sole thing that isn't wrapped: a small New Year's horn from the year 2000 made out of metallic paper with hanging silver festoons. I pick it up and inspect a smooth layer of dust that's settled on it in a thick coat. I sneeze. A spot Mami's cleaning crew missed. I go into what used to be my room and sit on the mattress wrapped in cling film. I drag my fingertips along its sheen, feeling like a haunting.

At night, at tía Perla's, we drag her plastic chairs and table to the threshold between her house and indoor patio. We open the sliding doors to catch some backward breeze from the fan whirring in her dining area. We want to hatch our plans for the disinterment, but tía Perla's husband, Juancho, is with us, and he's not in our circle of confidence, which only extends to Mami, tía Perla, her son Fabián, and me. We don't know why at the time, but Mami has decided that tía Nahía—her other sister who had the shared dream—is not to be trusted.

In tía Perla's backyard, Mami says, *Did I ever tell you about the time I spent an hour waiting in line at the grocery store?*, then tells us about it at length. Tía Perla beams—*That reminds me!*—

and describes a time when she overcooked a fillet of fish. This is a game. We are recounting the most boring experiences we can think of, trying to get Juancho to go to bed. I share how I once tried (but failed) to find a spot to nap at the airport, and Fabián explains to us how to fix a toilet, but begins by enumerating the parts we'd see if the tank lid were to come off. Discreetly, I bite into my palm. I cannot look in Fabián's direction, because if I do he will burst out laughing and I will spit out my wine.

Fabián is tía Perla's youngest, and since I am the younger of Mami's two, Fabián and I share a special bond. We've played together all our lives. Only Mami and tía Perla keep a straight face. Juancho sighs and announces he is feeling tired. We watch him stand, wait for the sound of his retreating footsteps. As soon as he is out of earshot, we stifle our laughter and begin. Tía Perla beckons us to come close.

Right after the tías shared their dream of Nono, a prospective buyer called tía Perla from Bucaramanga. Tía Perla and Juancho own a brick factory in Cúcuta that has not been doing well, so tía Perla jumped at the opportunity for new business. But once in Bucaramanga, she was so worried about Nono, she canceled the meeting and went to check on his grave.

You won't believe what I found, tía Perla says. We look at her and wait. *There was a candle burned down to a stump, and little papers stuck in the grass.*

Of the grave? I ask stupidly.

Tía Perla has been back to the cemetery several times. She's always discovered papers stuck in the grass. Everyone seems to know what they mean, but I am slow to realize that they are prayers, which would mean people have decided Nono's grave is miraculous.

There are miraculous graves all over Colombia. They don't belong to anyone special. Sometimes they belong to children, curanderos like Nono, murdered women sympathetic to women's troubles, or men of science who I imagine would be mortified if only they could learn of their afterlife fate.

There are several miraculous graves in the Central Cemetery of Bogotá. The most revered belonged to Salomé, a sex worker who used to sell votive candles at the cemetery's entrance, and who was buried during an eclipse. The story is that a man she knew was going through a difficult time. Even though he was desperate for money, he bought her flowers. He prayed for her help. On his way out of the gates, he came upon a bill on the ground. With it, he purchased a lottery ticket. It turned out to be the winning number.

Like that, with one person's miracle, the cult of a grave can grow. Salomé's popularity reached such heights that the cemetery administration decided to relocate her outside the city, but Salomé's devotees simply took their prayers to the grave adjoining, a mausoleum belonging to a family by the name of Morales, whom nobody knew anything about. There, to this day, people address the Holy Souls of Purgatory, inscribing passionate, run-on sentences on the walls:

> *Help me Holy Souls to get a stable job and I promise I'll pay*
> *for a church service dedicated to all of you.*
> *Holy Souls of Purgatory I pray that L.G.B. leaves Yvone, the*
> *one who works in Zipaquirá, separate them forever and*
> *ever amen.*
> *Dear God I ask you with all my heart please let my period*
> *come.*
> *May my dad be well wherever he is.*

I know there must have been an original miracle that Nono granted—a first story, like that of Salomé's friend—which made people flock to him and request his posthumous help. I wonder whose life he blessed, and how.

In tía Perla's backyard, Mami says that a candle burned down to its stump is the sign of an insistent and possibly dark request. *Did you read the little papers?*

Tía Perla shakes her head. *They're too terrible to speak out loud—and that's why I burned them.*

Tía Perla says the disinterment is expensive, and when we pool our money together, it's not enough. Back in our apartment, I stab open whatever seems valuable, clean and photograph it, post it online, and hope someone will buy it. I feel urgently that I must raise the money. Mami's upper lip stiffens in worry. Each night, I am still many pesos short, and each night, we go to tía Perla's backyard, where we play a few rounds of the mundane.

Fabián and I can barely participate. We drink wine, listen to music, and watch the bats dive as Mami's and tía Perla's stories become more pointless, drawn-out, and absurd. In what feels like a Beckett play, tía Perla tells us about showing up for a meeting with a banker who never arrives. I make blinders out of my hands as Mami tells us how she thinks (though she is unsure) a car works. Juancho retires earlier and earlier, until, one night, he doesn't join us at all.

At liberty, we take turns asking each other, *Okay, but once it's dug up, what do we do with the corpse?*

Ever since the shared dream, we have been arguing about it. What does Nono want from his own exhumation? We have come to agree that he's desperate to be free of people's prayers, that he's tired of performing miracles. Tía Perla says we should bury the body at a secret location. Fabián says we should burn it. I say we should scatter the ashes in the ocean, where they will never be found. Mami has not shared her leaning.

Each time one of us poses this question to the group, a deep silence ensues. I can't see very well in the dark, but I know that, at the end of the garden, in the guava tree, a small hawk sleeps. Plants grow from every nook and cranny, and in between the branches tía Perla has left cups of water for the birds, and plates with rotting fruit for the hummingbirds, woodpeckers, gavilanes, and blue jays. But at this time of night, only the bats are feeding.

One night, Mami at last gives an answer. She says the key to what to do with the corpse is to be found in a story. To the rhythm of swooping bats, she tells one we have heard hundreds of times, one Fabián and I used to beg for when we were children, one we could tell ourselves but don't, because we like it best when Mami tells it. She's the one who remembers how Nono used to tell it, and so, for an hour, it is like we're hearing him again, even though Fabián and I can't remember his voice. I was only one year old when he died, and Fabián was four.

Far away, in the jungle, Mami begins, Nono happened upon a clearing where a lagoon spirit appeared. It took the form of a beautiful woman, bathing naked and washing her hair. The water-line swallowed her hips. Great rubber trees rose at the banks. When Nono saw her, he stopped in his tracks. He knew very well what she was. She wasn't the most beautiful woman he had ever seen, but a supernatural beast. Lagoon spirits do not stand on the ground; they levitate in water. If one lures you to wade in, you will find you have no footing. An eddy will suck you down, and you'll be drowned. Knowing this, Nono stood on the shore, waiting for the lagoon spirit to speak.

Come, she said, reaching out a spectral hand. *The water is fine.*

Nono lifted his hat. *How do you do?* He sidestepped along the banks, pulling on his donkey. *Fine day for a bath.* He hurried away. Nono knew the spirit was but a hungry mouth, a creature with a stomach for him. He rushed away into the jungle and the din of birds, pulse quickening at his neck.

Nono understood that the dangers in the wild forest were not the beasts, but the haunted places that allowed another reality in, where ghosts breach our plane and can drag us back to their dwelling.

Nono almost lost his body in the forest, Mami says to conclude the story.

I feel warm from Mami's storytelling and all the wine I've been drinking. I understand this brush with death provides a map to what's supposed to happen to his body. *Does that mean we deliver him to the sea?*

Fabián is smiling at me, but his eyes are closed, and his neck is resting along the angle of the back of his chair. He gives me a thumbs-up.

No, Mami says, a little exasperated, like I've willfully not been paying attention. *We deliver him to the forest, but in the form of ash.*

Ash! Fabián's eyes are open now, triumphant. *So we burn him! That's what I have been saying.* He shakes my knee. *See? I was right!*

I sigh at him in exaggerated annoyance.

A cremation, then, tía Perla says. *I always thought one day I'd be buried next to Papá.*

We must abandon everything we assumed before, Mami says.

We have all gone quiet. In the seconds that pass, I try to do what Mami asks. I try to let go of what I know. I try instead to picture where the forest can thin, where the present can wear out and the past can slide in.

As I close my eyes that night, an older story I know about a woman at the middle of a lagoon comes to mind.

It happened in the kingdom of Bacatá (now Bogotá). A Muisca tribal chief found his wife with her lover, and made her eat a meal into which her lover's sexual organs were cooked. So she drowned herself and her newborn in the lagoon of Guatavita. After her death, the Muisca said she appeared floating in the middle of the water to pronounce prophecies. Tribal chiefs covered their bodies in gold dust, and the best golden votives and sculptures were piled on a raft for her. Attendants rowed the raft and the chief to the center of the lagoon, and there, fringed by forest and fog, the gold was thrown into the water, and the chief dove, offering gold to a woman and her hunger, even from his body.

When the Spanish arrived, bringing death, greed, and devastation, they were told of a place high in the mountains where gold offerings were cast into the water. The white men took this to mean that, deep in the jungle, people had so much gold, they were in the habit of throwing it away. They arrived at Bacatá looking for a city made of gold, and found instead Guatavita. The Muisca knew the lagoon swallowed those who angered her. Those who tried to touch the bottom of her, to forcefully retrieve her treasure, never came back. It was better to approach the water with tokens of devotion than to arrive with plans of extrication. Water is haunted for those who want to drain it, but not for those who seek to offer up their own hunger.

Guatavita sits atop a sinkhole, created by salt erosion, which tunnels back into the earth. The lagoon has long swallowed its gold, but even modern efforts to drain it have been abandoned due to massive, deadly accidents. Now it's protected land.

After the coming of the Europeans, some wondered if the lagoon woman was to blame for luring the white men to the continent and bringing ruin to her people.

But here might be a place where time thins, where the present wears out to let the past in.

Most of our water in Colombia is born in lagoons.

In English, "lagoon" means a shallow body of coastal salt water, separated from the ocean by a bank of sand, and lakes are inland. But in the ancestral languages of Colombia, there was only one word for water, and centuries later, we still use the words subjectively—laguna, lago. We consider a body of water and seem to decide whether it's female or male, haunted or mundane. Spain says a lagoon is shallower than a lake, fifteen meters deep or less, and this is the notation that Europeans tried to force onto the territory. But our water is ten meters deep and we call it a lake; twenty meters and we call it a lagoon. In the Chibcha language, after which most of our Native languages are based, the word for water is *sie*. Suffixes and prefixes delineated the meaning—whether the water in question was hot, was yet to be heated, had been used to dilute fermented drink, had engulfed a person, or made a pair of hands disappear.

In the stories that we tell as mestizos in Ocaña, hungry women lived beneath the crust of the earth. These women were fire-born and scaled. They slinked through the steam that seared the underground but left them untouched. They lived near lagoons, only lagoons, and broke the surface of the water when a person burdened by a desecrating hunger happened along. The men lived in fear. Lust was a hunger they knew they could not control, and they did not want to raise such specters.

Mamaria, Mami's grandmother, told her in secret: the women knew the stories too.

For many generations, the women had hiked—alone, in pairs, or in threes—to far-off lagoons where they would not be recognized. Once there, they hid their clothes—that is, they hid what made them human. Mamaria had done this too. The women addressed the water, the spirits therein, and asked for shelter. Where the men saw a trap made to bait them by their unmastered desires, the women saw a haven.

The foremothers waded into the circle of the water, imagining a transformation took place. They grew scales, breathed out steam. If a man approached, they would address him like what comes from fire, what aches to devour, and invite him in.

All that had been a source of danger to them on land—beauty, softness, intelligence, luster—became portents of power when inside a lagoon. Only an indomitable and fearsome spirit could cast such magic, could place such poisons into the air as to irresistibly beckon the men to come, to dare touch one foot to the water, to dare, to dare.

Mamaria said most of the time the women entered the lagoon and no men at all passed through the forest. The foremothers splashed, joked, and told stories, performed the holy rites of floating, of unloading cupfuls of water on each other's hair.

The foremothers warned—down the line to Mami, down the line to me—that once there was a woman who did not hide her clothes well.

The man who chanced upon her blanched, then glimpsed her discarded clothes hiding behind a rock. He dragged her behind a bush, beat her, forced himself on her, believing that he was imparting a lesson about a woman's place in the world. But what we took away from the story is that losing sight of your power is dangerous.

Mami is almost asleep when I turn on a light and wake her to remind her of what Mamaria said, and ask her if she thinks the woman Nono encountered standing in the water was actually a woman or a ghost.

Ghost, she says, baby hairs feathering at her hairline, her eyes shut.

Woman, I argue.

Mami doesn't like it when I disagree with her. She turns over. *Nono was a powerful seer; he would have seen past appearance who she really was.*

He was a man, Mami, I insist. *And she must have been especially radiant to fool him; she must have been an absolute splendor of power to behold.*

Mami stiffens at my challenge. Her back is to me, but I can still make out the topographies of her cheek, and by its lift I can tell she is smiling.

4

THE WELL

I n the mountains of Ocaña, in the streets of Chicago—two incidents, forty-three years apart.

In Ocaña, in 1964, the same well behind which Nona had
crouched in hiding from Nono and his machete was empty. The
ledge stones had been pulled apart. All that was left was the hole
that tunneled into the ground, which Mami's cousins wanted her
to see. *Come, Sojaila, let's go look at the hole.* Mami knew the well
water was gone: Nona had explained that construction workers
had drilled into the mountain, and were rerouting the groundwa-
ter into pipes so that the whole neighborhood could have water in
their homes. Mami was looking forward to that, to turning on a
faucet and watching the water spill, but she could not get excited
about some opening in the ground.

But you don't know darkness like this dark, her cousins protested. *It's really nice, you can almost lose your breath looking
down.*

Mami thought about it. The darkest dark she knew occurred
every new moon's night in the bedroom she shared with her sister Perla, when the silhouette of their curtain and mattress could
be only mutedly descried. Maybe she would like to know a darkness more absolute. The three of them, the cousins and Mami,
mounted the dusty slope to the cliff. Ledge stones lay scattered in
the grass. In the middle of it all was the hole. From where Mami
stood, she could tell by the richness of the dark that the hole was
deep.

The cousins skipped right up to the edge. Their long black hair dangling over the darkness. They yelled hello, and giggled as their words stretched and distorted on their way down. There was no telling where the hole stopped being a hole. Mami was too afraid to move any closer, but one cousin offered her hand: *Come, Sojaila, we'll look together.*

Mami liked this cousin. They passed whole afternoons playing tángara and hide-and-seek, stealing fruit from neighbors' trees, and taking naps at the haunted crest of Cristo Rey. Mami took her cousin's hand. Together, they stepped to the hollow. Mami stared at her toes touching that black circumference, at the light diffusing over the rows of stones that lined the well and had once shored up water. She leaned over to make sure, but she knew it was true: never had she seen darkness like that gnashing black which whirled and howled down the distance of that hole. Mami breathed in the damp, moth-eaten air. An updraft filled her ears, and then an eternal hush.

Just before everything goes blank, the last thing Mami remembers is a hand on the small of her back, giving her a gentle push.

In Chicago, I found a dress so beautiful, the silk so rich and lush, I didn't care that Mami made an international call to my cell phone to warn me that the dress was bewitched. Earlier that morning, I had e-mailed her a photo of the dress and a hastily composed message—*I present to you the new love of my life.* It was a black Vera Wang, which I bought on impulse during a flash sale. I was entranced the second I laid eyes on it. I wanted to be enveloped in it, for the black to hide even my toes, for the train to leave a stygian wake behind me. I rolled my eyes at Mami over the phone, annoyed that she could not acknowledge the beauty of the dress, especially when I had already taken it to the seamstress for alterations and couldn't return it.

It's new, *how can it be bewitched?*

You listen to me, Ingrid Carolina: that dress will turn you into a widow.

I sighed. *A dress. Will make my husband die? I'm not even married.*

Just listen! I'm telling you to stay away from that dress!

I heard *you,* I said. By which I did not mean "I will listen to you."

When the seamstress called to tell me the dress was ready to be picked up, I got on my bike and pedaled as fast as I could to make it to her shop before it closed. I never arrived. On my way there, a car door opened in front of me, and I crashed. The last thought I had before denting the door, twisting in the air, and cracking my head on the pavement was of Mami, of how delusional she had to be to believe that a black dress could have such power as to undo me.

Nono was hacking into a cocota tree when a desperate need to find Mami gripped him. He could hear a thin, ghostly version of her voice calling for him: *Papá. Papá.* He dropped his machete, left it stabbing the grass, and sprinted to the house to ask each of his six other children if they had seen her. Nobody bore word of Mami. Nono darted outside to the dirt road. The houses of Cristo Rey were built on cement foundations two feet above the road, so that when rains flooded down the mountain the houses remained intact. Nona's family all lived next to one another, uncles and second cousins all around. Nono peered down the road. It was possible Mami had gone farther down the mountain to have breakfast at a stranger's. Mami was always behaving like a stray cat. When Nona sent her out to sell pineapples, Mami enchanted whoever crossed her path with stories, and after a while, when it seemed natural, she let them know her favorite food was fish and that she would come eat it if invited.

Nono hopped down onto the dirt road and made his way to

Mamaria's; he spotted Mami's two cousins sitting next door, dangling their feet over the road, staring off into space, quiet. He bounded to their side. *Have you seen Sojaila?*

They looked at each other. *Sojaila?* They said the name as if trying it on their tongues for the first time. *I have not seen Sojaila. Have you? No, I have not seen Sojaila—you, either? No, not today. Not today, no.*

Nono ran from house to house searching for Mami. Mamaria had not seen Mami, neither had Mami's uncle Jorge, nor had Nona's cousin Moncho. Nono dropped to his knees and clasped his head. Seeing him distraught, Moncho told him, *You know, I think I remember seeing her with her two cousins, going up that cliff.* Moncho pointed to where the well used to be. Nono nodded, then leapt down the winding road and into the forest. He jumped over fallen trees and dodged low-hanging limbs until he reached the area where construction workers had dynamited the face of the mountain to dig a passage that led directly to the bottom of the well. The workers had left their headlamps behind, and Nono grabbed one, turned it on, and entered the tunnel, bracing his hands along its cold walls. Nono tiptoed through the tunnel, freezing at the smallest sounds. He longed to hurry, but he feared stepping on a snake. At last, the bottom of the well was in sight. He could see a little bulk, stilled on the ground. His headlamp cast a trembling spotlight over it as he drew near. Nono hoped to see coarse fur, leathery ears, and the sharp tusk of a sleeping boar. But, no, it was a girl, and the ground was wet with her blood. Nono prepared himself to touch the body. He grasped the shoulder. The girl fell back into his hand—it was Mami, wearing a crimson mask of burbling blood. With trembling hands, Nono checked her pulse, which throbbed, then her neck, to see if it was broken. He popped her dislocated shoulder back into place, and, after lifting Mami as best he could and placing her neck in the crook of his arm, he hurried her out and up the mountain, back to their house.

———

My ears replayed the crack made by my own head as it hit the pavement. I imagined my brain—pink and coiled—pitching forward in fluid. I brought my hands to my head and pressed, as if I could stop my brain from hitting the cranium. When I broke my eyes open, there was a man in glasses pulling me to my feet. I saw a bike, mangled, and his open car door, mangled as well. I gathered that this was how I had ended up on the ground.

The man asked if I was okay. He touched, then kept, his hand at the small of my waist. I brushed his hand away. *I am fine, I am going to ride away now.* I picked up the bike, straddled the seat, and pressed my feet on the pedals, but the wheels did not move. The man smirked. His brows pushed lines into his high forehead. He pinned the front wheel between his knees and yanked the crooked handlebar back into place, then replaced it in my hands. I had not known that a twisted wheel would impede my movement, but I did know about the hulking smile of a man. I rode away, not looking forward, not looking back, not heeding his call to hold on a minute, to sit down, to wait.

The blood from Mami's broken face wet the pillow of the cot where Nono's clients usually reclined. Nona shrieked at the door, begging Nono to take Mami to a *real* doctor. Nono upset his jars filled with oils and unguents on the side table, looking for something to clean the wounds. He called for his sons to take Nona away— her screaming was interrupting his thinking. It took three sons to drag Nona into a back room and lock her in. Only then did Nono realize that he needed to stanch Mami's bleeding before cleaning the wounds. Nono stopped blood the old way, with saliva, and with asking. Nono knew what the hospital doctors would do. They would stitch the skin together, knot it into zippers. Putting Nona's screaming far from his mind, he set about rearranging the meat of Mami's skin over her bones. The skin couldn't overlap, but it did have to almost touch. He then rinsed the wounds, wrapped her face in gauze, and blacked out the windows with sheets. Nona's muffled curses continued to roll out from the locked back room. Nono left for the mountains to gather supplies: young cane sugar and plant filaments to build a drip system to feed Mami his home-made serums. At home, he prepared and administered her herbal medicines and stayed by the cot, praying over her. In his sleep, he searched for her through black hallways to tell her it was safe to return to her body—but Mami was nowhere to be found. She was in a coma, and Nono did not know how to bring her back.

At the intersection, I got off my bike and stared, mesmerized, at the street signs—Madison, Halsted. Not only did I not recognize the names, it suddenly dawned on me: I had no idea where I came from or where I was going, what city I was in, what my name was, and I did not even know the year.

Somewhere, somehow, this struck me as funny. Nay, hilarious. Was I laughing out loud? I half reached out to stop someone to ask them the year, and if they didn't freak out maybe the city, but I pulled back in a giggle, thinking, *This is life imitating, life imitating* . . . I did not know how the rest of that sentence went. Bewildered, I followed the rut of that phrase until a man I recognized as the one who had just flung his car door in front of me passed me by, whistling in his coat and hat, walking a small white poodle. Then a sentence popped into my head, the way words sometimes do of their own volition, just pop into your mind: *All good science fiction begins this way.*

It's a story where . . . It was on the tip of my tongue, but I couldn't focus because I was raging with electricity. I was air packed together in sheer consciousness. I closed my eyes. I gave in to the current. I exulted on the street corner. There was the noise of traffic, the bustling of people. I was euphoria standing in place.

When I opened my eyes, how much time had passed? All appeared to be the same: people waiting, then crossing at the red light. Cars going, cars idling. *I am so, I feel so* . . . There was nothing to do but wait for this wave of devotion to pass. *Devotion to what?* I closed my eyes. *I am so, I feel so . . .*

In her coma dreams, Mami was a ghost. She hovered over her own eight-year-old corpse. It had been laid out in the open air of a cemetery. Whatever had killed her must have been internal—a sickness or a poisoning—because her body, as far as she could tell, beneath the pretty white tulle of her funeral dress, was unmarked. The people of the town she never heard named surrounded the corpse with flowers and offerings and prayed to it for miracles. It amused Mami to see them tear at their hair and sob into the earth. She sensed that they were crying not because they loved her, but because her unrotting skin defied the passing of days, and her brown locks that smelled of flowers rang fear into their hearts.

As the days passed and the corpse failed to produce the usual stench of death, a priest arrived to exorcise the body of the demons causing the aberration. When the priest left, the townspeople lit candles around the corpse. Afterward, they buried the body by a great tree close to a creek. Then the demands began.

How did it work? She wasn't sure. People's demands bound her. She could not free herself from them unless she complied. The townspeople tied their requests to the limbs of the tree, pieces of paper shivering like shoelaces. Mami was on a constant errand run. Some people asked for food, and she lured cows into their gardens. Others asked for protection, and she stood vigil as they slept. It was exhausting. The only errand she could not fulfill came from the woman who had been her mother, who demanded day after day that she come back to life.

I only knew the things my body told me: that there had been a before—a place where I had borne some unidentifiable weight on my shoulders and against my chest—and that there was a now—a dizzying, unbounded place where I had laid my burdens down. *You are now a blank slate,* I told myself, then tried to remember what a blank slate was. An understanding settled on me like mist. It was the state of being born into the world, new and untouched by experience and time. A bag strap was digging into my shoulder. I considered the bag. It was white and worn, with little printed stars. I knew it contained clues to my old life, so I took it off and strode to the trash can. I remembered that there was such a thing as the ocean: a blue and infinite-seeming place I suddenly desired to find. I would throw the bag away, I decided, go to a port, scam my way onto a boat, and, out on the water, where no questions would be asked, I would continue living as a blank slate.

I raised the bag over the trash; then I made eye contact with a woman through a glass storefront. At lightning speed, I understood the glance I had just given her—noncommittal, arrogant—I had given to myself. I was looking at my reflection in a darkened window. I was a woman. My hair was black and in disarray. I watched with astonishment as my own eyes (harried, unbelieving, wide open) communicated back to me every inch and ebb of what I was feeling. People walked around me, staring through me like I wasn't even there, like a miracle was not just unfolding before all of our eyes—because it felt miraculous, the seeing of myself for the first time. I inched to the window. I examined my face—the thick eyebrows, the brown skin, the wide nose. *What heritage is written on that face—South American, Middle Eastern, Caribbean?* I had no idea. I ran my finger across my brow, caressed my own cheek, played with my hair. *God, my eyebrows are so thick.*

I started to panic. It was proving difficult to remain a blank slate. I needed never to look at a mirror again. But it was addicting, seeing myself. I glanced, then looked, then gazed into my own iris. It was brown, and where light streaked in, caramel gold. My nebula of experience was located in the body I observed. What a strange fortress it was. I studied the reflection. The reflection studied me. I was patient and serene, wondering what key, what code might help me break the lock. Then, like turning a corner,

I was terrified, choking. Air was mud, stuck in my throat. Soon my mind would unhinge and open to madness. Out of the corner of my eye, I saw people crossing the street to avoid me. That was me, screaming. That was me, dropping to my knees, gasping for breath. That was me, a threadbare thing, fixing my nails into the crack of the pavement, latching on to a little piece of the world.

Every day, Nona sat next to Mami's cot. Every week, she clipped the growing nails of Mami's fingers and toes, cut the mat of stringy hair that fell over her chest. Nono cleansed Mami's wounds, pulled the split skin that had puckered to lay it flat once more on her face. He plastered her skin with mashed petals and seeds and saps from trees and tinctures, so it would heal without scarring.

When Mami at last opened her eyes, the dim light of the room assaulted her, but not more so than the strangers at her bedside, the young boys and girls and pregnant woman who were not townspeople she recognized, who could apparently see her, and who looked at her with such alarm and repulsion, Mami at once feared what they saw. Her hands flew to her cheeks. Her fingertips met with soft pads of gauze. Her whole face was wrapped. The little boys pressed Mami's hands down against the bed, imploring her not to touch anything, and the pregnant woman with her bulging stomach crowded what little space Mami had. Mami kicked and wept. She screamed for a mirror, and for answers: who were they, what did they want, why were they holding her captive? She screamed until she passed out.

How long have I been screaming? I was not sure, but my voice was hoarse. A man approached. He was old, had a bad foot, and leaned on a cane. I watched the rhythm of his progress—cane, foot, foot. He stopped next to me. I witnessed his effort as he bent down. His mottled, wrinkled hand with knobby fingers roamed around his pocket, then extended a twenty-dollar bill to me. I did not take it, so the old man lifted a journal that had fallen out of my bag. He placed the bill on the pavement and the journal on top as a paperweight. Then his hands, long-fingered, with knots at the joints, came together at his chest, and he bowed, once, twice, three times. Like I was a goddess. *A goddess of what?* He rose and limped backward a few steps, still facing me, like time itself was going back and back. He turned around. He crossed the street. He was gone.

Mami understood there were two realities. She preferred the one where she was a ghost with errands, able to pass through walls and enter rooms unseen, over the one where she was confined to a derelict, dark room and a pregnant woman who insisted Mami call her Mamá. The woman's children took turns telling Mami stories to prove to her that she was flesh and blood.

My name is not Sojaila! Mami cried. *I have no siblings! I am a ghost!*

When she closed her eyes and went away to the place where the villagers lived, Mami applied herself to being their ghost. She trained herself to move things with her mind by practicing on glasses of water and pushing them off tables. She made her mind a pinpoint that could grip solid things. That's how she got enough strength to retrieve a long-lost locket from under a chest to return to a townsperson who had made the request.

When Mami opened her eyes, one of the pestilent children was seated by her bed, reciting the same tiresome things: *My name is Ángel. You like it when I teach you karate. We run in the hills together. We chase frogs. We climb trees and spy on the neighbors. We used to make pies out of mud, and then we'd pretend to eat them.* Other times, it was the pregnant woman, listing lies: *Your name is Sojaila. I am your mother. You were born in August. You are the fifth of seven children. See, now I am carrying the eighth.*

Mami had been making headway in her life as a ghost, but she wasn't really free. She was enslaved to the townspeople and their incessant requests. In the other world, she was imprisoned in the dark room by the pregnant woman. Here or there, she longed for liberty. She learned how to appear before the townspeople, and she learned how to make them hear her. She said to them: *You must accept I am dead, and you must let me go.*

When Mami opened her eyes, the man who claimed to be her father was by her bedside, swallowing smoke, and exhaling the smoke up and down along her body. The smoke was white and pungent. It sharpened her senses. To this man she pleaded: *Please, bring me a mirror. Hold it before me for five seconds, one second, half a second even. I need to see.* But the man continued inhaling, exhaling, like he could not hear.

With my cheek on the sidewalk, in the stupor following the terror that had assaulted me, I noticed there were things I knew and things I did not. I knew that I had been born from a woman and a man. But I was ignorant about who those people were.

A shimmering ocean arrived, covered the street, lapped at my face. Then it peeled itself back and revealed an abyss. I saw myself lying down, not on the city sidewalk, but at the bottom of a drained seafloor, still wet and rich with debris. Ahead, just beyond reach, there was a crack in the oceanic crust, and inside the crack, gleaming, rolling lava. A different origin.

I sat up, searching the street. The ocean was gone. People walked past, a blur of legs and shoes. Behind me was the black window. I was resisting its gravitational pull. If I turned, I would be face-to-face with my reflection and the attendant hunger to know who I was. The desire to look consumed me, as did the opposite impulse: to never look into a mirror, to find the ocean and never leave it.

I sat, burning, at this fork in the road.

If I couldn't choose both, I decided, I would choose neither. I would return to my life and keep my blank slate a secret. I pulled my bag closer and fished around until I came upon a phone. Somehow, I remembered how they worked. I called the last person I had dialed—PAUL S. Who was he? I had no idea, but the phone was ringing, and his name was on the screen, and then I was speaking. *Hi, Paul, how are you?* To my own ears I sounded put together, but something in my voice must have given me away.

Ingrid? What's wrong? Where are you? Are you okay? Where are you?

I burst into tears at the sound of my name. Slowly I was building a catalogue of sorrows. I held my head and, weeping, told Paul I'd been in an accident and that I couldn't remember where I had come from. To calm me down, Paul listed the details of my life— that I had a sister, that my sister was his fiancée, that I was in Chicago, that I needed to call Jeremiah, my boyfriend, that I needed to get to a hospital. I memorized the facts Paul volunteered. *I know all of this,* I heard myself say. *I think it's the adrenaline. It's not letting me think straight.* I marveled at the fact that I knew the word "adrenaline," that I could so quickly invent a lie that called into question the lucidity of my mind while actually being enthralled by its intense focus. I learned, not without disturbance, that I was good at language, and therefore a master of manipulation.

The eighth child had been born. Mami could hear it bleating in a distant room. Her cuts had sealed and she no longer needed bandages, but Mami was still not allowed to walk, even around the house. Every day, she sat up in bed to find the windows darkened, and the chair by her bedside occupied: it was one or the other of the pestilent children, guarding her sleep. One day, the older boy, with gelled hair and feminine hands, set down a tray on the side table. When he turned his back to Mami to pour her tea (which they forced her to have, even though, as she was tired of explaining, a ghost like herself had no use for it), Mami flung her sheets aside and ran out of the room. It is difficult for Mami to say what happened next. She must have erupted into the hall, then come abruptly to a stop—but what she does remember is the shock of the polished oval hanging on the wall as it came to life. She remembers the scalding seconds of her life coming apart, of seeing on the trembling silver surface her skin, blue-black and swollen, one of her eyes on her forehead, the other melting against her cheek.

I am a monster! I am a monster! She hid beneath her bed, and there, willed herself to sleep, to see what miracles she could perform for the townspeople, whose needs she would now do anything to meet—she didn't care at what cost.

I lied at the emergency room. The doctor shone a light into my eyes, took an X-ray of my brain. He avoided the word amnesia, but everything he asked seemed a dance around it: *Are you having trouble remembering anything? Is anything strange?* I tangoed in response. *No, everything is normal.* The doctor narrowed his eyes. I needed him to sign my release. I smiled, glanced at his pen poised over my paperwork, then stared directly into his eyes.

The man who was supposed to be my boyfriend escorted me to my apartment, where I lived alone. I marked time to the metronome of others. I danced to the punctuations of what I thought was expected of me. I didn't care how far I had to go, so long as I could continue being a blank slate. I loved its strange vibration, and I didn't want anyone to fix it. I was at every moment soaring. I didn't care that I was lost to my past, since I was absolutely found to myself. When the boyfriend stripped that first night and lay down naked in bed, I understood I had to do the same. I dropped my clothes. I got in bed. He pressed his chest into my back. My eyes filled. On the fitted sheet, I descended to an inner nadir. I felt numb. I was a blip. He draped his arm over my stomach. Then his body relaxed.

You don't want sex? I asked.

No, I want to hold you.

The boyfriend had to wake me up every hour to make sure my brain was not swelling. He was supposed to ask me simple questions, like *What is one plus one?* That was the doctor's example in the emergency room as he checked a box on a form. At night, in bed, I felt like a game-show contestant. I had to study my answers, but it was hard to stay afloat. *One plus one is two, his name is Jeremiah, my name is Ingrid, the city is Chicago, the year is 2007. No, 2008. No, 2007.* I drifted off to sleep so easily, I didn't even notice I had fallen asleep.

My shoulder shook. I heard the boyfriend's voice: *What is your name?* It was dark in my apartment—or were we in my apartment? If I answered correctly, I could go back to sleep. *Ingrid,* I said. Something was wrong, but I couldn't remember what. Sleep was white fuzz; it wanted me so badly. I had to stay awake. I fought the marshmallow of nothingness, but soon I was consumed by it.

The boyfriend shook me again. *Where are you from?* Nobody told me this question would be on the test. *Leave me alone,* I huffed. *I'm sleepy. Just tell me where you're from,* he insisted. For once, I couldn't think of how to fake what I didn't know. Then I remembered what was troubling me. It was the million-dollar question: *Who was I sleeping next to?* I felt unsafe. *I'm from Colombia,* I answered in a jolt. Memory could return through association, I noticed, then chided myself for the observation. My purpose was to remain a blank slate. I had to play the role of girlfriend well. I snuggled my back to the boyfriend—his body strange and unfamiliar. I closed my eyes.

In my dreams, there were colors—the morphing skies of a sunset, the iridescent sheen of oil. I watched volcanoes erupt in the ocean. The ocean receded, just as it had before, on the street. I had no body. I was a ghost, strolling along the deserted seafloor. I knelt by a writhing fish, over the crack in the ocean floor. I lowered my ear to the crack, ignoring the heat blistering the side of my face. I longed to discover what the sound was, here at the beginning. It felt like only a second had passed when the boyfriend shook me again. *Tell me what my name is.*

Mami heard the crashing of the mirrors as they were destroyed. She imagined her eyes—deorbited—floating against the blue-black of her skin, shattering with each smashed mirror. Two young girls arrived at her bedside. They said they were her cousins. The older one buried her gaze in the ground. The younger girl asked, *What do you remember from when you fell?* Mami didn't remember anything. *Were you with me when I fell?*

No, said the one. *Yes,* said the other.

When the cousins left, the mother took Mami by the hand and led her to the kitchen. *This is where we cook.* She pointed to the adobe counter. A log fire blazed beneath and flamed through a hole on the surface, licking the underside of a pot of gurgling potatoes. The woman who called herself her mother still did not fathom that Mami was a chimera who needed no nourishment. Mami looked at the mud walls, how here and there on the blue wall shone clean squares from whatever had been hanging there. Mirrors. *This is what we eat,* the mother said, pointing to the potatoes, the basket of eggs, the stack of corn in the corner, but Mami could only see those bright squares on the wall, empty spaces that were somehow still haunted by reflection.

I knew myself in flashes: a blur of fingers, a motion of legs. I was sunlight, I was air. The mirrors in my apartment bespoke the borders of the body. We forget mirrors can be violent, reflecting the cage that we are. That was a face, a pile of hair, the ticking clock. Being reminded that I had a body made me anxious. I shrouded the mirrors in sheets. How infinitely better it was to be a ghost.

Three kittens mewled after me in the apartment, batting at my heels wherever I went. There was a bulky bamboo bookshelf in the living room, vintage orange furniture, and so many plants I felt like I was navigating a jungle. The kitchen was jam-packed with utensils and pots piled on racks piled on other racks. *What do the kittens eat?* I would need to figure that out. Surely the kitchen was where their food was kept.

I stayed in bed. It was entertaining being such a void. I was a terrain without history, witnessing itself. Time unspooled. A deep silence droned through me. My body told me here was a rare and divine occurrence. I listened to the silence, and what at first seemed like a product of my own quiet I discovered, in time, did not come from any self I knew, but thrummed from some alien part in me, some darkened water beating itself to life.

When the sun burned orange through the windows, I wondered if there were more layers to the mind I could peel back. Did the mind have a center? Was the center the darkened water? What would it take for the darkened water to speak?

Lying in bed, I jotted down a list of questions, composing them with the absolute assurance that the right words, phrased in just the right way, would cause the final curtain to fall, would bring me to the source material from which I was made, would bring me to the beginning.

Notepad in hand, I tried, *Who are you now that everything has been stripped away?* But the darkened water was quiet. *What are you now that everything's been misplaced?* But it remained solid and aloof and remote to me. The cats transformed into silhouettes as I drafted question after question. No matter what I asked of it, I was met with an uncanny silence. I was hushed by its expansive dark. The sun had gone down by the time it occurred to me that maybe the mind's language wasn't inscrutable silence but wordless abundance. I listened with attention, the way I might to a language I held no fluency in, and then, only then, was I swept from plateau to plateau of the unnameable.

It was late when my cell phone rang. MAMI, the screen announced. When I answered, the woman who was my mother launched into a plea for me not to wear a black dress, and while she talked, I marveled at three things: one, I could understand Spanish; two, the sound of her voice was familiar; and three, though I couldn't recall my mother or my boyfriend, I could still picture in detail the black dress.

The gown had a plunging neckline, an empire waist, and a long train. Folds of black silk covered the breasts, and the silk curled just barely at the shoulder. This was the dress my mother was now predicting would trigger a series of events that would turn me into a young widow. This was the dress I now remembered I had been on a mission to retrieve when I had my accident. *Por favor*—she was saying, *no seas terca.*

Am I stubborn? I wondered. *Is losing your memory like being widowed?* I realized I hadn't spoken at all since my initial *Hello?* I didn't know what kind of rapport I shared with my mother, but I plowed ahead: *No, I am sure. I am keeping the dress.* I noted that I did not for a second consider revealing to my mother that I'd been in an accident and that I had amnesia. Aside from my desire to remain a blank slate, when it came to my mother, I observed I was petty, and I simply did not want to allow her to relish the satisfaction of being right.

She was, after all, correct. My rush to get the dress had facilitated the accident. Yet her prophecy was off: I hadn't lost a husband, only my old self; I'd been widowed, then reborn. And it wasn't the terrible thing she implied, but actually the best thing that had happened to me. I was boundlessly rich in loss. I noted with curiosity the definite emotional reflexes I harbored against my mother, a woman whose voice I recognized but who was, otherwise, a mystery. *It's just a dress,* I told Mami at last. *Stop trying to jinx it with superstition.* I hung up.

My legs were unstable, so I crawled to the kitchen to hunt for a clue that would lead me to the dress. The three kittens leapt after my feet. I found their dry food in a lower cabinet and poured the kibble directly onto the floor. The cats attacked the pile, feral. If I could manage to make coffee, I could figure out where the dress was. I pulled myself up by the countertop and stood before the espresso machine. It had silver accents and bulky knobs. I tried to decode the curious hieroglyphs—*cup with waves, mushroom cloud, smaller cup.* I drank a glass of water and slept.

In my dreams, I hovered now, without form. Clouds traveled by, the ocean boiled. The waves hissed, and orange lava broke the surface. It oozed on top of the waves, filling the air with steam, solidifying into layer after layer of black land. This was land being born. Creation required an initial violence, a brief cataclysm.

The father was some sort of doctor. Sometimes his patients came to see him about boils, rashes, coughs. Other times what ailed them was not so apparent. Some people, Mami could see, trailed veils of shadows, gray-skinned people, beasts baring fangs. Neither the patients nor the father remarked on their presence. Once, Mami made the mistake of lifting a finger and pointing to a chair, telling the father: *Better treat him first, he's bleeding from the stomach.* The father gaped at Mami. The woman sitting next to the bleeding man glanced at Mami, at the father, then at Mami again. *There's no one there,* the woman whispered. *You don't see him?* Mami asked. *He's wearing jeans and a yellow plaid shirt?* The woman knelt before Mami. *That's my son! That's my son! He was shot in the stomach! That's what he was wearing when he died! Does he have a message for me?* Mami looked at the man. Blood pulsed out of his stomach, and his eyes rolled back. *He's dying.* The father rested a hand on the woman's shoulder and raised his other palm for the woman to stand up. *We'll see what we can do for him.* The father led the woman to the front room, his consulting room, and Mami sat rooted before the now empty chair, the bleeding man now vanished, her body heavy with the knowledge that she was alone in this ability to see.

It was a new morning and I had a to-do list: eat something, feed the mewling cats, find my way to the dress. The boyfriend called on my cell phone. *I have to work late. Are you still okay?* I said that I was. *Are* you *okay?* With no memory, the only conversational strategy I had was to behave like a mirror. He replied that he was, then we made plans to see each other the following day.

In the living room, I discovered a receipt for the dress in the

white purse with little printed stars. *The Dress Doctor, Since 1982.*
At the top was an address. As I read it, a memory began to intrude,
arriving like a wave. I lowered the receipt and waited. The seamstress's face fizzed into being. Her hair, to be exact. Silver and short
and beautifully curled. I saw her fitting room next: a small space
enclosed by black velvet curtains in a print of repeating roses,
heavy, with long golden cords. I recalled the elegant feeling of
stepping onto the cream-colored platform at the center. There was
a soft spotlight, and as soon as I stepped under it, I was flanked by
three images of myself in my underwear. I remembered: no matter how quickly I turned, I could not catch the reflection looking
at me when I was looking away. It was a game I had played as a
kid, but why? I remembered hearing the woman in the adjacent
stall detailing the changes she wanted made to a dress she was
wearing to a cocktail party.

At the hospital, I had also been in a curtained-off space. The
curtains were blue (or maybe white) and thin. Voices sounded
through the walls of fabric there as well. Behind me, someone
whispered in what sounded like German, and far off, there was
laughter, and farther still, one person was shrieking.

I did not want my memory to return. I felt the heft of those few
details on my shoulders. I was slowly becoming more flesh-and-
blood. My eyes watered with frustration, and then a feeling came
over me—a wordless, high-pitched terror that squeezed into my
lungs. Its grip was of lesser intensity than what had happened to
me in the middle of the street when I fell to the ground. I moved to
untangle the emotion, but the high-pitched terror was subsumed
by a routine nothing. Like forgetting a name or a face, the texture and shape of the terrible thing disappeared. *Anxiety attacks,*
came an involuntary thought. *That's what they're called.*

The anxiety attacks came and went over the course of the day,
and I feared I would be unable to pick up the dress, but I gave
myself no choice. I was quick and efficient. I found my address
on an outstanding bill on the counter. I had memorized my own
name by then, had repeated it to myself fifty times a day, but it

still didn't seem to belong to me. Like the address, the apartment, my mother, it belonged to a life I did not remember agreeing to. I dialed the saved number in my phone labeled TAXI and read my address off the bill. I handed the driver The Dress Doctor's receipt to show him where we were going, then rocked back and forth in the back seat, hands pressed to my temples. I asked the driver to wait for me while I went inside, then clutched the dress to my chest the entire way home. It was late when I returned. I hung the dress on a padded hanger. *It's so pretty. See?* I ran my finger-tips along the fine silk. *My mother is delusional. There's nothing supernatural about this dress.* I lifted the train. I fluffed it. I let it fall. I pushed off my clothes and slipped it on. I knelt, smoothing the gown around me so that it cast a perfect black circle, as if I were in the middle of a hole. I pranced around my apartment. I watered the plants, I sashayed to the windows. I let the train slide on the floor, even though I knew it was dirty and that the cats might attack.

It was clear: Mami had returned without a memory but could see and hear the dead. The father bade Mami to sit near the door of his consulting room so she could tell him what she saw. Sometimes Mami kept the visions to herself. Other times she pointed to the dead and described them to the living. Eyes dangled from slimy threads, blood poured from severed necks, veins glowed black through the skin. Some ghosts were beautiful. A woman smiled in a sundress. A boy skipped rope from wall to wall. A grandfa-ther bowed, taking off his hat. Soon the father's clients came to see Mami as often as they did him. In between sessions, the father made Mami stick her face into a bowl of ice, and applied crushed plants to her skin. He didn't say much to her, only that the swell-ing was going down, and her skin was healing without scarring, and soon she'd be as beautiful as before the fall.

The father had saved one mirror from destruction, a little

round shaving mirror that fit in the palm of his hand. He placed it beneath Mami's pillow before she went to sleep, saying only, *This mirror is to help you remember.* In the morning, he retrieved it.

When he left her with the mirror that first night, Mami took it out to check if his words were true. Maybe the swelling had gone down. She noticed that people didn't look at her with as much disgust as before. She held the mirror up and shut her eyes, afraid. Little by little, she allowed them to open. By the pale moonlight, she studied the contours of her face: sharp cheekbones, thick eyebrows, eyes that pooled with an ebony intensity. There were no scars except for one, still knitting itself along the sharp edge of her chin. She tilted her head to admire her nose. She gasped. One nostril was slightly bigger than the other. She wondered if it had been like that before, or if the father had made a mistake in putting her face back together. She forgave him readily, holding the mirror at arm's length. She was beautiful and would be beautiful again.

Mami snuck the mirror back beneath her pillow. The father had protected her from what she hadn't been ready to see. Looking into a mirror was an act of timekeeping. Nono's mirror had shown her that her face carried a history. She could see the marks of how she carried what she had lived, which she did not yet fully know. And she could cast her mind forward too. Over the image reflected in the mirror, she glimpsed another—her face many years from now, on which she could peruse, if she wanted, what joy and tragedies lay in wait. But she did not want to. These were things she had the will to ignore. That night, when she dropped her head onto the pillow, stuffed her hand beneath it to clasp the mirror, and fell asleep, she began to remember. She dreamt of the moments leading up to the fall into the well. She remembered there had been a hand.

In my dreams, I climbed down the crisp, hardened mounds of what had once been underwater terrain. The sooty wrinkles on the rock face were important. They spoke of a history of motion. The water was recently gone. The seafloor as far as I could see was littered with gasping fish. Everywhere was a foreboding hush.

Naming was one power I had.

Every darkened air I called *Night*.

Each body, an *Exhaustion*.

And the word for the yellow triangle of light that fell on my feet when I opened the fridge? *Reckoning*. The bruise still purpling my thigh could be an *Altar*, and every window with curtains drawn was *Condemned*.

I did the bare minimum to keep all the wheels of my life in motion. From my correspondence, I understood I had been hired by a journalist to do a translation. I opened the document, unsure I could perform such a task. It was a handwritten letter from a prisoner. I began by translating the first word, then found I had an automatic facility of pouring meaning from one language into another. It was like walking, something I could do unconsciously, and being in between languages, inhabiting another's voice in a letter addressed not to me, was soothing and familiar, a ghostly existence.

During the two hours I worked, I came to love the hush that opened between languages. There was a lag in translation, a no-place where, as my mind conjured meaning in one tongue and found the equivalent in a second tongue, a portal opened. Between languages, there was a wordless territory where everything was still unnamed, and, therefore, nearly eternal. Meaning was all there was. And language was doubled, and also erased. Wordless abundance.

I spent three hours translating the prisoner's words, then sent my work to the journalist. I typed into an online search bar, *what do people in relationships do*, then texted the boyfriend that I wanted to see a movie. *I'm writing now though don't text me.* Writing was another thing I was supposed to be doing. There was a window open in my computer with a draft of a novel. It took place in Bogotá and Los Angeles and was about two girls and a kidnapping. I could not remember writing a word of it. I scrolled and deleted paragraphs at random. I typed *good jokes in Spanish* into an online search engine, and texted one to my mother, then told her I was busy.

Having gone through my duties as quickly as possible, I stared at my brain.

Because I had no past or preoccupations, no thoughts emerged. I was a quiet that grew into a buzzing. I possessed nothing, which felt like possessing everything. Hours passed, and I listened to how the blood coursing through me made every second new.

I remembered things I wasn't sure were real. Some recollections contained glitches—in one, I am at a bar, speaking in English to people who only speak Spanish; in another I am young, walking around my neighborhood in Bogotá looking for trouble, but I am wearing a dress I know I bought as an adult in Chicago.

In the beginning, I consulted my journals, trying to fact-check, but they held no answers. Journals, I assumed, were bare-all accounts, but mine were vague. One page read, *I have gone to bed with an empty heart for three nights in a row. I feel that air fails me.* The rest of the page was blank.

Another page: *Cramping a blanket, nails digging.*

There were strange lists:

Memories of What the Sky Looks Like from the Back Seat
    of a Moving Car
Ways in Which Pets Have Died

Other pages were full of overheard conversations.

The only memories I knew were uncorrupted were those first moments in the street after the accident, when I had complete amnesia, and the weeks since. The moments of being on the street with amnesia were the most vivid memories I had. I had paid attention breathlessly as the world was being made. I brought each moment to mind again and again, knowing that they, too, in time, would deteriorate.

Right after the man caused my accident and helped me up from the ground, the heat of his touch at the small of my back named the lumbar spine. The arrogance in his eyes taught me about power. The pads of his fingertips upsetting the cloth of my shirt lectured me on wildness, and on the fact that there was such a thing as a claim on a wild thing.

Amnesia was like living at the world's edge. Majestic, and incredibly lonely. You can't cuddle up to the end of the earth.

I tried, for as long as possible, to call up the unimaginable freedom I had felt in my body before knowing I was a body. For many weeks, if I closed my eyes, I could still taste what it was like. But slowly, the feeling dulled, and now all I remember is a concept.

The stupid things people say are true. Ignorance *is* bliss.

I had no power over my memory returning. Bit by bit, I fell asleep and awoke, unwillingly, with new memories. I remembered throwing my head back in laughter in a bar. I recalled how, once, when I was walking back to my apartment very late at night, my boots sank into the snow and the slush leaked into my shoe, deadening my toes. Wind whipped my hair on my face in a speedboat. I woke up one morning knowing the plot of *Moby-Dick*. The five zones of the ocean.

I could not remember emotion. I could not remember loving my mother or my boyfriend. Like a cracked-up scientist, I wrote in a notepad: *Maybe emotion is what comes at the end, after an accumulation of memory.*

One day, I woke up with an image seared in my mind: Mami pulling tarot cards. The cards were spread before her in a gentle arc, and she was drumming her fingers in the air over them, looking for the ones she had to turn. I held my head before the flood of memory that came:

Nono could move clouds.

Mami could appear in two places at once.

Mami had fallen down a well. She had lost her memory. I fell into deep bafflement.

My mother had lost her memory too.

Every muscle in my body seized. I was asphyxiating. I gasped for oxygen that never seemed to find my lungs. I tucked myself into a ball. Renamed the event *growing symphony of Terror*. I entered a fugue state, then, gracefully, I took leave of my body. I watched myself from above: a human specimen suffering from an alien affliction. I stood in awe of the terrible.

By the end of eight weeks, like this, torturously, I remembered all.

You have two life lines, an old woman told me when I was eight. We were idling around the Plaza de Bolívar on a Sunday night in Bogotá. Mami, Ximena, and me. Mami let go of my hand to photograph my sister, who was chasing pigeons into flight, and in that moment, the old woman grabbed my hand, looked at my palm, and exclaimed. I don't remember her face, only what she said: *You will have the choice of two lives. One is more exciting, but you will die young; the other—* Mami pulled me away and made us cross the plaza at great speed, past abuelos sipping coffee and children scattering breadcrumbs before the birds. The woman gave chase, demanding payment, but Mami yelled over her shoulder, *Nobody asked you for a reading! Leave my little girl alone.*

I had been haunted by the woman's words, questioned every decision I made, wondering what exactly would lead me down a life that ended too early. Now I felt the prophecy releasing its clutches. But was this the long or the short life?

I uncovered the mirrors in my apartment and sat down. I remembered this too: I was someone burdened with trauma. There was no way to unknow. I forced myself to learn all there was left to discover.

Even though Mami acknowledged that her existence as a ghost and her existence as a bed-bound girl were separate realities, she understood them both to be real. Nono instructed her to choose a reality, but didn't tell her which. Mami's grandmother advised her to choose her physical life, because if Mami went around believing herself to be a ghost, what school would take her, what lover would kiss her, what life could she have?

Mami told her grandmother that if she was to live in her world, her condition was justice. She wanted whichever cousin had pushed her into the well to pay for her injuries, her amnesia, this return.

When the cousins were confronted, they had a story of their own. The hand that had pushed Mami into the well belonged to neither—it had simply bloomed into being from the air. The hand had been almost pretty, slender, see-through, with bluish nails.

The adults didn't know what to do. The cousins' mother forced them to sit at Mami's bedside and ask for forgiveness. Their apologies were not heartfelt. Mami became uninterested in justice. She liked the cousins' story, about the ghost hand, and asked them to describe it to her again.

There was the edge of a garment, the cousins said, a pinch of elastic at the wrist, and a billowy gauze that fluttered all around just beneath the sheer, clear-blue knuckles.

It was then that Nono began to read Mami's fortune. He used a deck of playing cards, but sometimes he stared into water. Its surface doubled Nono's face, easily refracted by the wind of his voice.

Nono told Mami that he was in possession of secrets that larger forces than himself prohibited him from teaching her, but that he now thought had chosen her on their own.

In the privacy of his consulting room, as Nono predicted what lay ahead for Mami, he narrated what nobody but Mami has ever heard: what steps he took, what words he recited, how he pointed his mind in order to pull back the veil and reveal her forking paths. Mami remembered then that this was a knowledge she had always hungered for. She wondered if her father was revealing the secrets to her for the reasons he gave, or whether they were a lure to make her choose the world of the living. Mami couldn't be sure without asking, and she didn't want to ask. She did, however, watch and learn. But it wasn't the future that Nono divulged that made her want to stay, or his revealing of the secrets: it was the soft worship of her in his voice.

I am not the same person as I was before my accident. Nor is my mother since hers. We are both women transformed by the exit and the return. In this way, we alone understand each other: we know what it's like to wake up disassembled and witness, hour by hour, the invention of self.

Once, we were empty, pristine, expansive—pliable and open as only the new can be.

Then we mourned the slow rigor mortis that made us one person and not another. We bemoaned the grooves of thought that surfaced, the tracks our minds insisted running on, catching always at the same places. We regretted the re-emergence of unfortunate personality traits—Mami's short temper, my self-absorption, Mami's vanity, my pride.

When we returned to our minds, not everything was in its place. Crucial pieces were mislaid, important moments misremembered, different conclusions drawn, cornerstone thoughts lost forever.

I came back together out of order. I remembered our family stories first, the circumstances of our leaving Colombia second, and, when it was already too late, when I had already learned to hold us in devotion, I recalled that Mami had always called for my silence.

I was telling an Iranian friend about a particular use of salt, a ritual we observed, when Mami's forbidding face flashed and hovered before me, and I stopped speaking mid-sentence. I excused myself and locked myself in the bathroom. I opened the faucet, stared at the water running, and recalled, and thus lived again, or lived then for the first time, Mami's urgency as she loomed over me, explaining that we were people who had survived through secrecy, and needed it to remain safe. Once, I had acted like this meant that we could only be who we were in the shadows, that palatability was more important than living our lives.

I tasted a searing, purifying outrage. My allegiance to Mami's desire for concealment went up in flames. I stared at the empty space inside myself that marked where shame used to be. Shame had once been a foundational emotion I had built myself on top of. Now that foundational stone no longer fit.

There was a difference between keeping knowledge secret, and living in secret. I could do the former, but I would not do the latter. I shouldn't have been telling my friend about salt, but I had done nothing else wrong. Whatever parts of Mami's shame or worry I had unconsciously absorbed, or willfully taken, were gone.

When Mami returned to her mind, for her part, her sense of vulnerability vanished. She didn't see herself as a child, let alone as a child in need of others. Food and love and shelter were things she could get from anyone, if only she cared to reach. She forgot that she was supposed to be primarily tethered to one world. She didn't care if she lived or died. She preferred the company of flowers. She swatted her mother away and roamed under the dappled light of the forest and sat by the anthills to chat with the insects. She fed on flower petals, leaves, and plant stalks. She grew thin, she fell asleep in the branches of rubber trees. She began to appear in two places at once.

And so, in those places left vacant by the erroneous reassembly of our selves, the remnants of our amnesias lived like a brood of wasps.

Everything has a cost.

There were frequent aftershocks.

I dissociated. In the middle of the day, I forgot who I was. My own emotions became strange, as if they did not belong to me. An implosion took place, then the unbordering of the body. At night, I relapsed into amnesia. I relived the same scene, stuck, unwittingly, in a loop.

Late into her teens, Mami dissociated too. *Don't talk to me, don't touch me, you don't know who I am.*

Eighteen times that first year, twelve the second, and now on random occasions, I sit up in bed, not knowing who I am. Though I can't recall the dream that's jolted me awake, I know that the next waking moments are a continuation of it. I think I am a ghost until I look down and see I have a body. I can't remember my name, what city I am in, what year it is. I am a gallop of fear.

The scene always goes one of two ways.

In one, my bed is empty. Silence heaps around me. I cling to the bedsheet and do not move. I think I am dying. I have to survive one second, and then the next. I remember numbers. A technology that can guard my navigation through time. I begin to count to one hundred. Each number is a continued attempt to outlast my distress. I get to fifty-six. What is it about the number fifty-six that calls to mind my mother? I am not sure, but I see Mami's face, and in a moment I remember: 1956 is the year Mami was born.

In the other, silence heaps around me as I grow conscious of a figure, slumbering directly next to what I suddenly understand to be my body. Dreams harden his face. I am a woman. He is a man. I know no despair like the one that comes when I sit up and move away because I am naked and he is naked too, and he— is my brother.

I cover my face.

I am heart-stricken and liver-sick.

I try to perceive whether there is semen.

I try hard to remember the instance of a condom, a pill, a sponge.

Sometimes there is semen. Sometimes there is no semen.

I cringe at what our mother will think.

Then I realize I cannot bring her to mind.

That's when a thought comes gurgling as if through water:
I've done this before.

Even the gestures, I realize, are replicas of other nights.

It is here where the two scenes converge.

As I reach the number fifty-six and recall my mother's face, as
I realize Jeremiah can't be my brother and I don't have a brother
in real life, as my own gestures evoke the feeling of theater—that's
when I remember the accident, the not-recognizing my apartment, and in a series of superimposed images, across the years,
I see myself sitting up in bed night after night after night after
night, *remembering myself* sitting up in bed night after night after
night after night.

Each time, the realization that I keep performing the same
scene crushes me anew. I am an actor in a play I wrote for myself
in a dream I cannot remember. I run through the lines, the stage
directions, perform the emotions, until someone, offstage, unseen,
unheard, yells *Cut*.

They say Mami's aftershocks during that first year after her accident, her slips back into believing herself to be a ghost, were what
caused her to splinter in two. A different doubling. When Mami
dissociated, her family retreated and left her to her whims. *Otra
vez se enloció? Who knows how long it'll last, better stay out of
her way.*

Mami's dissociations were difficult to predict. When the family planned a cookout at the river, Nono deemed it necessary for
Mami to stay behind. It was safer if she uncoupled from reality in
a familiar place. At home, he would know where to find her—in
the forest of Cristo Rey, sitting by the trees, sleeping on grass, talking to the plants.

No one thought to stay at home with Mami—that kind of thing
was just not done. Theirs was a village that could at any moment

be ravaged by war or calamity, making it essential that children learn how to bear their own burdens, or else they might never survive. So, instead of taking her along, Nono told Mami to keep an eye on his patients and ensure their safety while he was gone.

Nono's patients filled the house. By the back patio Nono had installed makeshift walls between four cots for his overnight patients. The first cot belonged to the woman given to fits of rapture who had conversations with unseen people. The second cot belonged to the grandfather who had recently started to cough up blood. Next to him was the woman who couldn't be near knives or she would murder. (Nono's instruction: *Just don't let her near knives.*) And, finally, there was the quiet man who could not pee.

Even though Nono had left Mami in charge, he enlisted this man to keep an eye on her. Mami was furious. Either she had executive power or she didn't.

When the family left for the cookout, Mami threw herself on the mattress she shared with her sister Perla and fell asleep in a brine of fury. Outside her door, the man who could not pee pulled up a chair. He turned on the radio and settled in with a *Bristol's Almanac,* the farmers' almanac printed in New Jersey and distributed throughout all of South America, the only piece of literature in the house. He was halfway through the little magazine when Mami's bedroom door burst open and Mami flew out. *Niña! Wait!* He attempted to stand and intercept her, but his illness had left him slow and infirm. Mami disappeared into the sunlight at the door. Worried about what the curandero would do to him for failing to keep his daughter in the house, the man hobbled after her. It was no use—she was gone. The man closed the front door, yielding to the idea that he might soon have to brunt the worst of the curandero's anger. He shuffled back to his seat and opened the almanac. He was nearly at the magazine's end when, once more, Mami's bedroom door creaked open. Again Mami emerged, but this time she looked fresh from sleep, doe-eyed, tousled, yawning. The man strained to his feet and fell to the ground. Mami rushed to his side. The man put up his hands as if defending himself against a gale.

He thrust the side of his wrist against his opposite forearm, forming a trembling cross. *I rebuke you, Satan!*

What happened to you? Mami giggled. *Did you see a ghost?*

Seeing that she was making fun of him, the man pushed himself to his feet and went into Mami's bedroom. *How did you sneak back in?* He palmed the bare walls, half lifted the mattress, paced by the barred window. He froze before a pile of clothes on the mattress, on top of which Mami had been sleeping. He groaned and lowered himself to his haunches. Mami stared. *What now?*

These were the clothes I saw you wearing when you flew out of the house!

Flew out? I've been in this room the whole time.

The man rubbed his face, then shrugged. He held out his trembling hand so Mami could help him straighten and lower him back into his chair. From his seat, he explained that she had undergone a splintering, and that she had appeared to him wearing the outfit on the bed. *We'll tell your father when he returns. This kind of thing must be common to your family, no?* He looked toward the kitchen. *Did your mother leave dinner?*

A man of few words when it came to magical occurrences, Nono was impassive as he listened to the story about Mami's splintering. He thanked the man for watching her, clapped his hand on the man's back, and asked, *You know how to gut a fish?* They turned toward the backyard, where the two would sit on stools and split the animals and save the innards for the dogs, but before walking away, Nono looked over his shoulder and gave Mami a wink. Nono himself could splinter—except, Mami said, he could do it on purpose.

After Mami began to splinter, Nono taught her how to prepare the doses for his patients. He pointed to his jars, instructed her on which herbs were good for what. He showed her the steps required to mash them, bless them, prepare salves and tinctures and drafts. When his restlessness took hold and he couldn't resist the call to wander the mountains, he left the business in her hands, telling her he would come visit the patients whenever possible.

Mami cared for the ill in his absence. She looked in on them before and after school. Sometimes the patients greeted her with the question: *Where's Don Rafael? I thought it would be him bringing my dose. He came by with my medicine last night.*

Knowing Nono had not yet returned, Mami suppressed a smile. There was one question she wanted to ask, but could not: Did the patients touch Nono, and if so, did he seem real? Was he warm to the touch or cold? The temperature of the apparition's form seemed to Mami an important detail, something that could teach her about the nature of the other side. She chatted with the patients about the weather, the chickens, the other patients. When enough time had passed, she allowed herself to inquire further:

When my father came to see you, did he give you your dose in a glass? Did you hold the glass?

He gave me a glass that I drank from—but I don't know where it went. Why do you ask?

When Nono returned from his journey, he brought Mami animals, as usual. She sat at his feet, playing with the monkeys. He told her stories about his travels. They never once discussed the other's doubling.

After my nightly amnesia lapses, I felt half in my body and half gone. I thought of my mother and her splinterings, trying to fathom my own predicament. Mami's doubling was a worrying event we all lived with, but Mami herself never expressed concern about having a splintered self.

While I was growing up in Bogotá, it happened that every time Mami grew intensely angry, feverish, or tired, Nona would call us from 251 miles away, in Cúcuta, to report that she had seen Mami appear. In the house that Nono and Nona built with their own hands, Mami would materialize—caressing the furniture, turning a corner, shuffling down a hall.

For a long time, I thought Mami's apparitions were just stories the family told. Then, when I was thirteen, I saw one of Mami's clones. I was heading down the stairs to the first floor of our house in Bogotá when I saw her sitting at the dining-room table, even though I knew full well she was upstairs in bed with a fever.

Mami? I called from what I hoped was a safe distance. I lowered myself onto the stairs and spied through the white wooden balustrades. The apparition did not look up when I called to it, but continued to stare at the round glass table where Mami's tarot cards (or the clone's tarot cards, I should say) were spread out in the shape of a star. Everything about the apparition was a faithful copy—down to the charms that hung from her hoop earrings (the right one a pyramid, the left a sphinx). The clone plucked a card from the tarot stack, turned it and placed it by the others she had uncovered, and jotted something down on a piece of paper. I ran away.

In her bedroom, Mami's brow was sweating. I shook her awake. *I just saw you, Mami, desdoblada! You were sitting at the dining table.*

Mami, pale and slick, turned over and groaned. *Oh, let me sleep, please. Sometimes that happens to me. Can't you see that I'm sick?*

Nona agonized that Mami's uncontrolled journeys outside of her body were a sign that death was soon to come. *Ve, negra,* Nona told Mami, *stop this nonsense. What if one day you get locked outside of your body?*

After talking to Nona, Mami brought me her complaints. *My mother's delusional.* She clicked her tongue and waved her hand in the air like she was shooing away an especially pesky mosquito. *All these years, and nothing's happened; it's normal.*

I remembered: after Nona passed, Papi became the person who sees Mami's clones the most. Papi regularly travels on his own for work, and he is often startled to see Mami walking around his temporary housing, engaged in the most menial housework. Late at night, when Papi is lying down on the couch, or early in the morning, when he is drinking coffee before going to work, he sees Mami walk by. She sweeps the floor with a broom. She waters the plants on the balcony. She sits in the living room, putting her feet up on the table. For some seconds after she's materialized, Papi forgets that Mami did not travel with him. He presumes it's the *real* her. But the straw of the clone's broom doesn't rustle against the cold tile. The spray of her watering can does not make pattering sounds as it hits the soil. Sometimes the clone lingers, cleaning a mirror, blowing the steam from a cup of coffee. Other times she disappears quickly into the nothingness from which she came.

I tried to pretend that the relapses I was experiencing were ordinary, just like Mami's doublings were ordinary. If I squinted, I could almost find something mundane in the full unloosening of my identity, the dispassion with which my brain shed its memories, the automatic compulsion with which it suddenly retrieved them, dragging me through a veiling and unveiling of who I was, like I was to learn something from it, from that particular experience of dissolution and nucleation. But then, on the eighteenth time of waking up into amnesia, and into a reality in which I had slept with my brother, a fluster of nerves, a searing of shame, something in me finally broke.

A full year after the accident, I cried and confessed: I kept waking up into amnesia, I had lost my memory in the bike accident of a year ago, I pretended that I hadn't lost my memory, I'd been trying that whole time to get to the bottom of what it was to be a person.

A thing nobody asked was: *Why didn't you tell me?*

Something everyone said was: *Of course.*

Mine were people who knew me more profoundly than I knew myself.

Whereas I had expected my family to feel angry, hurt, or betrayed by my silence, their shock rallied around the fact that the accident had been more serious than they thought, not that I had kept its consequences to myself. When I asked her about it, Mami said that for there to be hurt there would have to be surprise, and nothing about what I had done was surprising. My family seemed to understand my reaction to loss in a way I couldn't. They seemed to already know that I would seek loss as if it were abundance,

Mami, pregnant with my sister. Bogotá, 1982

that I would treat it like a honed edge I could break myself open on. And their concern over my well-being eclipsed everything else.

Jeremiah was entertained by the self-possession I had exhibited during a time when I had no self; my sister was interested in fact-checking my memories; Papi wanted me to get more X-rays; and Mami went astray into the thought that our lives were doubling again. All she wanted to know (just as the tías would once they found out) was what I dreamt.

Now that she knew I had lost my memory, Mami began to call me every day to tell me the stories of our family, stories I simultaneously recalled as she spoke them into being.

I felt like a groundskeeper. In Mami's words I looked for what she was already forgetting, what was already fading from her recollection. I tended the grounds I knew held space for my self-reflection, committing it all to memory.

My mother fell down a well. I crashed into a car. Air for both of us, then the shock of solid ground. Losing our memory was a blissful dying; regaining it, a painful return.

We live now with our splinterings—Mami with her clones, and me with waking up into amnesia in the middle of the night.

Though I had received a warning to stay away from the dress, nobody warned Mami off from the hole—unless the moment eight years earlier when Nona hid behind the well from her husband and his machete was a warning. Maybe Mami's fall down the well had been eight years in the making. A price exacted, a payment for a life not taken.

As a newborn, Mami was saved because her mother placed her in the orb of her mother's mother's hands. I climb out of amnesia the moment I remember my mother. Mothers are entry and exit. As a girl, Mami toed the dark circumference. As an adult, I bought a dress that made me the center of a circle of my own. A circle from a circle from a circle.

5

THE AFTERSHOCKS

It is ninety degrees at night in Cúcuta, and Mami and I only have one fan. We drag it from room to room in the apartment. We're always together, fanning ourselves, threatening to shave our heads, rubbing ice cubes on our shoulders, vying to escape the heat. We take turns beneath the cold spray of the shower, stepping under it with our clothes on; then we pad along the halls of the apartment like wet cats.

I worry that we might experience aftershocks while we are together. I dread that Mami will splinter and her apparition will condense in unnerving stillness before me when I least expect it. I fear that I will relapse into amnesia in the middle of the night and step into an appalling new loop, with Mami at the center. I don't want to know what story my brain will invent. I recite incantations of memory: *The woman next to you is your mother. The woman next to you is your mother. The woman next to you is your mother.* I barely sleep.

Mami and I are still trying to raise the last of the funds for the disinterment. We have gone through all the obvious valuables, and are now auctioning whatever we come across. In a great flurry of emerald-and-silver-tinted plastic, which comes off in strips, we unroll each shrouded thing. Heaps of wrapping soon become great hills impeding our movements. We remember where we had each object we unpack—whether in Bogotá, Cúcuta, Argentina, or Venezuela. The few things that came from Bogotá are as precious as a miracle. We can't understand how they made the journey to Cúcuta—we left Bogotá in such a panic.

There is the cookie tin filled with individually mummified ceramic rabbits, a set of floppy discs, and my baby blanket. We spend hours looking at each one, dazed by the past and the heat. I run my finger along the pink silk edging of the blanket on which I slept as a baby, on which I threw myself countless days after school, which somehow made it to this apartment.

Mami has never told me this story before: Seven months after I was born and just two months before he died, Nono leaned over my crib and gathered me up in this blanket and into his arms. *Thank God,* he breathed. *The good genes have been passed down.* He joined his mouth to my ear, covered us with the tent of his hand, and whispered a long string of words. Mami listened to his susurration, watched the movement in his jaw, but when she asked what he was saying, Nono said not to worry—he was only delivering some of his knowledge down.

Knowledge long lost, which I try to remember, which Mami says I should try to forget.

Here is a gold protection from when you were a baby, Mami says, giving me a tiny charm of a fist. *Your grandfather had it made for you in gold, because gold is the language of creation.*

I examine the little gold amulet. It weighs nearly nothing on the palm of my hand, small enough to be an accessory for a doll. The amulet is a protection against the evil eye. It is called Mano Figa, and originated in Etruscan Italy. The settlers brought it with them to the New World. But I know that what Mami has said about gold is what the Muiscas believed; I've read books about it. When I ask Mami, she remains uninterested in the roots of what she's told me, saying only that it's one of the many things the forefathers said.

Sometimes I feel like I am handling random pieces of a broken plate. Like we have inherited our before, but only in fragments.

We are a biracial people who lived in secret, and nothing fits. The broken plate is what we are.

There are curanderos from the tip of Argentina up the continent to Mexico, and into the parts of the United States that used to be Mexico. There are as many curandero traditions as there are geographies—healers who use hallucinogens, herb knowledge, dreams. Sobadores focus their healing practice on holy oils, which are old recipes, through which they can massage illness out. In Colombia, we don't call Native healers curanderos, though they are medicine men. Among ourselves we say, *I went to see a Wayuu woman,* or *A Kogui man helped me with my pain.*

Though they manifest differently, all curandero traditions agree on the understanding that illness is tied to the spirit, to the things we live through, and the things we carry. But Native healers root their practice in tradition; curanderos have lost that direct connection and are fond of improvisation. Their style of healing depends on their personality, and the original traditions of each area. Some curanderos are spiritual surgeons, for example. They heal in an operating theater and don a doctor's white coat, fish out scalpels and pincers from metal trays, cut the air above the body of their patients, and sing old healing songs, blowing out smoke and taking out cancers, of the real or metaphorical kind, in their invisible surgeries.

In California, where I now live, I've seen notices for curandero classes packaged into three-week intensives, which anybody can take; in South America, however, the knowledge continues to be guarded, and cultural lineage is a prerequisite of practicing.

Nono healed through potions, herbs, dreams, and stories. He treated ailments, then looked for invisible wounds, important wellsprings of pain. Part of what made Nono a popular curandero was his ability to speak what his patients left undisclosed.

You were molested by an uncle, he'd say.

You carry a pain that belongs to your sister.
You witnessed a man die, and blame yourself.

His clients, prompted, then divulged what they had lived, and Nono listened with attention. Stories held important information. Sometimes a person could be healed by Nono's recasting and retelling what he'd been told but with subtle alterations, which provided escape from hostile places that had long required leave-taking. Sometimes an exorcism was the medicine needed. Other times Nono healed clients in dreams. At night, he focused on finding them, and his clients in turn would begin to dream of him. Sometimes in real life, Nono inhaled the illness off a person, sucking the air from their face and inviting their illness into his body, where he could survive it and heal it on his own.

Curanderos, above all, have to be able to heal themselves.

In Cúcuta, when Mami tells me I should try to forget whatever knowledge Nono whispered into my ear as a baby, I know it's because she can see that I have barely survived my own disturbances. But I don't know how to go about forgetting what I don't remember.

Mami and I are in the middle of unpacking the mini bar when Papi calls over the Internet. He is at an oil site in Libya, halfway through a five-month post. He is lonely. We know because every day he sends us short e-mails.

Hello, Family, I hope everyone is well. The way we react to the things that happen to us today define us in the future.

Let us all be happy as we are now and even more. More happiness for everyone.

Papi's company knows he is lonely too. They have offered to fly Mami in for the last two months of his contract. Because Papi is waiting for Mami's visa to go through, when he calls I assume it's about her papers. I put the phone on speaker, lay it down on the floor, and continue to unwrap Papi's set of gold-rimmed whiskey glasses, which, unbeknownst to him, I plan to sell online for the equivalent of thirty dollars. Papi doesn't know we are selling our belongings in order to pay for Nono's unearthing—but Mami says, one day, when it is over, we will tell all, and it is better to ask for forgiveness than permission.

Mami is sitting on a rug, having just woken up. She is twirling her hair and drinking the iced coffee I made her that morning, shaking her head and sucking her lips dramatically each time she sips to let me know I didn't add enough sugar. I fail to suppress a smile, then turn back to my work at the mini bar.

The reason Papi is calling, he announces, is that he's just seen Mami appear.

Mami's clone has, just a little while ago, materialized on the second-floor mezzanine of the company rental, tossing chimerical bucket after bucket of water on the wall. Papi watched her appear from directly below, on the first floor, where he was working on some graphs in the living room.

Most of the time, Papi avoids acknowledging Mami's clone, but he felt such curiosity about what she could be washing, he raced upstairs to look. By the time he reached the mezzanine, Mami's clone was gone.

Papi asks, *So—what were you washing, Sojaila?*

Mami thinks for a second. *Probably cleaning the space for my arrival.*

Oh. Okay. Satisfied, Papi hangs up.

Mami and I laugh. We retell Papi's story to each other and make fun of him for hanging up so quickly; then I call him back. When he answers, I ask him how the clone's water behaved in his vision. *Well, hija, how else does water behave? It wet the walls! It dripped down! It puddled.* I smile, imagining the water dripping from the second floor into the living room, lapping up to the couch that

Papi has told me encircles the whole room and has tasseled round pillows arranged one after another.

Do you ever think you're hallucinating?

It's a possibility, he says. *But I have seen so many strange things in my life with your mother . . . I really think she has powers.*

My mouth drops. Countless times, I've asked Papi about Mami's powers, and he has never given me a serious answer. *More powers in a fried egg,* he'd say, or *You don't believe in all those canalladas, do you, hija? You and me, we're intellectuals.*

If I consider that when my mother and father first met he was a communist, an intellectual, a youth leader, an avowed atheist, his confessed belief in something as ephemeral and abstract as Mami's splintering doesn't add up.

Because I can't let go of Papi's crossing over into belief, I try to bait him with a term I've just learned. I suggest that maybe his hallucinations are hypnopompic in nature. I came across the term online while researching epilepsy-induced hallucinations, which Paul, who my sister had now married, was experiencing. Hypnopompic hallucinations, the kind that can manifest as one is waking up from a deep sleep or seizure, are considered unexceptional.

Papi doesn't wait for me to finish. *But it doesn't matter if science can explain what I am seeing—because it doesn't verify whether what I am witnessing is happening* in *or* outside *of my brain. Can science tell me that?*

I have no answer, and Papi tells me that seeing Mami appear is how he knows that Mami is taking care of him. He feels loved.

He tells me of another recent sighting. A few months earlier, Papi was in Villahermosa, Mexico, giving presentations and holding meetings. He fell asleep early one night, and when he opened his eyes the next day, Mami was there, in his hotel room, diaphanous, standing at the foot of his bed. Sunlight filtered through her hair, and through her he could see the white wall behind her and the tan shade of the hotel floor lamp. When the apparition began to blur, Papi sprang from bed and rushed to its side. *Hold on, Sojaila, at least give me a kiss!*

The apparition's edges sharpened, like an image shifting into focus through a camera lens. It smiled, lingering. Papi leaned and, closing his eyes, he planted a kiss on the apparition's lips.

I am barely breathing, unaware of the whiskey glass in my hand. I ask Papi what it felt like, to kiss an apparition.

I am not sure. He is one second silent. *Maybe it was like kissing the air.*

Having overheard him, Mami stretches out on the cool tiles of the floor. She smiles, turning on her side, delighted.

Thank God, she says, petting her widow's peak. *My powers are still what they used to be.*

That afternoon, after we sell the whiskey-glass set and a fancy lamp, I do some calculations, and we celebrate. We now have the money to pay for the unburial. Mami and I take all the cash in an envelope to tía Perla, who tells us she'll schedule the disinterment for the next available date. She urges us to go pack, to be ready to leave at a moment's notice.

Back home, Mami and I fill a suitcase with black clothes. We stare into the open mouth of it. So many things have begun to resemble holes. Tunnels. Graves. Places where my sight drops and my mind follows. I am staring into the black of the suitcase, thinking of my grandfather's bones as they must lie in his casket, in a mimesis of sleep, when Mami asks, *Did you bring any obsidian?*

I blink. As a matter of fact, I did. I root around for my obsidian earrings in the bag where I keep my jewelry. I show Mami. She examines the black-faceted teardrops. Mami has obsidian earrings too. She takes hers out, and we stare at the pairs in silence. They are remarkably similar—same size, same teardrop shape—except mine are framed by small golden hoops. This keeps happening to us: we keep doing things independently, but identically. I want to ask Mami when she bought her earrings. Her answer would lay to rest the question of who is the original between us, and who the copy. I realize with dread that I must be the copy. I was born of her, and that concludes the argument before it can really begin. But if I inherited her moles, and the one on our shoulder blades is switched, hers on the left and mine on the right, then not only am I her copy, I must be her mirror image too.

Mami presses my earrings back into my palm.

She picks an already folded sweater from the suitcase and whips it in the air. Dust motes wheel in the light. She says: *Obsidian was one of the earliest mirrors. That is why we must wear it to the disinterment.*

Mirrors rarely come up in our conversation, just as our shared experience of amnesia is a subject we seldom broach. They belong to a family of things that feel too hot to touch.

I watch Mami refold the sweater and fit it back into the suitcase.

What? she says without looking.

Will stories in our family always repeat themselves?

I am asking about Nono and Mami appearing in two places at once, Mami and me both losing our memory, the moles. But Mami doesn't ask me to clarify. She simply shakes her head. *Qué vaina.* Then she winks. *Better watch your back—as far as I know, stories happen in threes.*

That night, I forget to do my incantations against amnesia and fall into a profound sleep. I wake up to Mami gripping my forearm. *Did you hear it?*

Hm? I raise my head, then let it drop.

The footsteps.

I sit up with a jolt, trying to remember if I locked the front door. I strain my ears and attempt to pinpoint the sounds of someone stealing through our apartment, but there is only the buzzing sound of night.

Mami says, *That was Nono. I'd recognize his footsteps anywhere.*

You mean—

In the dark, Mami throws the sheet aside, staggers to the door.

I think about stopping her from opening the door to a ghost, but I keep still as she grips the door handle and pulls.

The hall is empty. Mami stands before the pulsating dark. I don't know what she's waiting for until a breeze surges through the door. Mami turns to look at me. All I see is her profile—her face hidden—as the hall becomes a throat of sound, a whoosh, a howl, a high whistling that pulls at the ends of my hair.

6

THE DISINTERMENT

The call arrives from tía Perla: *It's set. We leave today.* Tía Perla tells us that Fabián is driving, and they'll be in Bucaramanga, where the unburial will take place, that evening. I buy airplane tickets for Mami and me. It's only a forty-five-minute flight, and it's not too expensive. The hotel is outside what I have budgeted for us, so when Mami goes out to buy what she calls *disinterment supplies*, I put more things for sale online, and hope Papi will forgive us.

On the airplane the next day, I rest my temple on the window and think, *My grandfather's bones, my grandfather's bones, my grandfather's bones.* I look down at the silver stretch of the Chicamocha River, which from this height looks like a great silver snake gliding along the base of the green-tufted mountains of the cordillera.

On Mami's hand there's also a snake, but this one is gold. The ring coils around her thumb, glints at me, its glimmer catching my eyes when I am not looking at it. I know it's some sort of amulet.

Mami, I say. I want to ask about lagoon spirits, who are women with scales, and snakes, both of them born from fire. I want to know if they come from the same fire, or different fires. I want to ask about the golden snake she wears, which I know next to nothing about, but Mami doesn't hear me when I call her. She is lost in thought, filing her nails.

After a time, Mami blows at the white dust accumulated in

her nail beds. I watch the powder spiral into the air, and then I breathe it in.

The following day, when all of us arrive at the Jardines de las Colinas cemetery, where Nono is buried, I am thinking about dreams. Dreams as the burrow of the great beyond. Subterranean hillways, narrows, tunnels. In my family, we study dreams and seek to decode their architecture. We greet one another with the question *Did you dream last night?*, and if we want to ask after someone we love, we do so by saying, *Do you know what so-and-so has been dreaming these days?*

Dreams are why we speak of Nono in the present tense, because, even though he's dead, we continue to see him in dreams.

Dreams are how we find ourselves in this strange homecoming, at the bottom of the mountain of El Cacique, where we have buried our dead, on a sunny day, wearing black, ready. We have on face masks and latex gloves, and powdered sulfur inside our shoes to ward off what Mami calls *cemetery ethereal larvae*. None of us has heard of *cemetery ethereal larvae*, but the words are enough to paint a picture. We follow Mami's instructions and coat the insides of our shoes in the neon-green powder, even though it smells like a swamp and crunches against our socks with every step.

We meander up among the gravestones. Cousin Fabián and I fall behind Mami and tía Perla, who don't exactly remember the site of Nono's resting place. Fabián and I are nervous. We are trying not to giggle and are doing our best not to step on anyone's grave, but when we do, we check to see who it is we've disturbed. At a polite distance away, we speculate about their deaths. For example—the woman who was buried back in the 1970s by her husband, the only surviving relation marked on her tombstone: did he kill her, or did she die in childbirth? We deliberate. At the first crest of the mountain, Mami and tía Perla have stopped. We come to their side and stop too.

Before us is a dug grave.

The earth that filled it is heaped next to it in a mound. I think: *How strange to shovel earth out of earth.* And then three gravediggers, whom I had not noticed before, step forward and nod. They are wearing face masks and gloves, like us, but also yellow boots and royal-blue jumpsuits. They would seem sinister except that on their heads are thin, gauzy hair caps, which give them more of an intimate, soft, domestic look. One of them raises a solemn gloved hand, and commands our silence and respect. He announces they are ready to uncover the casket but warns us to stand back, in case of methane gas. I don't move. How can I explain to him that this is essentially the first time I will remember meeting my grandfather, even if it is just his bones?

Fabián must sense my unwillingness, because he glances at me before arguing with the gravedigger, *But we have our faces covered.* Fabián is a veterinarian, so he has clout—of some type.

The gravedigger says that if there's gas trapped in the grave the face masks won't do much to protect us from fainting or even spontaneous death. I remain unfazed. Dying at the sight of my grandfather's bones somehow doesn't seem to me like the worst fate. Like any good Colombian, I know I must die, and so I yearn for a good death, an exit that is both meaningful and dramatic. *It's been twenty-eight years, señor.* I speak loudly but it comes out muffled through the mask. I know it's been exactly twenty-eight years, because that's how old I am, and I am as old in life as Nono is in death. His body has been disintegrating at the same rate at which my body has been growing. We are two at the edge of the known and the unknown.

One of the gravediggers nods and shrugs to the others. *I bet there's no more gas.*

All right, says the one. *But if I tell you to stand back again, you must.*

I give a little grunt of approval, though I am not sure I will obey.

The gravediggers lower a yellow rope into the grave. One of them disappears after it, then climbs back up. He's hooked the rope to the concrete slab sealing the tomb. The gravediggers heave, lifting the slab, and drop it onto the grass near a neighboring tombstone. Immediately I rush to the edge of the hole and stare down.

It is so black I can't tell what anything is.

The one gravedigger steps up to my right, clears his throat by my ear, says, *You could have died.* Then he says for everyone to hear, *The casket has disintegrated. The corrosion is high. We'll have to pull the body out part by part.* He steps back to fit one arm at a time into a yellow butcher's apron.

I continue gazing down into the black. After a while, as my eyes adjust, I see pieces of a lilac ribbon. It amazes me how such color has survived, but it shouldn't: the ribbon is plastic. I blink. Suddenly I spot the skull. Then, among the clumps of earth, I see white finger bones.

Everything snaps into place.

The finger bones are peeking out of a graying coat sleeve, and they are wrapping delicately around the base of a turquoise cross. Here and there, I can see the cloth of Nono's pants emerging from the dirt. The white finger bones holding the last movement of my grandfather's body feels like something I am not supposed to see, so I turn away and close my eyes. Tía Perla is standing next to me. She tells Fabián the cross they buried Nono with was bronze, and Fabián explains that it is blue now because it has oxidized. *Notice all the things the cross has stained blue: Nono's chest, the coat sleeve, the earth.* Mami is quiet too; then I hear the sound of her camera shutter.

The gravedigger wearing the yellow apron climbs back down into the hole, and the other two stay up top, receiving parts. There is a long steel tray for the remains lying on the grass. They transfer my grandfather to it in handfuls. The first things to be placed on the tray are small bones and more colored ribbons, but then it's small pieces of paper, which get carried to the tray along with lumps of earth or cloth and unidentifiable matter.

Mami and tía Perla begin to count the papers.

I know the papers are the requests people sneaked into Nono's casket the day of his burial, like the ones tía Perla found half planted in the grass atop Nono's grave after the shared dream. When a curandero dies, it is customary to leave him with encargos. The curandero will then carry his people's errands to the afterworld, where his powers are said to multiply. But in his last days, Nono said his powers were waning. His load was too heavy, and he took to drink. He had asked Mami to keep any and all requests and prayers away from his casket. But family members and strangers alike disguised their requests behind flower arrangements and roses. The day of the burial, Mami and tía Perla intercepted at least forty requests. They repeatedly announced Nono's wishes to be left in peace. They grew furious, then dejected, and finally resigned themselves to people's disrespect. They supervised the long procession of mourners.

At the time, Mami unfurled and read some of the prayers she had intercepted. She wanted to know what was being asked of her father. Of these, there are three that she remembers:

Don Rafael Curandero of Ocaña, by this paper I hold you
    from your rest until you give me a house.
Rafael Contreras look over my children; they are in so
    much need.
Rafael by my will you will dwell among the souls in
    purgatory until you grant me revenge.

At the cemetery, I hover over the steel tray and look at the papers, wondering how many wishes were fulfilled. I have no way to find out. I had imagined I would be able to read them, but as I bend over, I see they have turned crinkly and black. There are at least thirty of them.

The gravedigger in the yellow apron is crouching at the bottom of the tomb. He is looking at nothing, it seems, but then he sweeps aside dirt and pinches at two points.

He pulls, and a light linen coat emerges. He places his hand beneath it, at the middle of its back, and as he does so, a matching pair of pants begins to surface. He pulls at this until he can slip his other hand beneath. I imagine he is trying to keep all the bones together. It is a logical, simple gesture, but I am shocked at how compressed Nono can be, leveled inside a coat and pants, draped over this man's arms.

The man in the grave swings his arms up to the man aboveground, and they transfer Nono from one pair of arms to the other—because the suit is not a suit filled with bones, but, to us and to them, for this brief moment, a person.

The man aboveground drapes the coat along the length of the tray, but the pants are loose and fold underneath. Nono is headless: just a linen suit he wore on his wedding day, dusted in decay. Then the skull is added, and, as a finishing touch, the shoes. All the ingredients of humanity on a tray.

After a while, tía Perla says, *How black the skull is.*

It's normal, Fabián answers. *It's the humidity.*

For the next twenty minutes, I don't know where the gravediggers go. I don't know what anyone is doing. All I am conscious of is that I am kneeling on the grass in front of my grandfather's bones, inhaling the scent of deep, dark earth that wafts off his remains.

I am hearing all of the stories retold to me. I can almost hear his voice. His bones are a conjuring.

Fabián, tía Perla, Mami. Bucaramanga, 2012

The gravediggers. Bucaramanga, 2012

Nono. Bucaramanga, 2012

II

EXHUMATION

—◡—

And I circled the well until I flew from myself
to what isn't of it.

—MAHMOUD DARWISH

Let me call my anxiety, desire, *then.*
Let me call it, a garden.

—NATALIE DIAZ

Mami's stories are peppered with the recurrent words En la vida real . . . En sueños . . . , *to mark the crossings her stories constantly toe. Dreams are as important as waking life. One story leads into another and the next, spiraling out and then in, until, at the end, we return to Nono and his bones, though in some measure we have not left them at all.*

In real life . . . , *she begins.*

7

MIDNIGHT

In real life, just after I was born, in 1984, exactly at midnight in a fluorescent-lit hospital room in Bogotá, Mami lay sore and spent on the cot where she'd just given birth, gradually losing the movement in her arms.

At first her fingers became still, then her forearms, and finally, by the end of the month, her shoulders. Soon her arms hung helplessly at her sides. She could not will them to move.

In the days after my birth, the doctors kept Mami under their care, calling her a *mystery of science*. She had developed advanced arthritis from one day to the next. On the hospital cot, the nurses placed me over Mami's chest, and Mami maneuvered me with her knees until she got me to latch on. This was all practice for when Mami went home and had to feed me on her own.

I know that inscrutable things happen all the time to women after childbirth. I have heard of reappearing wisdom teeth, extra nipples blooming where there were none, skin peeling off as in a sunburn.

But everything to my family is a sign.

While the doctors ordered X-rays for Mami's hands, Mami's sister—whom Mami has now been mad at for tens of years and only refers to as *The Same as Always*—stood outside her hospital room and speculated (loudly enough to be overheard, and with anyone who happened by) that a midnight birth bespoke the devil and that Mami was a witch who had paid for her powers with the mobility of her arms.

In the telephone-gossiping circles of the family, five of Mami's siblings said Mami's sudden-onset arthritis was suspiciously suggestive of God's disfavor. Tía Perla argued that it was an outcome of malnutrition. Tía Nahía wondered if the arthritis could not be karmic payback for something Mami had done. Tío Ariel countered that it was obviously the consequence of Mami's knowing the secrets. And while Nono placed the blame with Papi's family, whom he accused of hexing Mami, Papi's family, for their part, prayed that it would all end in divorce.

At the hospital, as I finished feeding and the nurses tucked me into a nearby crib, Mami strained to pick up the sounds of my distress. They never came. I didn't cry when I was hungry, didn't cry when I soiled my diaper, didn't cry when I couldn't sleep.

Mami likes to tell me: *Even then, you'd rather die than ask for help.*

She heard the wailing of other babies, and that's how she remembered to check on me. She tells me I did like to laugh, though. I laughed and laughed.

Mami was not perplexed by the decreased mobility of her arms. She had expected her second childbirth would take something from her, just as the first.

When Mami gave birth to my sister two years earlier, it was the visions of ghosts that went. Nono said it was normal: to give life was to lose some of it. But Mami was lonely without the ghosts. When she shook a stranger's hand, she no longer saw if they had any translucent companions. There were no women levitating across rooms, no bedeviled children. There was also the matter of her business. Without seeing ghosts, how would she broker deals between the living and the dead?

People paid Mami good money to do exorcisms. Whenever Mami was contracted to fix a haunting, her clients expected a show. They presumed she would sprinkle holy water and burn bundled herbs. Instead, Mami borrowed a tall drinking glass, filled it with tap water, set it on a table, and sat across from an empty chair. Mami was a lazy exorcist. Instead of doing the actual work of driving ghosts out, she held negotiation talks.

Listen, she began, within earshot of her clients. *I don't want to be here. You don't want to be here. But we have a problem. I need the money. So here we are. The people here want you out. If I reach out to one of your loved ones and get them a message, will you leave?*

The negotiations could take a number of days. Some ghosts were wicked, others stubborn. Others lived, unaware, in a loop. While most jobs required little effort on Mami's part, they did call for her expertise and training—anyone could, after all, light a candle, but only Mami could get the desired result. And when the ghosts left and the hauntings stopped, Mami's clients marveled that she had *quote unquote* done nothing but set a glass of water on a table to make it work. In the end, it didn't matter if ghosts were invisible to her. All it took to negotiate was to listen.

But on the hospital cot in Bogotá, as Mami lay ruminating about ghosts, wondering if the movement in her arms would return, tuning her ear for my crying—that's when she realized she had lost that too. If she put her ear to the wind, to the place from which the thin, ghostly voices came, she heard nothing. The spirits who bothered her at night, screaming into her ear—they were gone. There were no voices whispering now, no pleas, no threats, no rants against cold and hunger. The silence disturbed her.

Hearing and seeing ghosts were abilities that could come and go, Mami knew. What was divinely given could be divinely taken. The secrets—the instructions for harnessing what abilities she had left, the knowledge of prayers and plants, the rituals and observances—those she still retained, and in this she took refuge.

When Mami was discharged from the hospital, she continued to frequent the radiography floor. There, in dark rooms with small, grated windows, doctors exhausted their tests, gathered their evidence, ran up her bill. They provided a diagnosis, then disclosed there was nothing they could do. Like many others who were failed by Western medicine, Mami turned to Nono.

The doctors called the frozenness in her arms arthritis; Nono called it paralysis. Nono began by treating Mami in dreams. He trekked, in sleep, to forests where she was rosy and napping amid daffodils; to her apartment, where her eyes were tinged yellow; to the hospital where she had just given birth. In those varied dreamscapes, Nono prepared her an infusion from a mysterious plant he hadn't seen before. As Mami drank, Nono tried to examine more closely the leaves and seeds, but his sight blurred and, at last, he stirred awake.

In the apartment where Mami and Papi lived in Bogotá, the phone rang and rang. When she felt like taking the exercise, Mami bent at the waist, unhooked the receiver with her chin, fit the side of her face onto the telephone, and spoke. Her sisters and brothers asked after her health. Her friends hoped to hold the newborn. And Nono craved to prove that Papi's family was responsible for her paralysis. Each day he called, divulging more. Mami had been fed a poisoned meal. A plate of spaghetti, soft chicken, and queso antioqueño. There was a red sauce, Nono offered another day, into which a tincture of cassava root had been stirred. Papi's mother had done it. Mami knew cassava root was poisonous, but even though she admitted that her mother-in-law *had* served her such a meal shortly before she gave birth to me, Mami couldn't imagine that Papi's mother was capable of such hatred.

Papi's family did, however, detest Mami.

They were many shades darker than her, but some had been born with piercing green eyes. They said of themselves, for this reason, that they were white.

Papi didn't think of himself as white. His hair was too black, his eyes too caramel, his skin too dark for him to call himself anything but brown. His family called him Negrito, just like Mami's family called her Negrita. It was a term of endearment, but it was also meant to cut, to signify *lesser than*, the darkest children.

Papi's family hated Mami because she had never aspired to fit in, didn't go to church, refused to learn her place, and then there was the chaos that had ensued when Papi and Mami visited them two years earlier, in 1982, after my sister, Ximena, was born.

Papi and Mami got to his family's after nine hours on the road. It was late at night. Papi's family surrounded him and rushed him inside, placing a glass with ice and whiskey in his hand—leaving Mami at the door with her baby. Two of his sisters stayed up to see to the topping off of his drink. They soothed and cooed. Why had he abandoned his family? He no longer sent them money to pay for rent and groceries. They could barely make ends meet. He knew they struggled to find employment. They loved him so, and so they could say it: the woman he married had emasculated him. Papi spat, annoyed. *I'm a new father, not less of a man.*

Prove it, his sisters dared. *Beat your wife in front of us.*

Mami stared at her drunken husband, and when he remained quiet one second too long, she rose and entered the bedroom where they were to spend the night, made sure my sister was tightly bound in the soft terry of her baby blanket, then came out and unsheathed a machete that had been hanging as decoration on the wall. She licked its blade on the cement floor, making it spark, inviting him to try to lay one finger on her. The commotion woke up everyone else in the house, but in spite of the women's pleas, not one of the seven men who set foot into the room dared step an inch closer to Mami, either to overpower her or to retrieve the weapon. Finally, the men clucked, and concluding that this was not their problem, they returned to bed; Papi announced he was going to sit for a moment to think, then began to snore on the couch. The women, too, retired. Within seconds, the house fell into a deep, expectant silence, and Mami, satisfied, lay down next to her baby and found profound rest.

She awoke to a chorus of whisperings. Papi's family was in the kitchen, discussing her inability to be a good wife. Mami breezed in, poured herself coffee, and handed Papi the baby. She sat among them, agreeing, adding that she was born to rule, and she was born to recline. Anybody who thought differently was denying their eyes.

Now, bedbound and reclining in a way she hadn't envisioned, grieving the loss of hearing the dead, Mami was stuck at home in their rented apartment in South Bogotá. A small one-floor place in the middle of an unsafe neighborhood, it was the best they could afford. Meanwhile, Papi's sisters were in town, luring him into bars. He assumed they were celebrating his fatherhood, but after a round of drinks, they introduced him to attractive women who just *happened by*—white and conservative, dreaming of keeping house and rearing children. Papi rejected the women, but he was hurt by his sisters' allegations about his *diminishing masculinity.* He obsessed about proving his power—to himself, to his family, and most of all to Mami.

There are stories in every family whose harm we are supposed to keep under wraps. In mine we call these stories *secrets of ultra-tomb.* They're the kind you take to the grave. But Mami is a tumba abierta. Every harm she's supposed to bury, she speaks.

I am an open tomb as well.

Papi locked Mami inside their apartment. Each weekday, he poured his coffee into a thermos, left Mami's liquefied meals out on the counter for her, got his briefcase, turned the key from the outside, and went to work. Mami had become able, through Nono's nightly visitations, to lift and move her arms, though bolts of pain coursed through her body. Stinging, she tried the knob and found it bolted.

Why did you lock me in? Mami would ask when he returned.

The door's been unlocked all this time, Papi said, twisting and releasing the handle to prove his point. *Did you think it was not?*

Mami has said to me, *Who your father is to me as a man is not who he is to you as a father.* Nona said as much to Mami about Nono when Mami was little, and Mamaria to Nona when Nona was but a girl. But while Mamaria and Nona could not escape their lovers' abuse, Mami refused to let Papi win, and she mocked his attempts at control.

Twenty minutes after Papi locked her in, Mami would lean out one of their second-floor windows, the one without bars, and, tensing her lower lip, give a shrill whistle. She had befriended a neighbor, who waited for her signal each day and brought a ladder to lean against her sill.

Before escaping the apartment, Mami cast a prayer of protection, leaving me and my sister under the watch of her ancestors, which is to say, of her ghosts. (For years, these same ghosts would be our babysitters anytime Papi and Mami wanted a night out alone.) Mami climbed out the window and navigated slowly down the ladder. Because she couldn't grip the rungs, she had to rely on her sense of balance. At the bottom, her neighbor, a young and handsome music teacher who didn't leave for the public school until the afternoons, waited for her. *Leave him,* he regularly entreated. *I'll answer for your children, if that's what you fear.*

Was Mami afraid? If I ask her directly, she says she was not. She had always had a surplus of admirers, men who offered to take in her and her babies and give her whatever she wanted, and a community of friends who offered her the same. Papi's efforts to control her made her laugh. *Pobre güevón,* she said then, and still says on occasion now. He was insecure and immature. He wanted to exude authority and power, but these were qualities he did not have. They were, as it happened, the very air that Mami breathed.

Released from the locked apartment, Mami would go out with her friends. They picked her up at appointed times and took her for coffees and smoothies. At nearby discotheques, where they played salsa during the day, Mami danced cheek to cheek with other men. When milk began to seep through her bra and shirt, this was the alarm that let her know it was time to return.

Mami was intent on generating an abundant supply of rumors. The discotheques she frequented were near where Papi's friends went to work. She knew it was only a matter of time before word reached him, and when it did, he'd have to wonder if he had really locked the door or just dreamt it; he'd have to question his reality, just as he'd feebly tried to make her do.

One day, Papi came home and pored over the lock. He bolted and unbolted it, then took a screwdriver to the mechanism. Mami went to laugh in another room. The sounds of his confusion as he disassembled the lock bubbled softly around her like a spa pool. Finally, he came to tell her the lock was broken and a locksmith was on his way.

A few days later, when Mami was still riding the high of this poetic justice, Nono called. At last, he'd struck upon the medicine she needed. He had seen it in a dream. At a valley along the cordillera where filtered sunlight fell over a meadow tall trees blossomed with red, sweet-smelling flowers. He had gone in search of that valley, and had returned today with bags of the flowers ready. He'd bought a ticket to Bogotá and would be at her doorstep within a week. A farmer near Bogotá who wanted to rid his land of a hex was hiring Nono and paying for his ticket. He would see and touch her one last time before he was called to go.

Y eso? Mami asked. *Where are you going?*

She heard him inhale.

To where they never return.

8

WHEN YOU UNEARTH HAUNTED

TREASURE

W_hen you unearth haunted treasure, you're supposed to trace a circle on the ground; recite the sequence of creation in order and in reverse._

These were incomplete instructions Mami once overheard Nono give his nephew, who was going treasure hunting for the first time with the men. Mami wanted to know the secret about hunting for enchanted treasure, but Nono had refused. Ten years old, she stood breathless on the other side of his closed office door. But she never heard more than the first three steps. Nono must have sensed her. He flung his door open and discovered her there, crouching, listening in.

There are many types of haunted treasure: Secrets long buried, come to light. Knowledge long lost, then returned.

Even Nono would become something we'd unearth.

In Ocaña, enchanted treasure exudes supernatural light. It is said to glow only before a chosen person, or indiscriminately during Holy Week. Wherever it is buried, it breaks out through the soil in golden beams.

Some treasures are colonial-era sacks full of gold coins, known as guacas. These were buried in a time of war by people on the run who no doubt hoped one day to return. Older, Native burials of gold artifacts and nuggets are called múcuras. They were made as offerings to the deities of the earth, or stowed with loved ones for their use in the afterlife. There are more guacas than múcuras, and only guacas are cursed.

The intention with which something is laid into the earth matters.

When the Europeans arrived, they stared after the gold that Indigenous people wore, clasped on their arms and septums, plating their chests—how the sun fevered brightly on the surface— and lost their minds. They died in droves, slogging through jungle and river, racked with a bottomless hunger, in search of more and more Indigenous villages to raid, more of everything to loot and claim as theirs. They skimmed from what they stole for the Crown, buried this in secret to keep for themselves, and thus created the first guacas.

Now those who don't know or don't follow the procedures for unearthing guacas can become infected with the ghost disease, a spectral variant of what the Europeans suffered from, and which spread all over the continent.

From then to now, Colombians have had plenty of occasion to bury their valuables. Armed militias, embattled with one another or the government, have roved the country on and off for most of our history, collecting made-up taxes in order to finance war or enrich themselves. People hide what they have in the earth, so it won't be taken as war tax. People fleeing modern wars also bury what they have. Those pots full of bills, rings, earrings, and bangles rolled into cloth are also known as guacas.

We call our perpetual state of war the Conflict, and nobody really agrees on when it began. The government starts the count fifty-seven years ago, when it began its war against communist-allied people. Other people maintain it began seventy-three years ago, with the civil war previous to the current one, and the magnicide that caused it: the killing of Jorge Eliécer Gaitán, a presidential candidate on whom the poor and oppressed had laid their hopes. It wasn't our first magnicide. By then, the assassination of our political leaders was so common that we had already invented a word for this type of murder.

Others believe the Conflict began one hundred years ago—with the violent skirmishes between dispossessed farmers and land-owners in the coffee-growing regions of Colombia that led to the magnicide, that led to the civil war previous to the past one, that led to the current war.

Recently, the government declared the current war over, book-ending the conflict by signing a peace treaty with FARC, our larg-est guerrilla group. But neo-guerrillas, police, and paramilitaries still continue to enact the same violent cycles as before, resulting in massacres every month.

I am with those who say we have lived in a state of violence since colonization—that the conflicts between farmers and land-owners of the 1920s are echoes of the founding of the New World. The agricultural system of the 1920s—as well as its inspiration, the colonial encomienda—kept (or, in colonial times, enslaved) a peasant workforce of Black and Indigenous descent in a highly destructive and orchestrated oppression while lifting up landown-ers of European lineage.

Stories of people finding guacas make it from time to time to the local newspapers. In 1995, a farmer in Antioquia found three gua-cas, a rich bounty that ended up ruining his life. By the time he talked to the reporter, he was on the street pulling on a cart, hav-ing lost his home, his job, and his family. In Ocaña, in 2007, a con-struction worker found a múcura. He was finishing up pouring a layer of foundation when the ground erupted into a glow. Alone at the site, he edged toward the mysterious radiance. He pushed aside a rock to get to it, but the light disappeared. The man leapt after the rock, which tumbled down the hill. When he picked it up, he saw it wasn't a rock at all but a Native vase filled with gold nug-gets. The base had cracked, releasing the gold. The man gathered the gold into his shirt, sold it by the pound, and, with the money, moved and bought a house in Medellín.

Everywhere in Ocaña, the land seems to hold once-loved, precious things. Everyone I have asked in Colombia knows somebody who has found treasure, as well as somebody who lost their mind after impelling a treasure's haunt.

When Mami was a young girl, every year, Nono went questing for haunted gold.

His younger brothers, Nil and Manuel, arrived, always by burro, a day before the beginning of Holy Week. Nil told Mami ghost stories, sagas about his encounters with lagoon spirits and a mountain ghost called the Whistler, which materialized only as a sound. If the Whistler was heard as if far away, it was actually near; when it sounded near, it was far. Manuel was more reticent, but he was Mami's favorite. He arrived with a parrot perched atop his head, and an iguana lazing about his burro's back.

The brothers drank that night, and the next day, in the darkening evening, they decamped with rifles, divination tools, aguardiente, amulets, and staffs of command, which, in Nono's lineage, were given to those who became curanderos and which were fashioned after inherited Indigenous traditions. Manuel, Nono, and Nil climbed the mountain, wandered the hills, shared the bottle of alcohol. They were boasting of all they would do if they ever saw signs of treasure when, at a horizon of night, a glare flashed into view. They ran to the spot. Drunk and excited, they dug. One meter down was a pot of gold.

Or who knows what really happened?

The men forgot to follow the instructions for unearthing haunted treasure, and afterward, they each told a different story. Nil said he saw flames licking the underside of a pot at the bottom of the hole. Manuel said he blinked and the gold disappeared, the pot was empty, and then there was no pot at all. Nono said the hole heaved out a dark and terrible whirlwind, and he shrank before it and sprinted away. Though he knew what to do, he was drunk, and therefore helpless. Manuel and Nil hastened after Nono, yelling, hysterical, until they slipped back under the forest cover.

Nobody knows if there was ever really gold in the pot, or what the ghost was, or anything at all. The three of them slept in a cave, and the next morning, when they retraced their steps to search for the hole they had dug, they found nothing.

What is known is that, after that night, Nil began to dig holes.

He opened small pits all over his garden, then around the perimeter of his house. He was rooting after an ever-migrating metallic noise that nobody heard but him. Coins fell and filled his ears in a waterfall of sound. Wherever he heard it, that's where he dug. It was the same pot of gold they had seen in the mountains, he was sure, calling to be unearthed.

Whereas the sound had first appeared outside, now he heard it inside his house. There it was, in the wall dividing the kitchen and the living room. He hammered a screwdriver into the wall, triangulating for the sound, until he opened a wide cavity. Next, he removed the tiles in his kitchen and dug. No matter where he shoveled, he found a void.

The sound of falling coins haunted Nono too. There was no cure for it. This is what happened when the process of digging up a guaca was botched. Nono descended to the plaza to look for the witches' mail and get word to his brother Nil. He recited his message to the old woman: *Nil, my brother, I hope you are well. The only thing left to do is to try to outlast the ghost and resist its provocations. It's important you never dig for the gold while infected with the fever: the ghost will only become more powerful. If we can withstand the haunting, without caving in to temptation, it will release its treasure.*

The woman, a professional, remained impassive as Nono recited the message and, giving a curt nod, received from him a few coins. Mami remembers her cheeks, how they were leathery and deep brown, creased by age, and, she imagined, continually kissed by sun. Nono continued to ignore the call of the gold, whose din increased as he lay down. He let it become a noise that mingled with the calls of the birds, the racket of crickets at night.

When Nono got word back through the witches' mail, a few

weeks had gone by. Nil's wife reported that her husband was in a deep delirium; was there nothing Nono could do? Similar reports came each week, until Nil edged back to his usual grasp of reality, though the digging never ceased.

It was around then that Nono woke up sure he did not hunger for the gold. He heard the waterfall of coins, but they no longer dredged up feelings of avarice; he could let the moment pass, knowing he was free of the ghostly infection. Then, later, while he was collecting curative herbs for patients from his garden, he heard the metal tinkling beckon again. The sound grew louder as he wandered through the forest of bushes with ruby-red coffee berries at the back of his house. Beneath vines hanging from a palm tree, he shoveled. A fountain of clear water sprang from the earth.

Crystalline, Mami called it. *Holy.*

Nono built an adobe fountain there and called it healing water. He dipped his hands in the water when he wanted to cure someone. He sent word to his brother through the witches' mail, telling him to come. Nono figured he could probably heal Nil with the water the treasure had released.

While Nono waited for his brother, the people of Cristo Rey came to see the water and receive its blessings. The local Catholic priest, who, unlike the Catholic church, didn't see anything wrong with how Nono healed or prayed, came to their house and held Sunday mass by the fountain, to pay his respects to the miracle.

For some reason, Nono's other younger brother, Manuel, never heard the sound of coins. Nono and Nil didn't know why he had been spared.

When Nil finally turned up and tethered his burro by Nono's door, it was Holy Week again. He was thin, and his eyes drifted nervously from ground to sky. He was distracted, chewing at his lip, asking Nono if he did not want to go treasure hunting again. Nono flinched to see his brother so frail, and led him directly to the water. There Nono prayed and washed his brother so he would be released from the haunt.

Some say Nil got better right away, others that it took many days until he became the man he was before.

But a year later, Mami woke in the middle of the night, needing to use the outhouse, and walked with a candle through the dark halls. When she stepped outside, she discerned a tall figure standing in the middle of the backyard with a shovel—a terrifying ghost.

Mami dropped the candle. She had been sighting ghosts for four years now, ever since her accident, and still they always managed to startle her. She was in the habit of needing to relieve herself in the middle of the night, and it was especially then, when she was alone and sleepy, that they appeared. One night, she'd had to walk through the living room as it became animated with ghost murmurings of the twenty mysteries of the Rosary. Another night, pale shins pierced through the ceiling into the kitchen, and the relaxed toes of the ghost who must have been stuck between floors twitched sleepily. It didn't help that there were also real manifestations that could be easily mistaken for apparitions: once, a shocking casket, which unbeknownst to Mami someone in the village had left for safekeeping overnight with Nono, took up space in the middle of the room. Mami was never sure what she might encounter, whether in this plane or another, and she was always on edge.

Outside, Mami bent to pick up the snuffed-out candle. Ghost or not, she really had to go. In the dark, she walked toward the lighted figure, deciding that she could at least find out who the ghost was, or what it wanted. But as she drew near, she saw it was only Nil. His lantern was on the ground, throwing light up on his chin and nostrils, making his face askew. Mami was relieved. She was about to mutter a greeting when Nil wiped his brow, unaware she was there. He was staring at the ground. His shirt was wet and clung to his chest.

And opening at his feet was a deep hole full of nothing.

———

Nono had warned Mami to be careful about unearthing what had been long undisturbed.

Who was to say what happened to something after decades of being in communion with the dirt?

If a guaca released a haunt, a person could become infirm, sweat, turn in the night, hallucinate, and sleepwalk in search of relief for excruciating hungers. To unearth haunted treasure, a person needed to have the stamina to sit with pain as if in a garden.

It was only then that a haunt unsnarled its grip, and surrendered its treasure.

9

BLACK SMOKE

Nono arrived on a weekday in April of 1985 at Mami's door. He sat erect in her dining room in a wool poncho and his aguadeño hat, reporting no turbulence on his flight. He had heard whispering in his ear, *Rafael, you are going to die,* and thus he understood that he'd be dead by the time the rainfall season let up.

Nono was always announcing his own death. When Mami was young, every time he caught a bad fever he called his children. *Children, line up by the bed, because I am going to give you my last blessing.* Mami's siblings sniffled throughout the many years of that repeated scene. They bowed their heads as Nono put a hand over their crowns and whispered, *May God always be with you.* Mami had been devastated at the prospect of Nono's dying, but then she grew bored, and, later, irritated. *Papá,* she told him, *either die or don't—but leave me out of it, every year it's the same with you. I'm going back to sleep.*

There were many warnings of death. A knock on the door at night. A dream of getting married with a spouse whose face could not be discovered. A one-second drag in the movement of one's image in the mirror. A ghost veil lowered over the soon-to-be-deceased.

In the intervening days, as Nono had been traveling and on his way to her, Mami had heard disembodied knocking on her bedroom door. Now, as she beheld Nono across the table, she saw a smoky black film glazing over her father's eyes. The ghost veil.

Of all Nono's children who happened to be born with a gift, tía Nahía is the one most able to see the ghost veil. While Mami can only perceive it in the eyes of someone soon to die if she stares with attention, tía Nahía can spot the veil from a distance, concealing a person's whole face. She sees it even when she's in the middle of something else: running errands, paying for vegetables, talking on her cell phone. In the 1990s in Cúcuta, when tía Nahía lived with Nona in the family's last house, their neighborhood came under guerrilla occupation. When Nahía stepped outside, everywhere she looked were people whose heads were cloaked in black smoke. Two out of four men playing dominoes at the curb were marked for death; so was one of the women washing laundry in the middle of the dirt road; and so were the children chasing one another down the street. Tía Nahía stopped going out. She adopted a fluffy white dog and spent her days lingering idly about Nona's garden, where she was safe from knowing.

At her dining table, Mami's joints ached as she reached for Nono's hands. He was cold and sweaty to the touch. His hands carried tremors. She knew that he was going through alcohol withdrawal, and that he was heartbroken.

Seven years ago, after Nono and Nona separated, Nono had fallen in love with another woman, and five years ago, that woman had disappeared. The woman had lived alone in the forest. Nono described her to Mami as solitary, earthy. Mami did not breathe a word, but the witch Nona regularly saw told her of it.

Nona hated the idea that her estranged husband could be happy with someone else. She paid the witch to tamper with Nono's destiny, so that his and his new love's paths would never cross again. This is what Nono said, and also what Nona confirmed. When Nono returned to the forest, the door to his lover's house was open and everything inside was broken.

People in the nearby town said it had been paramilitaries.

This was war.

Men raped and pillaged. Sometimes the paramilitaries kidnapped women and took them to their camps. Sometimes the men made money off the women's forced prostitution. Sometimes the paramilitaries coerced women to participate in improvised beauty pageants where the top prize was being chosen, and therefore enslaved. Sometimes the men got carried away and had to disappear the corpses.

Nono was bereft. He accused Nona of asking for the death of the woman he loved. She denied it, said she had not *asked* for the woman's death.

The never-to-be life with the woman he loved was a knowing that undid him by the hour. He moved to Bucaramanga to be far from Nona and near his third son, Ariel. In Bucaramanga, Nono continued to heal clients and spent all the money he got on rent, women, and drink. He downed whiskey with tío Ariel in taverns. In each other's living rooms, they would sing ballads about loneliness and heartbreak, distracting themselves with plans to hunt treasure.

Mami was not ready for Nono to leave her. She had two baby girls and hands she could not use, and her gifts of seeing and hearing spirits had gone. She had at least handled Papi's abuse; the new front door lock that had been installed could be unbolted from the inside; and she had continued to torment him, filling his ears, apropos of nothing, with stories about how guilty men often saw dangers where there were none, took leave of their minds, and precipitated their own demise.

But Mami did not want to burden Nono with her problems. Instead, she asked about what plans he had for fixing the hex.

Farmers were always wanting to hire Nono. When droughts prolonged, pest control didn't work, the economy soured, or animals got sick beyond the scope of Western medicine and strategy, they turned to him.

Once, in Ocaña, when Mami was twelve, Nono brought her along on a job. No explanation for what she saw—in a field of cacao, birdsong, and Nono stepping in a dance. Caterpillars dropped from the trees to the ground.

Now, in her living room, Nono told her the farm he had been

hired to fix had cows with worms, and stalking paramilitaries. Nono had plans to feed blessed tobacco to the cows, and against the paramilitaries he would bury around the periphery of the farm small satchels of disorientation, the contents of which I am not at liberty to disclose.

Mami and Nono sat in silence. Nono fanned his fingers over hers. *I can see that you're sad. Think that I am going on a trip. Just like when you were little and I packed my bags to go live away from you—like that. Think that I am going; but never believe that I do not exist.*

In the kitchen, Nono spread the bundles of red flowers he had brought for Mami. He set to the work of boiling and blessing the greenery. The tree pods were oblong and tawny. Nono cracked them to get to the small seeds inside. He ground the seeds into a fine powder, and from this and the leaves he made drafts. He balanced cupfuls of the bitter water on Mami's lips and tipped them back so she could drink. The tang of it was awful and sharp, like nothing she had ever tasted. *Like lightning,* Mami told me.

In the weeks that passed, Nono's drafts made the pain in Mami's arms decrease. The inflammation of her joints eased. Mami wept in relief. She was nearly able to grip with her hands. Exuberant, Nono and Mami went out and spoiled each other, Nono clasping my sister by the hand and Mami carrying me in a wrap. They weaved in and out of museums and parks, bought each other clothes and perfumes, feasted on ice cream. They put on boisterous shows for shopkeepers and vendors as they fought over who would treat whom, passing back and forth the only credit card they owned, which was Mami's, and which she would pay off for many years to come.

At home, Nono helped Mami care for me in her bedroom. He placed a number of pillows on her lap, and then me on top. With the help of the pillows, her knees, and her shoulders, she could get me to feed. She didn't fully trust her hands yet, so, to show me love, she brought her lips to my scalp and licked. She licked, as if she were a lion and I her cub.

Mami and Nono told stories.

Once, when he was in his twenties, a fiery orb buzzed after Nono through the jungle. He hid inside the hollow of a tree and waited out the night. When Mami fell down the well, Nono heard her voice, even though it was not possible—he couldn't have heard her voice. Once, when Mami was seven, Nono took the family to the river and Mami complained it was boring, there were too many people, she could scarcely breathe. Tired of her whining, Nono unloaded his gun several times into the sky. A shocked silence settled on the riverbanks, and then one hundred people fled. Everything but the river was still. Mami glanced at the overturned pots, blankets, and food, and complained again—now the river was empty, there was no one to look at, let alone speak to.

In Mami's bedroom, Nono confessed that the reason he had revealed the secrets to her wasn't that she had returned from amnesia with abilities to rival his own. Rather, it was because of everything else that had happened right before she fell down the well.

Unwisely then, when Mami was seven, Nono had encouraged Nona to raise Mami to be a wife.

Mami needed to learn obedience if she was to have a good life, but when Nona ordered she collect her brothers' dirty laundry and wash it, she refused. She argued that her older brothers, who were fourteen and twelve and ten, had biceps three times as large as her own—wouldn't it make more sense for *them* to wash *her* clothes?

Her older brothers were cruel. She climbed to the treetops to escape them. She watched from above. Each weekend, they asked one of Mami's sisters to play hide-and-seek, lleva, and marbles. One sister fell victim to their tricks. The real game happened around a bucket of water into which they dunked her head until she almost drowned. The sport was in watching her feet—how her kicking grew frantic, then weak, then slow. They allowed her to come up for air just before it was too late. They implored for her forgiveness, then called her queen, promised not to do it again. With Nono gone, Mami's brothers conducted themselves after the men around them—steely men, who flaunted an enthusiasm for brutality, and were guerrilla or paramilitary members, or the victims of these men. Violence touched everyone. Mami didn't tell Nono how his sons became worse men in his absence, but later, for many years after I turned seven, Mami would tell me this story over and over again. Unlike Nona, who wanted to teach Mami obedience, my mother wanted me to understand defiance.

Ours was a country, hers was a house, where a woman's life was worth little, and Mami's sister had the same power as her mother, which was in forgiving and absolving the men who hurt them. Men could hit women in her house, especially if it was to teach them a lesson. Sometimes Mami's brothers got into a mood. They accused her, a seven-year-old girl, of giving older men lascivious looks. They kicked her until she curled into a ball. Neither Nono nor Nona intervened. Nona advised her daughters, like many mothers did their own in Santander at that time, never to be alone in a room with their brothers, who, though they were blood, were men.

Mami had to learn her own violence. Once, she broke the lid of a toilet tank on the head of one of her brothers, giving him a concussion. Another time, when an older brother was looking to hit her, she sat on the floor and imagined her nails were jaguar claws full of a power that wouldn't allow any inflicted wound to heal shut. She filed her nails with a seashell into ten points. When her brother dragged her by the hair outside to the coffee jungle to lay his kicks into her, Mami carved so deeply into his arms and stomach, he was forced to let go. When Nono came home, his son had bled through his shirt. Nono tried to stanch the bleeding, but it would not: he watched it trickling from the wounds. Nono turned to Mami, who was smiling, and bleeding from her nose.

Sojaila, undo what you did.

No.

Sojaila, this is your brother. Undo what you did.

No.

Surprised by the scalding purity of her fury, he left the room. Mami told her brother, *I can make you bleed out.* When it seemed to her that her brother was appropriately afraid of her, she called Nono back, informing him that she was ready to allow the wounds to close. She remained beside Nono as he again breathed the words to stop the blood. When it worked, Nono placed his hand on Mami's head. She waited for a scolding, but instead, he cupped her hands in both of his and led her to her bedroom. *Sleep well, my little mountain beast.*

It was apparent to Nona, too, that Mami was more beast than girl. Who would marry such a creature?

Nona instructed Mami: *Each night, at dinnertime, set hot plates of food before your father, brothers, me, and your sisters—in that order. Then you can eat. On Sundays, collect your brothers' dirty laundry and take it outside to wash.*

After her directive was not heeded, Nona broke off a branch from the cocota tree. She pruned it of leaves and twigs and leaned it against a corner by the dining table. It was there at dinnertime as a visual threat, the tool Mami would get beaten with if she disobeyed. Her siblings glanced from Nona to Mami to the branch. Nono set his elbows on the table, locked his fingers beneath his chin, and closed his eyes.

Mami took a leisurely walk to the kitchen. Once there, she served herself soup and hopped onto the counter to eat. She was halfway through her bowl when Nona came to see about the delay, and dragged Mami into the little room where her bleeding and screams were usually extracted, but not her repentance.

The next night was the same: the branch in the corner, the order to serve the men first. This time, Mami waltzed into the kitchen, jumped onto the counter, lowered her underwear, and, leaning her bare bottom over the pot, peed into the soup.

The rattle of her urine splashing into the pot drew Nona and her siblings to the kitchen, where they were struck still and silent at the sight.

The little room filled with Mami's screaming; this time, her siblings thought she would be beaten to death for sure. They pounded their fists on the door, imploring for a stay of execution.

The third day, Mami decided she'd had enough beatings. Her anger chiseled a thought. She retrieved Nona's scissors from the sewing set and cut her own hair as close as she could to the scalp. She walked up to Nona and presented herself: *I am a boy now. I don't have to do anything you say.* Nona blinked.

Confronted with Mami suddenly masculine before her, flat-chested and brawny, Nona thought back on Mami's seven years. Nona would later say that she saw what those years would have been had Mami been a boy, that as a girl Mami had too much fight in her but as a boy would have been Nona's best son.

Mami was wild and untamable. Nona stopped asking her to do chores, her brothers left her alone, and Nono loved her even more.

A few months later, Mami fell down the well.

That was why, Nono now told Mami, he believed that, even if what the forefathers said was true, that women who possessed the secrets would suffer misfortune, Mami would outwit that too.

Later that day, right after Nono laid me down in the crib and was walking down the hall toward Mami in the living room, he happened to glance over his shoulder and saw a snake appear at the opposite end. It slithered quickly across the carpeted floor, carving *S*'s into the pile of the rug, into the nursery. Nono stalked after it, but it slid up the crib, beneath the veiled canopy. When Nono lifted the veil, the snake was asleep and I was giggling. Then the snake was gone.

Nono brought Mami to see me, told her either I had a snake spirit or the snake was an enemy whom I had entranced. He gathered me up in his arms. *Thank God. The good genes have been passed down.* Each time Mami tells me this story, I uncover something new. *Mi güichita,* he called me then, Mami says: my little sun. It's not a word I find in any Spanish dictionary, but one I came across in a haphazard collection of Indigenous words sampled among the tribes from the area of Santander in the nineteenth century by the writer Jorge Isaacs. Güicho. Sun. And the diminutive, I imagine, the -ita, must be a colonial adaptation, the Spanish suffix that means *little, beloved.*

Nono whispered a wind of knowledge into my ear. Knowledge long lost, which I try to remember.

When Papi heard about this, he yelled at Mami: I had neither a snake spirit nor an enemy—I was *newly born.* Papi addressed his anger at Mami because he couldn't even raise his voice at Nono or call him anything but *sir.* He still remembered visiting Mami in her family's house when he was a teenager—how Nono had opened the door, raised a rifle, and unloaded shots that sparked at his feet.

Papi felt that Mami's and Nono's worldview was dangerous. It was navigation through guesswork, and both of them, though astute and highly charming people, were also impulsive and quite possibly deranged. Papi wanted to explain to them both that hallucinations could happen during alcoholic withdrawal, that everything they called magic could be scientifically accounted for. It was easy to trigger someone into having a hallucination with a persistent suggestion, for example. Since Nono and Mami constantly talked about Nono's impending death, jobs they'd been on, and ghosts they'd seen, they were prone to seeing things that weren't there. That's probably why Nono had seen a snake, and then later, to Papi's own mortification, why Papi himself had observed a nurse walking down the hall, carrying a baby bottle full of milk after leaving the nursery, even though there was no such person in the apartment at all.

Mami told Nono: *It's the same ghost as before. Can you get rid of her?* She had seen the nurse, too, before my sister had been born and Mami lost the power to see ghosts. She had felt there was something sinister about the nurse, but, being pregnant, she had lacked the energy to deal with her.

As Nono went to smoke the ghost out, Papi sat with Mami

in the living room. He made her describe the nurse in detail. It wasn't possible that they had seen the same thing, and here was his opportunity to prove it. This is how doubt began to bore into Papi's mind. Mami remembered her well. *She was white,* Mami said, describing details of the woman Papi had not shared aloud. *She had red hair, small black eyes. . . . What else? She was left-handed. She carried things in her left hand.*

Each day that passed, Mami healed a bit more, but time also crept closer to Nono's return flight, a brutal juncture that yawned before her as the last moment when she would see him alive. She uncovered a clause in a dream: If Nono forgave Nona and sought her pardon, he would live five years more. He would be able to spend more time with her. Nono shook his head. He had lived all he'd been willing to endure. *If they told me tomorrow, tomorrow I'd go. There's nothing left in me to give that woman.*

On the morning when Nono left, Mami held him close. He would continue healing her through dreams, he told her at the airport, but she'd only recover fully after his crossing. *I'll keep watch over you from the other side.* With those words, Nono walked away.

Mami watched at the airport windows. Some distance away, Nono walked the runway. He climbed the mobile steps to the airplane. The wind played with the edges of his poncho. He entered the cabin, sixty-three years old.

I'll keep watch over you from here, Mami answered, speaking to the glass.

Nono points to the sky at the crest of Monserrate during the last trip he took to see Mami, two months before he died. One print is covered by an accidental spill of whiteout. Bogotá, 1985

10

MUD

In dreams, two months later, Nono appeared to Nona and made love to her in her bed.

It wasn't their matrimonial bed—that one, she'd taken many decades ago to the witch who had split up Nono and his new love. Nona had wanted the witch to help bring Nono back. The witch had said the matrimonial bed possessed a magic not even a man like Nono could resist. The witch kept Nona's mattress for seven days. After retrieving it, Nona waited a year, then lost faith Nono would ever return. She waited for night, then dragged the mattress up into the wild jungle, alone and in her nightdress, as far as body and rage allowed. When she looked up, hair plastered against her face, locusts rattled at her from the grass. She left their mattress there, deep in the forest, for the beasts and elements to tear apart.

Mami had bought Nona a new mattress since that night, and in Nona's dream, it was on that current queen-sized bed that Nono flooded her with pleasure, boring a pathway back to a softness in her she thought had long curled up and died from the hurt of his leaving. He brought her back home to her body through his body.

After the throes of lovemaking, Nono looked at her. There were the spots of hazel in his brown eyes she knew so well. He apologized for all the suffering he had caused her. He begged. Nona had always wanted him like this, supplicant before her, desperate for something only she could grant. And so, she grew cold, and drunk with power, she denied him.

The next day, when Nona woke up, there was dirt all over her sheets.

And mud in her underwear.

That was how Nona knew that overnight, her estranged husband had died.

She did not cry. She would tell everyone, *Now I know what it's like to make love to a ghost.*

11

THE BURIAL

In Bogotá, Mami opened her eyes and recalled a moment she didn't think she remembered but now suddenly did:

Some few seconds of consciousness when she was at the bottom of the well. She knew herself to be eight years old and disfigured, and in her mouth a celebration of blood. Darkness pushed in and erased the borders of her body. She was spilling herself outside of herself.

Soon she would become no one, but for now, there was a thought that was language directed at her father: *Come find me, I am dying.*

Far up in space, white glowed in a circle.

In Bucaramanga, tío Ariel towered above his father, who was naked and fallen on the bathroom floor, clutching the shower curtain.

It was night by the time tío Ariel called to tell Mami that Nono was dead. He insinuated Nono had been with a woman—something about the state of the bed and the state of the kitchen. Mami paid no attention. She had dreaded the news of Nono's passing since Nono foretold it; now it had happened. While tío Ariel related the details of the wake, her dismay was an eternity of air through which she dropped. The memory of the well that morning had been Nono, urging, *Come find me, I am dying.*

Nona made no plans to attend the funeral, but she did describe in detail, to anyone who called, the dirt on her sheets, the mud in her underwear, the dream, the shellshocked mantra, *Now I know what it's like to make love to a ghost.*

If he really had powers, Papi told Mami as he packed their bags for the funeral, *how come he died when he was about to take a shower, hmm? Para mí, que todo eso es puro cuento. Nobody, including your father, knows when they're going to die.*

Mami glared. Papi finished packing in silence, then left to make himself useful, to buy food for the car trip and enlist a neighbor to care for me, since Mami said it was not good for babies to be near the cold of the dead.

Papi drove all night and half of a day to get to Bucaramanga. Along the way, soldiers at military roadblocks pointed their guns at his tires and searched his car for drugs, kidnapped persons, or signs of guerrilla affiliation. They questioned Papi. Mami released her cheek to the frame of the car window and slept.

The body was in tío Ariel's house.

In the casket, Nono's hands were like great claws, rigidly clutching at a phantom shower curtain. His teeth were clenched. His jaw projected. His eyes would not close. The tías and tíos could not stand to look at him; there was such fright on his face. Mami rested her head on Nono's chest, forgetting for a moment this was a corpse and there would be no sound there, nothing but a ruined silence. She jumped back. Everything smelled like formaldehyde.

The tías and tíos were arguing over which of Nono's belongings were missing and which they wanted to keep.

Where are all his statues?

I claim my father's hat.

I should be the one to keep his rifle.

What about his amulets—where'd they go?

And that skull he kept in a corner of his office? Which of you took it? How did a thing like that disappear?

His gold jewelry is missing too!

Mami sat on a stool by the casket, trying to think of an herb, a prayer, anything that might compel a corpse to relax. But Nono had only taught her to treat the living. *If a baby is in danger of dying from the evil eye,* she remembered he told her once, *it should be placed inside the stomach of a cow, freshly killed.*

The family didn't want a closed-casket funeral. Closed caskets were for victims of violence—the dismembered, the disfigured, the drowned. Families were marked by closed-casket funerals. When they were held, people hypothesized about ties to guerrillas, paramilitary, drug traffickers. Gossip could be deadly. When guerrillas and paramilitaries descended into the state of Santander, as they did from time to time, they often demanded to know at gunpoint who sympathized with their enemies. All it took was one person pointing a finger. Supporters were rounded up and shot.

Tía Perla and Mami went out into Bucaramanga, hoping to find a curandero who knew about relaxing a dead body. They inquired at the pharmacy, then stood around in a park asking strangers. People made recommendations, but each time the directions to the curandero's place of business turned out to lead to Nono's. Mami and tía Perla laughed at the paradox, then wept. They resigned themselves to a closed casket and what it might mean. As a last resort, they got a cross blessed by a priest. They returned with it to tío Ariel's, and found Nono's brother Nil sitting on the same stool Mami had occupied, looking like a healthy, rosy version of their father. Mami enclosed him in her arms, nearly collapsed at his body's warmth, and was about to ask him if he had seen Nono and what he thought they should do when she cast an involuntary glance into the casket. There, in the recesses of silk lining the casket, Nono's eyes were closed, his hands relaxed, and his jaw unclenched. Nil replaced his hat farther back on his head. *He didn't look at peace. So I helped.*

What did you do?

Nil blinked away.

To keep herself from another teary outburst, Mami busied herself with the toddlers, my sister, Ximena, and tío Ariel's eldest, our cousin Gabriel, who were giggling, weaving in and out from under the table, beneath the casket, oblivious of the corpse.

Because the tías and tíos suspected Nono had other families (Nono had spent too much time away for this not to be true), they announced the burial through the local radio station on the same day it was going to take place, and only hours before it was scheduled. They feared a crowd of half-brothers, half-sisters, wailing women, a mourning party made up of strangers bearing his face.

Papá will hate us for giving him an underattended funeral, the tíos said.

Pobre Papá. Not even Mamá will be there.

The tíos carried the casket out of tío Ariel's door. Trailing closely behind, a small procession of Nono's children and other family from Ocaña followed, singing and praying into the street. After each city block, the mourning party grew. Nono's clients, Nono's friends, and people nobody seemed to know drifted from stores and homes, having just then heard of the burial. Some understood that a curandero had died and wanted to pay their respects; others wanted to see if they could not send the curandero off with a personal request for a miracle.

There is one surviving photo of the funeral procession in one of tío Ariel's photo albums in Bucaramanga, and when Mami and I bend over the print, looking closely at the forty-some people surrounding the casket, she cannot tell me who anybody is—not the man with slicked-back hair bearing a funeral-flower arrangement on the handlebars of his motorcycle, not the young man in a suit who seems dejected and is scratching the back of his ear. Mami says the number of funeralgoers was easily three times that amount. The family had no money for flower arrangements, and there had been no money to buy a plot in the cemetery. A friend of the family, Raúl, whose little girl Nono had cured of a bad fever, had offered his wife's plot. Nono's casket would be buried atop hers.

At the cemetery, as the funeral procession made the climb to the crest of the hill of El Cacique, Papi remained at the bottom with Ximena in his arms, walking the grounds. Funerals scared him. Nono scared him. Mami scared him. His two daughters scared him. At the edge of the cemetery, with Ximena wrapping her little body around his chest, he could pretend his was a normal father's life. Ximena did not understand yet what funerals were. As far as she knew, Nono was not dead, but sleeping. Not sleeping, but gone away. Papi whistled part of a song, hummed another, and taught Ximena the names of the flowers. He leaned her over them so she could smell their sweetness, and then he looked to the hill, where the procession was still inching along. He guessed by then people were taking turns before the casket, saying goodbye. He knew Mami would be guarding the coffin, trying to keep requests for miracles from going with Nono to the grave. Papi didn't believe in miracles, or in Nono's ability to concede them—what harm could a piece of paper perform against a body without a pulse? Still, he had fretted over Mami's grief about not knowing how to grant her father's dying wish. *Why don't you and Perla stand at both ends of the casket and keep vigil?* he suggested. Mami had seemed calmer then, having a plan, and Papi imagined she was at that very moment at the mountain crest, by her father, doing as he'd suggested.

In a moment, Papi would hear guns fired into the sky.

Nono wanted his farewell to be like that of a general, even if he had never fought a war.

Mami had no trouble fulfilling this charge. With only a day before the funeral, she approached a couple of army men who were on a break, smoking in the park by her father's house. She gave them a sample palm reading, and then traded a full reading for their presence at her father's funeral—but they had to come in full ceremonial garb, fire guns, and play trumpets. She told them, *If I see you perform the salute even halfway, so will I, when the time comes, give you half a palm reading.* The men stood at attention the whole time the priest was giving his service.

Ve, I never knew Rafael had fought in a war, Mami overheard the family from Ocaña say.

Yes, I seem to remember, must have been La Violencia.

Nono was not fond of priests. The priest was there more for the sake of the funeralgoers than for him. Mami didn't care much for priests either—to her, they were mere men pretending to be holy—and so, as the priest read from the Bible, always the same story about death and salvation, Mami lifted her gaze to the sky.

Above, clouds gathered, glowing at the edges, and quickly bruising.

Perla, Mami whispered, not taking her eyes off the sky. *Do those clouds look* natural *to you?*

Tía Perla said, between gritted teeth, *Don't you dare say one more word to me.*

Mami stared in silence as the clouds bulked.

Perla, Mami insisted, *look.*

Tía Perla glanced up, then away. *I think I'm going to have a heart attack.*

Tía Perla, who had never grown comfortable with the supernatural despite her upbringing, began to hyperventilate, attracting her siblings' attention, and in the murmurings that ensued, Mami took the opportunity to disseminate her question about the sky and the clouds. One by one, Nono's children looked up. Someone else noticed, and the observation was repeated in hushed tones along the tottering row of Nono's sons and daughters, whose reactions ranged from delight to terror, that the mob of darkening clouds was a phenomenon *only* happening above Nono's funeral plot; and down the hill, where another funeral was taking place, there were no clouds at all.

Farther down, where Papi stood, just as he was running out of the names for flowers he knew and was beginning to invent, there was sunlight.

Tía Perla held her temples: *What if he gets up and walks?* And just then the casket gaped open for a final farewell.

Everyone gasped.

Her siblings inhaled at tía Perla's words, but tía Perla and Mami were looking at Nono. They had guarded his head and chest well, and there were no little papers requesting miracles there, but his sides were stuffed with them. People had managed to sneak them in. It didn't occur to the family to stop the proceedings and dig the little papers out, and in their grief, they simply watched it all unfold. Sensing their anguish, the priest recommended, *My sons and daughters, take a fistful of dirt and throw it on the casket as it goes down; this will help your mourning.*

Not knowing what else to do, the tías and tíos complied. They threw dirt on the casket as it dropped.

That's right, my flock, take handfuls of dirt and say farewell.

With pain, Mami had closed her fist around black earth when it began to rain. *It's just raining on this plot,* Mami whispered to her siblings around her. *It's only raining on this plot.*

The tías and tíos saw that it was true. At the other funeral downhill, all of the six or eight persons attending had remained dry. Mami turned to the sky and allowed the rain to drench her face. Her brothers and sisters keened, and then she heard the knock of Nono's casket as it was released on top of what must have been the coffin of Raúl's wife. The priest, seeing but not understanding the wild eruption of emotion, insisted, *Take fistfuls of dirt, all of you, and throw them on the casket of your good father, for this is the way to say goodbye.*

The tías and tíos continued clumping and throwing dirt at their father in his casket, and then the final gunshots were fired into the sky. Mami released a last fistful of soil.

Slowly, the grave filled with earth and water.

Back in Cúcuta, Nona walked directly to her notebook of important facts. It was the one where she had recorded the date of her wedding, the place and time of the birth of each of her children, their baptisms, marriages, and the names of their children. She turned to the very last page, scratched the date, and wrote in all capitals, "RAFAEL CONTRERAS ALFONSO HAS DIED HE WAS BURIED IN BUCARAMANGA."

Junio 30/8

Murio
Rafael Contre
ras. Alfonso.
Fue sepultado
en Bucaramanga

12

THE CURSE

Many decades later, it would be said that Nono's death was what set loose the eerie trouble that had been stalking the family ever since, though nobody would use these words. If there was ever any term I heard it called it was *eso:* that which we inherited, that which could not be understood, that which struck some but not others, that which caused stories to repeat themselves across generations.

Many things could be called a curse.

Tía Perla's teeth, of a sudden, falling out.

A tío being kidnapped four different times by guerrillas, each time held for longer and longer periods.

The cells of Mami's eyes attacking themselves from an autoimmune disease that is supposed to strike only people with AIDS.

What are the odds? the family kept asking, reproach tinging their words. *All of this happening in one family?*

Tío Ariel knew some of the secrets, but not all. When Mami was a senior in high school, tío Ariel had two sons and no job, and Mami begged Nono to teach him anything that could help him put food on the table. Nono balked at the idea. Tío Ariel was no good for the knowledge. *A man whose knees tremble before a ghost cannot be a healer.* But Mami could be very convincing, and in the end Nono taught tío Ariel to move clouds, the most showy but arguably least useful of the secrets. Then, when Nono was soon to die and Mami needed a last set of drafts for her paralysis, he made another exception.

Nono trekked to the meadow where he had picked the red flowers before, the name of which Mami can't recall, collected some more, and left them with tío Ariel. *When Sojaila comes . . .* , Nono began. Tío Ariel interrupted: *Does Sojaila have plans to come?* Nono didn't say. He didn't want tío Ariel to know he was crossing.

Mami couldn't stay in Bucaramanga for treatment after the funeral, so, instead, tío Ariel and the flowers traveled back to Bogotá with her. The flowers, leaves, and seed pods were individually bagged, and the bags were knotted, but their cloying sweetness slipped past plastic and knot and made both Ximena and tío Ariel, who were riding together in the back, carsick. Papi had to stop often.

In Bogotá, tío Ariel prepared the leaves and flowers after Nono's instructions. How could something that had smelled so sweet turn so bitter once steeped? Mami plugged her nose and forced herself to swallow. She suppressed the urge to throw up. She followed the treatment. When, after a few weeks, the force of her grip returned, Mami should have been relieved at the independence restored to her, but every day she suffered a kind of selective forgetting and picked up the telephone from its cradle and dialed her father. She was full of news about her paralysis, full of missings of him, and she wanted to know what he had dreamt. Each day, the ringing dial tone traced the outlines of her grief.

Mami and tío Ariel consoled each other, but tío Ariel always had disaster on his face. He suffered from depression. He was an embattled man, seeming to overcome his worst, then not. Papi and tío Ariel drank together. At night, they grew somber and erratic, and high-spirited and red-faced in the day. It was under those intemperate moods that Papi proposed they take me to meet the Salto de Tequendama, his favorite place on earth.

The Salto is a gleaming waterfall with a drop of more than four hundred feet. It's an hour's drive out of Bogotá. At the top of the road, a mansion hangs at the edge of the abyss, and the spray of the falls rides the air. The mansion, built in the 1920s, was a train stop, a hotel, and later a restaurant. Year after year, it collected its ghosts: jumpers who chose the place.

The spot where the waterfall greets the river below is known as the Lake of the Dead. In the sixteenth century, the Muiscas, the original people of Bogotá, knew they would lose their territory and kingdom to the Spanish. Rather than being conquered, many chose to jump. What is a waterfall? A promised descent, a journey water takes to meet itself. The survivors told the story: instead of joining the water in its fall, the jumpers turned into eagles, and the eagles flew to the sun. Those who stayed behind regretted not leaving with the others.

For centuries, the bodies of jumpers at the Salto de Tequendama vanished into the whirlpool beneath the falls, into the Lake of the Dead. It was believed to be a vortex, a place of no return. The first body to be recovered from the falls was in 1941, that of a taxi driver. His friends, also cab drivers, steered their canoes and ropes and got close enough to smell the putrefying body and to see it, lifeless, tossing and turning beneath the tumult of the falls.

No one has ever sought to recover the bones that lie at the bottom of the waterfall, and people say to this day to be careful, never to stare too long into the Lake of the Dead, because the dead are constantly calling from the water. A hungry mouth, clamoring for a drowning.

Three weeks or so after the funeral, Papi pulled over and parked, and together we hiked up the road's edge: Papi holding Ximena, Mami holding me, and tío Ariel bringing up the rear. At the manor, Papi went inside to buy coffees and almojábanas while Mami and tío Ariel strolled to the broad stone balcony. They leaned over the banister and gaped at the steep drop of the canyon and the roaring whitewater. Mami grew transfixed. Her gaze took in the foam of the rapids below, the glaze of the rocks, and, by the crest of the waterfall, the blue-robed Virgin of the Suicides, who stood, opening her arms, overlooking the Lake of the Dead. The misted air gradually soaked Mami's skin; then her arms flinched and, on their own, went slack, a betrayal of her body that Mami's siblings would later identify as eso. I slipped from her grasp. In the hell of an eternity, during which Mami's hands did not work, not my limbs but the red blanket I was wrapped in stuck to her fingers. I dropped toward the white thunder, and Mami knew she would jump too.

Behind us, Papi was coming down the steps to the balcony. His hands were full of coffee and pastries, but beyond that, I don't know what he saw. He won't tell me anything else, and he walks away from me each time I ask.

Tío Ariel possessed an intermittent ability to perceive the future, and he said later that he had foreseen what was about to take place. That was why he was already kneeling, already sticking his hand through the stone balusters of the balcony, to catch me by the wrist as I fell. As Mami screamed, he calmly pulled me up. He paused once his arm met the thickness of the top rail, reached with his other hand, passed me from one hand to the other, and released me, safely, on the ground.

Mami says I looked like a small sacrifice to her, laid directly on the brick, a wailing red-faced baby girl with a dislocated arm stretching away at a cruel angle. Papi pulled at his hair in the roar of the canyon, and tío Ariel, who had also learned from Nono about setting bones, popped my arm back into place.

After what Mami called a near-disaster and what tío Ariel called the consequences of her knowing the secrets, Mami refused to leave the house. She was angry. The waterfall had tried to gulp her baby down. Tío Ariel advised her to abandon her practice of healing and divination, for her family's safety, and teach what she knew to him. Only then might she be released from the string of tragedies nipping at her heels. Mami accused tío Ariel of jealousy. Nono loved her more than him, believed her to be more capable. She had earned the secrets, while he was only privy to a few because of Mami. Tío Ariel packed a bag, bought a bus ticket to go back to his family in Bucaramanga, and left within a day.

This was not the first time Mami and tío Ariel had fought over the secrets. Back when Nono had taught tío Ariel how to move clouds, tío Ariel opened a consulting room. But he didn't know how to heal. Mami was finishing high school, and thankful to tío Ariel for saving her from an abusive relationship, the one before Papi. So, just as she had done for her father when she was younger, she ran the operation for tío Ariel's consulting room and moved into his house.

Unheeded, unrecognized, she prepared the drafts, cared for tío Ariel's patients, and carried out the actual work of healing. Tío Ariel delighted in her support, but as he sat in his consulting room, negotiating payment and treatment plans, saying *his assistant* would carry out his instructions, there came a day when he began to believe the charade that he was in charge. After Mami healed his patients, the patients presented her with tokens of their gratitude. Tío Ariel didn't immediately discover the tokens, but once he did, he stole them. He was the face and brains of the operation. He accused Mami of prostitution—what else would incite his patients to give her extra money and gifts if they had already paid him in full?

Mami allowed him to insult her, take her money, break her gifts only because she was biding her time for the perfect moment to exact her revenge. Tío Ariel's wife, Mariana, was scandalized at the thought of Mami selling sex under her own roof. She stole Mami's panties and half-buried them in the soil of their house plants so Mami would see what Mariana had done and come to understand that Mariana did not condone her actions either.

One night, when Mami was sure they were both asleep, Mami gathered as many of tío Ariel's belongings as she could, piled them high in the indoor courtyard, doused them with gasoline, and

The road to the Salto de Tequendama. Bogotá, 1997

Six years later at the Salto de Tequendama, my sister runs at my father, who takes this photo. Sitting on the ground with cousin Gabriel is tío Ariel. In front, also on the ground, is cousin Fabián. In the back row, from left to right, is tío Ariel's wife, Mariana, with their sons Ivan and Omar. Mami, still nervous that someone might tumble into the falls, grips and holds on to Omar's shirt. I am seated next to Mami, on the far right.

tossed a lit match. She walked away from the house in the middle of the night, the air thickening with smoke.

What did I tell you, mi animal de monte? Nono said, not surprised to see her arrive at his house as the sky was beginning to lighten. *He's no good for it. He'll lose his head.*

At the time, tío Ariel called for Nono to beat Mami for what she had done: his children had been in the house, after all, and if he had not woken up when he did, the whole house might have burned down. *You deserved what she did,* Nono said. Eventually, tío Ariel forgave Mami for setting his things on fire, understanding that he had wronged her. He wanted her to return, to prove he could treat her better, but even though she let go of her resentment, she couldn't trust him in the same way again. He was a man like all the men she knew: threatened by her, and interested in control.

In the absence of Nono's and Mami's guidance, tío Ariel bought an old book on Spanish witchcraft at a secondhand bookstore and used it to teach himself to communicate with spirits, invite them into his body, trade his sensory experience of life for their ability to foretell. He drank a whole bottle of vodka in a night, saying the only ghost who could tell him the future liked to enter his body and drink. It was the price he had to pay.

By the time of Nono's funeral, tío Ariel's consulting ghosts had begun to take residence inside his body without his permission, demanding more and more alcohol. The family remarked on his declining health, and with the additional news of my almost falling into the waterfall, the baby girl born at the devil's hour, questions that had long been coming were uttered for the first time: If the practices Nono had devoted himself to were good, why had he died looking like such a terror? If the practices Mami was devoted to were also good, why had she lost the movement in her arms? Why had the Lake of the Dead tried to take a newborn life? Why had tío Ariel, who had closely followed Mami and Nono, ended up becoming, clearly, an alcoholic?

Then, as always, missionaries knocked on their doors and gifted them with Bibles, fastening flyers on their door handles with rubber bands. They had experienced all of this before, but, with Nono gone and grounds for budding suspicions breaking open, the tías and tíos wondered if there might not be some substance to those frazzled believers' pronouncements that the end was nigh, that it was time to repent. They wondered which story was true. Was there a jealous Christian God who hated them and their father for being idolaters? Or was there a lineage of healers who promised knowledge and protection, and who were angry at them because Nono had defied their instructions that a woman never be taught?

The missionaries said divination was abhorrent to God, and God punished the wicked, and if the tíos and tías were witness to punishment, then this was their own call to reform. But the tíos and tías couldn't make up their minds. In a gesture they hoped might satisfy the two possibly aggrieved parties, they burned Nono's possessions.

His whole wardrobe was incinerated, as were his bedsheets, then his shoes. Each sibling kept something to remember Nono by, thinking they would be forgiven a small memento. But wherever Nono's belongings were kept, ghostly sounds materialized. All nine of his children, from Bogotá to Rionegro to Cúcuta, reported hearing jingling keys in the middle of the night, approaching footsteps, and at the bedroom doors, though the knobs didn't actually move and were not locked (as established and verified by many), the doorknobs made the rattling sounds of someone struggling with a bolt. A second wave of burnings took place.

Mami laughed at her siblings' fears. It was only Nono saying hello, looking in, treading the rounds of his ghost walk, making sure his powers were still observed. There was such a thing as a good haunting, she told them, but Mami's siblings remained unconvinced. And so the suspicion that Nono's practices were unholy took root, though it would still be many years before they took hold.

While I was growing up, Mami, Papi, my sister, and I traveled by car from Bogotá to see Mami's family in Santander. We saw Mami's family for only two months out of the year—in September and December, the months that Ximena and I had off from school. I was unsure if I believed in eso, but I could see why some tías and tíos might. More than what seemed usual, even for Colombians, we were a family surrounded by the strange.

Annually, as our car glided up from Bogotá along the Eastern Cordillera, into which the Northern Central Highway is etched, into the foggy air of the highlands, we used the newspaper as our road map, avoiding towns and areas where recent skirmishes and massacres had taken place, but this also made us feel that at any point we could suddenly take a wrong turn toward calamity.

We sweated through the infernal heat of the lowlands, and at night gaped at the cemetery, where small balls of fire could be seen floating above the graves, which Mami called ghosts, and Papi called photon emissions. It would be early morning by the time we pulled up to tío Ariel's house, where Mami shook us awake and told us to scoot inside.

The house had been a largesse presented to tío Ariel by an old man, a devotee of the Black Arts in the European sense, who had come to tío Ariel with a bad case of arthritis. Tío Ariel healed the man using the same medicine Nono had shown him for Mami, and the old man was so thankful to be rid of his daily pain that he immediately moved out and gave tío Ariel the keys.

It was a big house, three stories high, and with a basement. But under tío Ariel's care, it fell into disrepair. The roof needed new tiles, the paint peeled, and the basement smelled like urine. Ximena and I were afraid to stay inside too long, so, for the two or three nights we spent at tío Ariel's, we chased fireflies outside, ate random plants to see what would happen, then went to taverns to see tío Ariel sing.

Tío Ariel had a mariachi group. Mariachi music was a mestizo music, developed from centuries of revelry in Indigenous, African, and European spaces by the mixed people who crossed between them. Colombian rancheras were inspired by mariachi music, and tío Ariel sang those too. Standing at the center of the small stage, under a soft spotlight, he would transform. In the dark, starred by a million bright points that lasered toward us from a rotating disco ball suspended from the ceiling, we listened to the croon of tío Ariel's pretty tenor calling us beautiful, calling us heartbreakers. *Mujeres, mujeres tan divinas, no queda otro camino que adorarlas.*

During the day, tío Ariel massaged my arms with holy oils to cleanse me of what he said had tried to kill me at the waterfall. If my mother was touched by eso, I was too. His hands were meaty, too warm, and smelled of camphor oil and vodka.

Did eso exist? Mami said all of it was puro cuento, the purest fiction. She tried to teach me then: there is no such thing as a curse. Her life had been touched by tragedy and loss, but she didn't need to call it anything except what it was. A life. But Mami was always someone who laughed in the face of crisis, danced while grieving, forbade anyone to dictate the boundaries of her possibilities. I didn't understand all she was trying to tell me. How could curses not exist when everything around us was crumbling?

Mami said tío Ariel was not good at healing. He was sensitive, artistic, chaotic—a good man—but he was lost in the woods of his own demons and emotions. *What's needed to heal others is a clinical coldness,* Mami said, *a steady pulse.*

Sometimes tío Ariel got his whole family into his Jeep and we rode together the three hours to Cúcuta, where all of us stayed in Nona's house. Nona's home was beautiful. She and Nono had molded each brick in their own hands from clay and dry grass and water. Nono had baked the bricks in a little machine he acquired in lieu of payment for his work in ridding one farmer's house from a hex. He built new rooms whenever there was money. This meant there were two levels, with windows in strange places, doors that opened onto rickety stairs, and parts of the second floor with no banisters or walls, so that you could step right up to the frightful drop and jump. There were latticed walls which bathed the house in the shrill of crickets and mosquitoes, and for a time there was a dirt floor. Nona would throw buckets of water onto the dirt and get on her knees to make circular patterns on the ground so that the dust did not rise. The family walked on dirt patted fresh by her hands.

One brick in Nona's patio was said to be cursed.

The story is that one day, Nono had been drinking alone, and, as was sometimes his routine, he taunted spirits to come and try to take his soul if they so dared. The tías and the tíos (back then, all of them teens) were inside the house, sleeping. A howling woke the house—a windstorm that sounded almost human.

They ran to the patio, but the gate to the outside was stuck. They could hear two voices yelling, something indistinct beneath the moan of wind, but in the dark they could not see what was taking place. When it was over, the gate unlatched. They found Nono far down on the patio, shining a kerosene lamp on the mud, ordering them to stay back.

Near the house, by the gate, there was a single footprint, four sizes larger than that of anyone in the family. Nono said that this was the devil's footprint and that it was impossible to get rid of such a supernatural mark. Their only choice was to hide it. The next day, Nono laid a brick path over the area. Six bricks covered exactly where the footprint had been, but one of them, the one that had blackened as if singed after it was laid, was the one that was cursed. Nono said that if they tried to replace it the next brick would also singe, so nothing else was done.

Being young, Ximena and I used to sit by the cursed brick, playing on the ground with the puppies that were never in short supply. Nona's dog was always escaping and returning pregnant. We knew that the puppies would die, that Nona would drown them or kill them by smashing their furry heads into the wall. There was barely enough food in her house for people. One day we'd wake up to no puppies and blood seeping into the cracks of the cursed brick. She'd chosen that spot for convenience, because it was closest to the kitchen and the cement container in the garden where she collected rainwater, so she could therefore easily clean up, but still, it felt fated.

When Mami wanted to scandalize us, which was often, she would sweep her hand across the garden beyond the brick path at Nona's house and say, *This is a plantation of aborted fetuses.*

Whose?

We were rarely shocked as children, possibly because Mami was too often shocking.

Frog skeletons too, Mami said. *Your tía The Same as Always got into that type of Spanish brujería. She sewed papers with names written on them into frogs' mouths, and buried the frogs alive.*

We were intrigued. *What's that supposed to do?*

How would I know? I'm *not into Spanish brujería.*

In Nona's backyard, the relentless heat made us sweat, and the sweat made us glow. Tías and tíos were growing apart. Discord and doubt were in the air, but it seemed no different to me from before. They still bounced me on their lap, called me *Mamita, mi cielo, mi amor, mi turroncito de azúcar,* tucked strands of hair behind my ear, took pains to get me the very best of the avocados and mangoes that hung, bright bulbs, from Nona's trees. *Why couldn't you be born to me?* they asked. *You're such a sweet thing.* Then they sat in plastic chairs, smoking and drinking aguardiente, arguing over supernatural powers and to what degree they each had inherited them. Tío Ariel had a dexterity for setting bones, he could move clouds, and he knew how to let spirits set up house in his body. Tía Nahía could see the death veil. The Same as Always told fortunes by reading the embers at the tip of her cigar. But no matter what, Mami always won. Mami's siblings admired her, loathed and envied her. She burned too bright. I felt it was the honor of my life just to be her daughter.

All night, we awaited the mysterious conditions under which we could settle and, as we were fond of calling it, listen to the tongue. Mami would tell us a story. Usually, around the witching hour, after the adults had had a few drinks and we tired from running around, Mami would begin. Other people's stories began, *Once upon a time.* Mami's began, *Once, in real life* . . . She weaved the same stories we had heard countless times, but with such a collision of charm and tension and high drama that none of us dared move, not even to pee. Our favorite story, the one we asked for again and again, was about Nono and a black vulture. It was a story about being cursed, and breaking a curse.

Once, in real life, during one of Nono's travels, when he was walking the Andes range, he noticed he was low on drinking water.

The salt of his sweat stung his eyes. He wiped his brow. He shielded his face under the shadow of his palm, but could barely make out the distance to the peak. He knew he should have reached it hours ago, and that, once there, he would soon arrive at the road that led him back home to Ocaña.

Nono caught his breath. At his feet was a tiny dying shrub, nothing but a mess of brown stalks. He kept hiking. His burro trod with its tongue hanging out. Another hour went by. His skin had pebbled with sweat. Again Nono checked the distance to the peak. It did not seem to be any closer. He began to worry he might faint. He petted his burro, took a deep breath, and looked around. He would have to locate water, or else they might both die.

Next to his boots there was, if not the same shrub, a shrub similar to the dying one he'd spotted earlier. Nono stepped forward, but the shrub remained rooted and immobile, while the dirt glided beneath his feet like a conveyor belt. He broke into a sprint, trying to bound past the shrub, but no matter his speed, Nono could not get any farther.

From the tree above him, he heard the drawn-out hiss of a black vulture, a raspy, death-rattle sound.

This was a witch. The kind that turn into black vultures when they want to fly.

The witch ruffled her long ebony feathers and glared, her beady red eyes bulging from her black, wrinkled birdskin. Without taking his eyes off the witch, Nono squatted and felt the ground for a rock. When he found one, he tossed it into the air a few times, then flung it at the bird. He hit the vulture on the shoulder, startling it and knocking it off the branch. It came spinning from the tree, and then, out of the blur of feathers, a woman's legs and a mane of black hair appeared.

Clouds of dirt rose around the body where it landed. As the dust settled, he could make out a woman moaning in pain from the fall, her face curtained behind her hair. This was the witch protecting her identity. Nono cleared his throat as he stepped over her. He and his donkey had been released from her spell and could now advance on the trail. When he reached the peak of the mountain, Nono looked back, but the woman was gone.

Once or twice when Mami told this story, a black vulture flew overhead, the downdraft of wings beating just above our heads, too close. All of us ran—except Mami and tío Ariel. They pointed at us and laughed when we returned. Mami liked to say it was a warning. Witches hated being talked about.

In Santander, we called the black vultures chulos. Tío Ariel and Mami taught us the procedures for felling witches in case what happened to Nono happened to us. All of us children practiced together. We spent our daylight hours tracking flocks of chulos until we found them crowding big trees. Sometimes when we went through the procedure a chulo fell to the ground. Did it tumble out of the air inexplicably, or was it a witch?

We feared witches and what they might do to us. There was nothing more horrifying to us than the thought of an enchantment to trick you into believing you were moving forward when actually you were only marching in place.

Stuckness was something we noted. Our tíos and tías accrued debts and had to stay in bad relationships, bad jobs, dangerous neighborhoods. Our whole country seemed stuck too. At any moment, we might become victims of war.

Sometimes I was moved to tears watching Mami's siblings: with all that weighed on them, they played records and danced, shed their anxieties to drums and maracas and gaitas, rooting around for joy. Soon they would reach for my hands, guiding me to raise them with abandon to a sky that would soon glow neon. We lived in the midst of the incomprehensible.

When I turned seven, the kinship we knew as a family finally slipped. Mami's sister, The Same as Always, became a devotee of a charismatic church, and her enthusiasm for speaking in tongues and for the priest who got bitten by a snake and survived the poison was so palpable that it converted many other tíos and tías too.

The tías and tíos now divided into camps: those who wholeheartedly believed Nono and Mami were sinners, and those who did not.

Mami's siblings without powers had always beheld the lineage they felt perpetually shut out from with distrust. Now they adopted the Christian language of damnation. Tías who had never seen a ghost veil before relished their luck. Tíos who had been Catholic in name only became vehement born-again Christians and Jehovah's Witnesses. Once, we had enjoyed attending midnight mass together on Christmas Eve, watching with reverence as the single light-blue dome of the Cathedral of Cúcuta took incense and sound. Now, Mami's siblings reprimanded us for going to the *wrong* church, or for going to church while also practicing curanderismo, or they introduced us, at the end of the service, to strangers who were born-again or charismatic and who launched into endless-seeming proselytizings. Soon we couldn't be in the same room. Our evenings soured, always ended in the same fight.

They wrote us letters about our salvation, letters which they said came from a place of love, but which called Mami a witch and a demon, sometimes both. They assured us that Nono's gifts had been acquired through a deal with the devil, and that we were damned and going to hell. Mami, in turn, sat with her photo albums, painstakingly cutting out the image of each sibling who had insulted her. She sent her siblings envelopes full of their tiny faces. Over time, the images of the otherwise peaceful family scenes in our albums came to bear rows of empty silhouettes.

And Nona, who had received Bibles from many of her children, began to read Scripture daily. The book spoke of false prophets, and she grew convinced that Nono had been just that. Nona urged her children to excommunicate everything that had to do with Nono from their lives.

13

COINS

It was sometime during that season—after Mami had sent the cutouts to her siblings in the mail, when Ximena and I were a little scared and lonely, wondering if we might not be damned—that, in Bogotá, rain fell in sheets. The newspapers printed images of flooded houses, couches and lamps drifting in street rivers. After a year of drought, the rain was much desired, and astonishing. There is one photograph I particularly remember: a man lying on the fitted sheet of his mattress, wearing a sleeveless shirt and boxers. If you just looked at the way his hands dug into the bed linens, the tension in his eyes, it seemed he was having a nightmare; but really his mattress was riding downriver on a flood, along with buoyant objects from other people's houses and trash, and he was holding on.

Then, it happened to us. Mami was driving when rain began to patter and the radio issued a repeating warning to get to high land. Mami sped, swerved, taking side streets, rushing home. We had a small car, a Renault 9, set lower than most cars, and were still on the far side of the city. Soon we couldn't go anywhere. We inched behind a dull motorcade. Rain began to clatter on our roof and hood. We had neared a tunnel by the time the rain swallowed our tires, the water choked our engine, and our car stalled. Other cars, set higher than our own, raced around us, leaving us behind. The street grew deserted, and over the echo of rain I could hear my sister yelling for Mami to do something. Mami tried to turn the wheel, press her foot on the brake pedal, pull the hand brake. It was no use: the wheels were not touching the ground. Suddenly, a tide rushing from behind propelled us screaming toward the tunnel, the lowest part of the road, straight for a cluster of stranded cars trapped there. Another river current hit the rear of our car and spun us around. We bumped against the cement median and plunged into the dimness of the tunnel, sideways, knocking into one of the other cars. The collision caused some cars to move, and they gushed ahead. We were still. The tunnel was relatively quiet, the rain a far-off thing. Then the water rushed through the cracks at the bottom of our car doors. Mami said it was black water from the sewage, and I pulled my feet up onto the front seat and hugged myself.

A car riding a wave, as we had done, came from behind and bumped us, and we whirled half a turn until we were facing forward, surging farther inside the tunnel. We coasted past a couple sitting on their car roof, hugging each other in the dim light, and then we were out in the daylight again, under the racket of rain. We glided down the incline of the street, and slowed at the nadir of the road. It began to thunder. Rain lashed our car, drumming it into motion. Uselessly, Mami turned the key. A cab driver whose car was stalled to our right crawled out of his window. He was carrying a shovel and swimming against the current of the street river, toward the street median, a high hill that divided our descending side of the street from the opposing one, which sloped upward. I watched him dig into the median, trying to create an opening, I imagined, for some of the water to flow to the other side. In front of us, a young man repeatedly elbowed his car window, but the glass wouldn't break. Ximena was crying in the back seat. I cranked my window down, took off one of my shoes, filled it with the water lapping up now onto my seat, and tossed the water out the window, thinking, *If only I do this fast enough . . .* Mami scoffed at me. All at once, she seemed to become conscious of our predicament. She uttered a series of words that are not in any language I know, and which I am not allowed to repeat. At their pronouncement, the storm turned into a drizzle and, in a few minutes, ceased.

I leaned forward and looked up at the sky, then down at the water lapping against my seat. *Did you just do that?*

She didn't, Ximena said from the back. *It was a coincidence.*

Ximena and I feared a car might crash into us, and talked about what we might do, what might happen if we died.

You won't die, Mami repeated to us.

This must be eso, I said.

There is no such thing as eso, Mami said, turning her exasperated gaze to her window.

We were considering climbing out to our roof when a man in a working semi truck paused by my window and offered us a ride toward dry land. Mami agreed. He put down a plank he kept in his truck, between my window and the bottom of his truck cabin. I was the first to walk it. I noted the water had submerged the tires of the semi truck into which I was headed, but I concentrated on the wood grain of the plank. Past it, the water, still animated with current, was carrying sticks and garbage beneath its surface. For a moment, I wondered what would happen if I fell, what it would mean to drown in a temporary river. The truck driver's hands reached for me, then my sister, and my mother. Once we were all inside and ready to go, the truck stalled. The street river had killed his engine too.

We felt terrible. He had tried to help us, and now we were all stuck. He gave a curt nod, and we sat in silence, looking straight ahead at the aquatic road, waiting for something or someone to come to our rescue. Mami and Ximena and I were wet and shivering. It began to drizzle again, and we leaned to watch out the man's window as the water engulfed the seats of our Renault 9 below. The water crept ever nearer to the bottom of the doors of the semi truck.

There was no way the water would come inside the semi truck, Mami said. Timidly at first, then with feral imperative, we cuddled up to that stranger, bidding him to put his arms around us, to warm us up. He didn't seem to mind our animal burrowing. He received us in his arms, smiling to himself, and in this new, temporary family we had made, as we waited to see if this vehicle would flood too, Mami asked him to tell us the story of his life.

The man said he had grown up in the outskirts of Bogotá, his parents had recently died in a fire, and he was suffering from heartbreak. Not knowing anything about love or grief, I told him to trust that one day he would be okay, and Mami examined the lines on his hands to predict when he might fall in love again. When I had to pee, he pointed to the corner of the truck cabin by the door and turned away as I crouched down and relieved myself, watching the stream travel down toward his booted feet. I wish I could remember his face now, but all I remember are his hands, large and brown and covered with sun spots.

Eventually, the water grew tame, and firemen came in a raft to rescue people, but we waited for the tow truck and stayed where we were, huddled with the man. The semi truck made waves like a boat as we were pulled, the water spraying from our sides, the waves crashing against the median and rolling back to the road, all the way to the tunnel. I stared at Mami's face, her olive skin aglow, and wondered if she had really stopped the rain.

We parted ways with the truck driver once we were on dry land. We thanked him, hugged him, never saw him again. We had been in a drowning car, then not.

Mami hailed a cab, and as we climbed into the back, I thought about how, when we were still seated in the semi truck, waiting to be secured to the tow, I had peered out of the window and cast a last glance at our Renault.

It was flooded up to the radio, and the coins Mami kept in the center cup holder were floating on the water.

As we rode in the taxi, heading now for high ground, I knew that what I had seen was impossible, that the coins, being metal alloy, would most certainly have sunk.

I considered what Papi would surely say: that I had undergone a traumatic event and, in my altered state of mind, hallucinated. Ximena would tell me I was fantasy-prone. Mami would label it an enchantment. But I had experienced the unexplained firsthand, and I didn't need to call it anything. Maybe just unexplained. I felt alone in what I had seen, and scared by what it might mean, but with Mami by my side, I felt safe.

14

WATER

In my family, stories travel up and down. Lives contract and splay out like accordions. Only the characters, it seems, are different. What I know is that many people came from neighboring cities in the state of Santander to see Nono, and that, just as Mami grew up in a living room teeming with people awaiting his treatment, so did I grow up in a house in Bogotá with people clamoring for Mami's care.

Just as Nono had done, Mami set up a consulting office in our house right around when I was two or three years old. In the attic, over a round table, she draped a blue cotton tapestry printed with galaxies and moons and stars, and over this image of the universe she scattered her small hand mirrors, golden pyramids, and royal-blue cones of incense.

Mami's clients came, in ones and twos and threes, at all hours of the day. They were doctors, businesspeople, seamstresses, cooks, security guards, engineers. Some were regulars: the fashion designer, the psychologist, the lawyer. I liked to sit on a bed of pillows at the second-floor landing, down the hall from the stairs that led to the attic, trying very hard but failing to find a mental footing in the only books we had—the dictionary, the encyclopedia, *The Communist Manifesto*—but here before me, marching up and down the steps of my own house, was a more accessible and fascinating literature.

Mami's clients were a common sight in the house for as long as I could remember; and, that year I turned eight, as the understanding that some people thought what Mami did was wrong sunk in, I watched them closely. They walked slowly behind her, staring at me. I stared back. We looked at one another as if we were each an item in a cabinet of curiosities.

What I really wanted was to be inside the room when Mami gave her readings, but I was not allowed. Sometimes I eavesdropped behind the closed door. I heard Mami's commanding voice, her clients sobbing or gasping; otherwise, a resounding silence.

Once the clients left, I went to find Mami so she could tell me about their ailments. Psychic-client confidentiality doesn't exist, so Mami shared everything. There was the school-grounds caretaker who wanted to know about her son's father—not her husband, but a man she saw once and never again. There was the lawyer whose ex-wife had cursed him to die in a car accident; he came twelve days in a row so Mami could cleanse him of the hex, and then returned every weekend to have his fortune read.

Sometimes Mami had no appointments, and she let me sit with her in the attic. I watched her, spellbound, as she lit a tea candle and placed it beneath a small tin bowl to burn rose oil into the air. She smoked cigarette after cigarette. She is someone who has always loved to hear herself talk, and I have always loved listening to her.

Mami repeated to me the lessons that Nono had given her— *Good divination is the art of a good story.* I took notes as if I were in a classroom. I was eager and serious about learning, perhaps to a pathetic degree. Mami described the legend building, the assured guesswork about a client's desires, the bridging of what she clearly saw and what she intuited. *You have to speak in metaphors, in paradox, in symbolism,* she said. *You have to tell a story that will allow the client to experience the truth without your ever having to name it.*

I wrote everything down in a scrawl, trying to keep up.

The biggest thing I have learned all these years, Mami confided in a low voice, *is that nobody wants the truth, but everyone wants a story.*

Mami didn't always know not to tell the truth directly. She had seen her father deal with the truth through symbol, but when she first started out, she was so preoccupied with following the process of divination that she forgot to disguise the answers her clients sought. Instead, she rattled them out: *Yes, your husband is cheating on you. No, you should not go on that trip. Yes, he likes you, but I do not see him long-term in your path.* Her readings were brief and to the point. None of her clients came back.

The first client Mami succeeded in keeping was a young woman who had been disinherited by her father. Mami didn't reveal the simple truth—that she needed to extend forgiveness to him before he extended forgiveness back to her. *Some truths are so plain, people think they're garbage,* Mami says. *Nobody wants to be told: Be a good person, be nice to your family, be kind. But sometimes that is the answer.*

Mami told the woman that, the day her father disinherited her, he had pinched one of her plants in anger, and until this plant was cleansed and released into the wild, her father would be deaf to her entreaties. Apparently, as the woman confirmed, it was true that the father had been toying with a plant when he told his daughter she was to receive no more money and was on her own. Mami and the woman slipped on surgical gloves and drove the plant to a nearby river, where they cleaned it with river water and prayed. It was there that Mami instructed the woman to forgive her father. The plant was a metaphor, but the woman would never know. Mami had given her a tangible task in the face of a broken relationship, gave her a story, and the woman forgave her father through the living of that story. Eventually, he forgave her too.

Was it the ritual that worked, or the metaphor? Is a ritual a story enacted?

Rituals are what allowed Mami to help her clients, who came to her not knowingly but nonetheless burdened with a number of truths which they could not directly acknowledge and preferred to ignore. They were the sort of truths, Mami said, that, if dragged into the light, upset the frail balance of a life. *Those poor people,* I said once. *Those poor people nothing,* Mami cut in. *It happens to us all.*

I chewed on my lip, wondering what truths we ourselves were refusing to admit, and tried very hard to identify them—the specters hiding on the other side of a wall.

I was too mature and thoughtful for an eight-year-old, people were always telling me. Maybe it was because Mami had never protected me from knowing the types of things that children are not supposed to know. Maybe I was too withdrawn and sensitive. Maybe the national state of emergency and violence had forced me to grow up too fast.

I know that I was a child who was often afraid. Papi had taken care to find us a new place to live in the north of the city, far from police, newspaper, and state buildings that could at any moment explode. Still, guerrilla groups left car bombs in front of banks and ATMs as metaphorical attacks against capitalism, and Pablo Escobar's paramilitaries left bombs in random places too—where their enemies lived, or in stores and public buildings, as routine acts of terror that forced the government to the negotiation table. I lived in a nest of worry.

We acted as if it were a mere inconvenience if our windows blew out from bomb blasts, but later at night, the experience put a shake in my hands. I moved in my small world with restraint, a sea of calm, overcompensating for the fear I felt at the scent of burning creeping closer to our home.

I had no name for the quick patter of my heart; the labored breathing; the episodes in which I lost track of time and fell into holes of abject terror. When I told Mami I thought I was having heart attacks, she took me to a doctor. The doctor timed the beating of my heart, hooked me up to a machine, and assured us nothing was wrong. We didn't know the term "panic attack," because our people didn't get sick in this way, or if they did, we had no word for it other than "suffering." We came from a people who dealt with suffering by making offerings, relying on our community, defying it with joy. This worked, for a time. But our suffering returned.

Unable to rid myself of the growing anxiety I felt, I threw myself into academic tasks. I outperformed my peers, finding relief in theorems and math and grammar. At home, I spent nearly all my free time trying to disappear into my surroundings so that I could eavesdrop while Mami's friends described to her the horrors of being a woman.

Mami's work of healing was never over. Even when she was off the clock, her friends came over, seeking her counsel. If Mami's friends became aware of my presence, they asked, *Should she be here?* Mami gazed at me. *She's fine. She's a little adult.* Mami listened to the problem, dealt cards, read palms, administered instructions for rituals and healing, and I came to understand that some men were everlastingly violent.

I found it soothing to catalogue all the possible undoings I might one day suffer. Men might get drunk and hit you, cheat and then accuse you of cheating, force themselves on you thinking if it was marriage it was not rape. Men could control the money. They could get other men to lie for them in court to keep the children, and in this way keep you hostage in a life you did not want. My heart broke for Mami's friends, but I listened clinically, methodically plotting a way to escape a similar fate.

Because I was mature for my age, I thought I understood what Mami meant when she spoke to me about people not wanting truth, but always story. I thought she was saying no one likes to hear their own flaws or mistakes spoken. No one wants to hear about how they're the ones ruining their own lives.

Now I think Mami was saying something deeper—that there is violence in the truth. Once it is spoken, it cannot be taken back. Even when we want to forget what's been revealed, to leave it behind, we cannot.

Mami was kind in her handling of people's truths. With her friends and to her clients, she told stories in which the truth fell into the background, there for them only when they were ready to deconstruct or understand what she had disguised.

Mami was a popular fortune-teller because of this ability, but her main source of income came from filling empty plastic bottles with water from our sink.

After filling the bottle to the top, she held the mouth of it to her lips, flashed the whites of her eyes, and delivered a long murmur. Nono had taught her to do that—to bless water so that her prayers, buoyant in the liquid, could be ingested—even though he himself had mostly depended on dreams and the plant medicines he harvested from the mountains, which were always at his disposal.

In the city, Mami had no mountains to peruse. Initially, she bought healing herbs from a market in a warehouse called Paloquemao, on the eastern part of Bogotá, near the city's geographical center. Past stalls overflowing with flowers and produce, at a kiosk in the back, curative herbs tied in bundles hung from the rafters. Nothing was labeled, and if you asked what they were, or what they were for, you'd be met with a cold silence and a stare.

When I turned five, in 1989, while Mami was on her way to Paloquemao, a bus packed full of dynamite exploded. The bus bomb had been parked in front of the police intelligence headquarters, around the corner from the market. Mami heard the blast, felt the ground shake; then the air filled with screaming. Sixty people died.

So Mami veered from Nono's teachings and stopped using herbs.

To Mami, there were two different types of troubles: people could suffer from afflictions that could be treated, nursed back to health, and restored; or they could suffer ruptures that could not be mended.

These last required more effort, and Mami had to deal with clients who stubbornly insisted she make their ailments disappear. *Who do you think I am,* Mami said, cross, *a magician?*

From what she had seen over and over in her consulting room, Mami said people tended to harbor a resistance to change, a misconception about the nature of life and bodies, a desire to remain always *like new*. But without fail, what people truly wanted was to be free.

Whenever Mami's clients had troubles of the second order, the kind that couldn't be reversed, healing came from accepting that some things that touch us change us forever; and beyond that place of reckoning was a path of adaptation, a surge of creativity in the face of the new limitation.

For the price of fifty thousand pesos, about a quarter of our groceries, Mami's blessed water most often promised to rekindle marriages, turn up jobs, protect against the evil eye, carry out light exorcisms, help with depression and other mental instabilities, and remedy the pain of unrequited love.

She labeled the bottles, laid them sideways in a row, and stacked them in pyramid formations in the kitchen. Customers came and went, giving Mami money and stealing away with our tap water.

Mami was always pressuring Ximena and me to drink more soda so that she could have more bottles to sell. The whole thing was funny to us. As Colombian children, we had been drinking coffee since we could remember. In the mornings, before school, when Mami was in earshot, we stole each other's morning coffees, blew on the surface, and, returning them, said, *Here you go, you will get an A in math today!*

Ajá! Mami said, banging her hand on something wooden in the kitchen. *And who do you think is paying for the roof over your heads and the food on your table?*

We laughed.

Of all the people Mami healed, those she wanted to help most were Papi, my sister, and me. We also happened to be the most resistant to her aid. Mami was exasperated. *Do you know that people pay me to do what I'm offering to do for you for free?*

Papi had lost his job, betrayed and set up by colleagues he thought were friends. He spent his days on the second floor of the house, sitting in the dark in his bedroom, his back bent, staring off into space, unable to eat. Mami said to leave him be: he would eventually come around to allowing her care. Meanwhile, the bills piled up on the dining table. To this day, I am amazed that Mami put food on the table and paid our mortgage largely by breathing words over water.

I did what Mami said. I put Papi out of my mind. I did not worry about Mami's born-again siblings, whose display of love and aggression confused me. *Don't waste your time on people who don't love you well,* Mami said. I laid all my trust at my mother's feet, followed her around as she continued to expound upon the theorems of divination. She taught me how to do tarot card readings, what each suit and number meant, and when she could think of nothing else to teach me, she dealt the cards into a star and read her own fortune.

In the tarot, Mami was always the Empress, a woman wearing a crown of stars reclining on a throne with a scepter in her hand. Whenever she drew the card, she clapped in glee. *Oh! There I am!*

I loved to see how the stories bubbled to the surface in Mami's tarot. It wasn't the Empress herself who told the story, but the cards around her. They were the ones that unfolded each chapter of Mami's life: The poverty and violence of her childhood. The brutality and obsession she awoke in the men around her. The cousin who nearly raped her. The man she was forced to marry before Papi, whom she wasn't quite ready to tell me about fully. My father, with whom she finally made peace and a home. Mami told me about how he had locked her in the apartment, and how the man he was back then was gone now. He woke up to his sexist treatment of women, and worked hard so he could be a different man for us.

When Mami turned her attention to the area of the tarot card star that spoke of her future, she peered breathlessly at the cards, but she did not dare tell me what she saw. Even Mami was reticent in the face of a truth she had no control over.

To help with money, under Mami's tutelage, I read fortunes at school, using a deck of playing cards. Being a rookie, I only charged five hundred pesos per reading. In the beginning, I made an effort to do as Mami instructed, following her steps for divination. But as my clientele grew, I found I didn't actually have to do any work. I could tell from what people asked of the cards what they really wanted to know, which in my school was one of two things—who had a crush on whom, and who was cheating on whom. I knew all of it. I was a repository of information. I dealt the cards without looking at them, talked cryptically about symbols, relayed the information, and charged my fee, which as I grew confident, I exponentially increased.

When I brought my earnings back home and gave them to Mami, she laughed at my laziness and was also proud of my hustle. When I told her I was using deduction and not divination, she winked. *That's my girl.*

Those months, when I was learning divination and helping with money, felt long, and I completely forgot about Papi, until he didn't sleep for three consecutive days. My sister and I were worried. Mami said it was depression and she could fix it, but Ximena scolded her: *He needs a doctor. Take him to the hospital.*

Mami tsked. *What are they going to do? Medicate him until he can't think?*

She spent hours in the kitchen, murmuring over the surface of three glasses of water. I had never seen her pay so much attention to a single prayer. She needed the water to be potent, she explained.

Before, Papi had rejected anything Mami had prayed over, but now his insomnia made him compliant. She said, *Drink,* and he tipped back each glass and swallowed every drop. That afternoon, he fell into a deep sleep.

Qué les dije? Mami beamed. *My water works.*

It's a coincidence, Mami, Ximena said, flashing her eyes in annoyance. *He had to fall asleep at some point.*

Except that Papi then went two days without waking up. Even when we shook him, we couldn't make him come to. He moaned. He tossed. We couldn't make him keep his eyes open. We got worried again.

Ay jueputa, Mami said, running to the kitchen. *I overdid it.*

I laughed. In the kitchen, Mami turned on the faucet and held a glass beneath the stream.

It's because I used the wrong word, she explained. *This time, I am going to bless the water with the clear objective of making him alert.*

While Mami filled two more glasses, the water rising over the top and spilling onto her hand, she said: *You have to choose the words accurately, you see. You can't be inexact. A vagueness on your part, and kaput.*

You can't be inexact, I repeated in my head, stowing away more of what would become the best writing lesson I will ever receive. *A vagueness on your part, and kaput.*

Now go, Mami was entreating, setting the three glasses before her on the counter. *I must begin.*

The water meant to make Papi alert got him out of his slumber, but didn't have any other obvious effects. Each day Mami gave Papi a different diagnosis. One day, she prepared water to reconnect him with his purpose. Another day, she prayed for the water to help him locate his voice. Finally, she blessed the water so that his voice, wherever it was being held captive, returned to him. When Papi drank this last water, he threw up in the bathroom. He retched until there was bile.

Good, Mami said. *Now we're getting somewhere.*

Papi crawled back into bed, looking pale and exhausted. Mami dragged me out of the bedroom to leave him to his rest and closed the door behind us. *Now we wait,* she whispered. She made her way to the attic, and I went along. I waited until we were seated amid her trinkets and asked, *Wait for what?*

Hmm? Mami was simultaneously sucking on a cigarette and shaking a lit match in the air to extinguish the flame. *Oh! Your father? For his confidence to come back. That's what's wrong with him.*

Good divination is the art of a good story, *Mami said.*
Bogotá, 1981

It is? Why didn't you tell him?

Mami exhaled smoke. *I already explained this. You can only point the client in the right direction. You can't tell a client the truth.*

As I left Mami's side and went to my bedroom, I wondered what things Mami could see me struggling with that she wasn't telling me. There must have been some truth I was failing to grasp. I crawled into the space beneath my bed, suddenly short of breath. Mechanically, I counted to one hundred, a tangible task I had devised to tolerate and be patient before a fear and pain I had no name for. (This was a strategy which later, when I had no memory, I would devise anew, as if I hadn't thought it before.) At eight years old, under my bed, I tried very hard to think through what it was that I could possibly be ignoring, evading, burying deep—what, if acknowledged, would make everything collapse.

The next day, Papi woke up and started looking for work. He called in favors and got some preliminary interviews. The problem came, each time, when he had to explain why he had been fired from his previous job. *A colleague backstabbed me,* he explained the first time. *Nothing, in the end, was proved against me,* he tried in the next interview. Then he hit upon the right words: *I made the mistake of not being vigilant of the budget that people beneath me were handling. I will not make that mistake twice.* In a week, he was invited to visit an oil site and see if the project and company was a good fit. As with Mami, for Papi it was a matter of finding the right words.

My fortune-telling spot was under a tree, where prickly grass poked at my legs. We had to wear plaid skirts at school then, and knee-high blue socks. I sat there at the start of recess and worked through the break. There was always a line: kids my age, older kids, younger kids.

Because the information I had provided about crushes turned out to be so accurate, people began to ask after other details of their lives. I heard about divorced parents, older siblings' drug addiction, abortions, brushes with guerrillas and paramilitaries, death.

I dealt cards despairingly, for the first time understanding the responsibility of divination. It wasn't just about precision; it was about interpreting the language of grief and finding there a sense of direction that had eluded the client. But violence was nonsense. What possible answer could there be in the face of it?

That must have been why curanderos were often people who had survived illness, near-death accidents, loss. It took going to the abyss and returning to know how to open a path through wreckage. I was out of my depth.

I knew, from watching my mother, that I was supposed to create a ritual in order to shore up these darker questions. I was supposed to create a story.

Once, a classmate asked after her father, who was being held in the jungle by guerrillas. She wanted to get a message to him and asked if I could perform such magic.

Another time, a classmate told me his family was losing their house, and asked where he would be living in a couple of years.

What ritual, what story could I build to hold these confessions? Were these troubles of the first order, the ones that could be solved, or of the second, the ones that required surrender and adaptation? I declined both times, saying I was not advanced enough to help.

At home, Mami tried to instruct me: *When somebody shares their inner pain, they are sharing a burden. A good curandera knows to make space for the burden, but knows never to pick it up.*

I was always trying to pick it up. *I don't think I'm meant for this,* I told Mami.

Bemused, Mami replied, *I already told you that. I thought you were having fun.* She was doing something with her hands, maybe darning a sock. What I do remember is the intense focus of her eyes, her long lashes, her silky black hair, and what might have been a vibrant red thread poking in and out of black fabric. *It's not fun anymore?*

I shook my head.

So stop.

One regular client of Mami's was the most intriguing to me. She wore stylish ponchos and high-heeled leather boots. She was a trader, exporting which goods we weren't sure, but what she asked Mami never changed. She brought a calendar with handfuls of days circled and wanted to know which ones were auspicious and which inauspicious. My mother never asked, *Auspicious for what?* The woman said it had to do with shipments. I told Mami I thought the woman was lying; probably she was a wedding planner. Mami was sure the woman was lying too, but suspected she was hiding something worse.

Like what?

Mami wouldn't say. *What are we going to do? We need the money.*

While Papi was away, interviewing at the oil site where he would eventually be hired, the trader arrived with a big envelope. Mami pulled it out to show me: inside were three tickets for an all-expenses-paid vacation to Medellín.

What did you do to deserve that*?* I asked.

Apparently, one date that Mami had approved had turned out to be a great business decision, and the woman was thankful. Mami didn't think we should take the vacation, but Ximena and I begged her to accept. *You never take us anywhere!* we said. *Nothing interesting ever happens to us!* We reasoned that Papi was away and it didn't matter where we went or what we did. We got on the plane.

Medellín was very unlike Bogotá. It was warm and hilly, and the hotel was luxurious. We lounged by the pool. The hotel staff were overly attentive. We reveled in the freedom of the warm air, the fresh towels, and all the nonalcoholic daiquiris we could want. For the first time in our lives, we didn't have to worry about money. We greased our limbs with coconut oil and darkened under the

sun. We only had to shift in our seats and look around for someone on the staff to jog to our side.

When we asked at the front desk about sightseeing, we were
discouraged. Medellín was Pablo Escobar's turf, and he was on the
run from hired assassins, who were riding motorcycles in search
of him. *Stay here,* the people at the front desk told us. *We'll see to
whatever you need.*

When we got home, we found a message on our answering
machine. Papi was still at the oil site, and there was a chance the
job might be offered to him on the spot. Ximena and I clapped
in glee, but Mami stared as if from far off. She explained that our
getaway had left her with a bad feeling: *This all smells like drug
trafficking to me.*

When the trader showed up for her next appointment, Mami
thanked her profusely for the trip. The woman smiled and said
she was glad we had enjoyed ourselves. She pulled out the calendar with a new set of dates already circled. *Maybe you can help
me again!*

Mami said, half joking, *Thank God you're not testing your luck
by being a mule.*

Me? the trader said. *No, nothing like that! That's for the people
who work for me.*

Mami hid her shock, forced a smile, asked, *And business has
been good?*

*Yes! Ever since I've started coming to you, our people are almost
never pulled aside by the customs officers!*

The woman said she worked for Pablo Escobar. Mami gave the
trader dates one last time, and once she was gone vowed to never
see her again. Mami lit a candle for my father and prayed that he
would get the job. She thought maybe she should quit. Some people had always said it was bad luck to charge money for a spiritual
gift, and there would always be people like the trader who would
use Mami's abilities for immoral purposes. And her siblings constantly told her she was sinning. Mami felt attacked from all sides.

When the trader called, Mami excused herself: *I am retiring, and there is a lot of darkness in what you do. I will not be involved.*

Nothing about this business ever brings good luck, Mami told us. *What if my life gets torn apart through all this meddling?* Her eyes glinted with actual fear. I had never seen her like that. My breath caught.

It was damnable that we had taken money that came indirectly from Pablo Escobar. Those were his bombs exploding on our television screen, in malls and highways, in front of banks, under bridges, on airplanes. We had received blood money—worse, she had aided a murderer's business.

Mami prepared glasses of water for my sister and me. I was ready to decline, sure that my older sister would refuse first. But Ximena didn't protest. I think seeing Mami afraid rattled her too. I watched my sister drink her water; a moment later, she felt sick, and she retched in the bathroom until there was bile, just as Papi had.

I believed in my mother, but I could not grasp how the same thing that had happened to Papi had happened to Ximena—until I drank my glass of water and threw up and retched myself. I had not been feeling sick at all, but the water I had just swallowed came back up, and after it, an orange, foul-smelling sap.

Afterward, I felt clean and spent. My body tingled, and a deep rest overtook me. For a moment before falling asleep, I luxuriated in the physical sensation of the transformation that had taken place.

When Papi returned, officially with a job, Mami cut down on her clients, seeing only people she felt she could trust. We delighted in our good fortune.

Then tío Ariel's wife, Mariana, called. She wanted to invite us to her late husband's funeral. Tío Ariel was dead.

15

MEMORY LAGOON

On the night he died, that September of 1992, tío Ariel was drinking alone at home.

When Nono was still alive, he and tío Ariel busied themselves with the exercise of calling upon spirits and taunting them. Often Mariana woke to sounds of things crashing. The spirits who materialized were violent. Once, she raced toward the loud banging in the living room and witnessed a lamp hurled across the room by no one she could see, and Nono and Ariel hiding behind the couch, arguing over who would intervene with the ghost. After Nono's passing, tío Ariel had kept up the antics, and Mariana no longer got up to check if he was okay.

The night he died, tío Ariel called Mariana's name. When she stepped into their living room, he was red in the face and extending to her a knife. *I'm having a heart attack,* he breathed, then pressed the knife on the neck artery he wanted her to cut so that his blood pressure would go down. Mariana backed away. Weeping, she called an ambulance. Weeping, she watched him die.

Tío Ariel was one of the youngest siblings. His death was a shock. Half the family blamed Mariana; the other half blamed Nono. Mariana should have sliced into her husband where he indicated. Nono shouldn't have passed the secrets down to tío Ariel. They weren't right for him, and they had led him to drink. With this death in the family, Nona demanded that her children set aside their differences. She wanted everyone reconciled and together. Her children kept the peace, numb to one another and grieving, hugging, briefly blaming one another, parting ways.

In Bogotá, Mami agonized over ever having asked Nono to teach tío Ariel anything. None of us blamed Mami, but she withered before our eyes. It was almost like Mami couldn't stop hearing her siblings' condemnations, and they nursed on her until she had a crisis of faith. Maybe healing was okay, but telling the future was not. She had recently observed that her clients became embittered and addicted to her visions when she gave them access to the bits and pieces she could foretell of their future. She wanted to facilitate a deeper connection between people and the unknowable, but she ended up being mistaken for the connection itself. She was robbing them of their spiritual connection. Mami made rice and took it to her bed, where she ate alone with a spoon directly from the pot, falling into a deep depression that would last for the rest of the year, and which we would call, in hindsight, the Epoch of Rice.

That same September, Mariana might have been thinking of her late husband when she sent her sons Gabriel and Omar away, just as if she were sending them to a summer camp, to a distant farm where they could apprentice with a curandero. The training lasted a few weeks, but her sons returned to Bucaramanga without new abilities, and Gabriel couldn't remember a single prayer he was told. At the dinner table, however, Omar's voice would all of a sudden boom like tío Ariel's. He called Mariana *mi amor* and asked his siblings about homework, just as their father had done. Then he yipped and howled and scratched behind his ear like a dog. A few minutes later, he'd press his hands together and whisper litanies, and adjusted what seemed to be an invisible nun's veil. Years after, Omar would tell me that he had no recollection of the time during which he was possessed.

Mariana took Omar to other curanderos in Bucaramanga so

they could shut down whatever allowed spirits to pass through him as if he were a revolving door. Hospital doctors gave him pills, and Catholic priests sprinkled him with holy water. Eventually, the episodes Omar suffered became less frequent, then ceased.

At home, while Mami withdrew, Papi denied that Mami had healed him. Time and his own efforts were what had gotten him out of his anguish, misery, and insomnia. He was working during the week at an oil site in Chitasuga, a savanna an hour north of Bogotá, and came home to us on the weekends.

I sat with Papi when he leisured with a drink, as he played records and drew cartoon potatoes wearing top hats on the back of napkins. He scooped ice into one of his special whiskey glasses for me, poured soda, and splashed the tiniest bit of whiskey on top, just enough for me to pretend.

As far as I knew, drinking was a requisite of being a man. Everything revolved around drink, the amber gold floating a constellation of ice. It looked the same way whether the men were together or alone: the singing along to music, the raised fist in the remembrance of a broken heart, the eventual slumping and staring down at the surface of a table in abject desolation.

Papi said that Mami needed space, and that everyone was pretty broken up about tío Ariel. I asked him if he thought Mami would quit divination, and he told me that Mami was a woman who would never stop being herself, no matter what she decided.

Papi understood Mami in a way I failed to. When I asked him why he had liked her to begin with—they were so incompatible in what they believed—he thought about it for a moment, then said, *She's more alive than anyone I have ever met.* Though he reserved his doubts about her healing ability, Papi said it wasn't personal: he doubted all religion.

Papi and Mami met in Bucaramanga, where Papi was born. He was not at all impressed that Mami's father was a curandero. One of Papi's uncles was a curandero, too. He called himself Simón

Calambas, Curandero of the Mountain. But unlike Nono, tío Simón was running a con. He was married to a Wayuu woman, who knew Wayuu medicine but never gave it to outsiders, least of all to white Colombians. They were itinerant together, making their way from town to town, earning their living by selling fake cures. *Potions for love,* they announced. *For money, against sorcery.* Within minutes, a line would form. When they passed through Bucaramanga, Papi watched as money and colored bottles exchanged hands. The couple stayed in Papi's small bed, and Papi slept outside in a hammock. Like Mami, the family treated tío Simón's wife with disdain. But tío Simón was Christian, and the con of being a curandero was *just a con.* His sin of lying to people was one that Papi's family forgave him: he was taking money only from the lost and superstitious.

Each time he visited, tío Simón gave Papi a bundle of coins to collect wild herbs from which to make tinctures. In the family's kitchen, a little assembly line formed: Papi's mother holding a small bottle as tío Simón added aguardiente, then water, and tío Simón's wife mixed in different-colored dyes—and sometimes a worm, for flair. The different dyes denoted a system: the blue bottle was to ward off the evil eye, the red to steal a man's heart, the gold to win the lottery. The bottles were not blessed, and nothing was done to them except wiping them down.

My father is a curandero for real, Mami, age fifteen, told Papi as they were becoming friends. He was six years older.

Sure, sure.

I have the power to see too, Mami insisted.

No, I believe you, he said, not believing her for a second.

Papi and Mami were an odd pair. They were only friends because Mami had run out of guardians to answer the principal's calls when she got in trouble. She got in trouble often at school—for talking back, cheating, interrupting, wearing skirts that were too short, fighting, sneaking out. Nono went at first, but he tired of going to the school; then Nona refused; then all her brothers one by one. Papi had been the best student at the school in a decade, and since he was still involved because of his little brothers, the principal had asked him to act as Mami's guardian.

Papi took pains in tutoring Mami, to no avail. When he came over to her house, she tricked him into doing her homework. Papi was serious, mature. Throughout high school, he had earned more money than his father by tutoring rich kids, and these earnings paid for the family's rent and all his siblings' food, clothes, and school supplies. Mami was the opposite: free-spirited, careless, unreliable.

Papi had a strange way of talking. He told me a story when I asked a simple question, and when I asked for a story, he gave me science and philosophy.

Millions of years ago, he began, in response to my request for the most exciting story he knew, *at the bottom of the oceans, rivers, lakes—in all the basins of the earth—microscopic animals, algae, remains, and matter collected.*

He paused for effect.

Then, over hundreds of years, these remains were covered in sediment, then buried over for millions of years more. As the earth moved, they sank deeper and deeper. In the heat and pressure near the core of the earth, these remains were cooked into a soup. Now, when the earth shifts, sometimes this soup comes closer to the surface.

This was oil, Papi said, the deep-night substance that polluted the oceans and that we used as fuel. *Isn't that incredible?*

Papi said nobody understood the holiness of what it truly was: remains of organic life consumed over millions of years, kissed by what lived at the core of the earth, returned to the surface. Papi said nobody knew what lived at the core. It was an unmeasurable place. No instrument we knew to create could withstand the high pressure and volatility of what exists there. Scientists theorize that the core is mostly iron, which, along with other heavy minerals, is what would have sifted down to the planetary center. What we do know is that beneath the crust of the earth there's a layer of magma. Beneath that, it is believed there is a swirling sea of boiling iron encircling a solid ball of iron that is so hot and pressurized, it rotates slowly.

I thought about all that lay untold in the men I knew.

Papi and the tíos were proud of not breaking, of acting tough. Conversely, in the middle of the day, the tías cried over loads of laundry, spoke with a rawness that marked that hour in the afternoon as a forever-crater in my mind. And then, as if it had been nothing, they'd dust their hands, wipe their cheeks, bask in the lightness that came from having expressed a deeply buried truth, and move on. They began the work of cooking dinner.

What the men in the family couldn't see was that, in their suffering alone, they only made us, their wives and daughters, carry the weight of what they would not deal with themselves. Papi grew angry, restless, anxious, depressed, until we were hurt by his actions and Mami was forced to swoop in to help.

Papi, what happened to you in jail? I asked him when I was nine.

Nothing, nothing, Papi would reply, in a way that told me a lot had happened, more than he could say.

Before I was born, Papi was imprisoned for leading a coup d'état on the government palace in Bucaramanga, back when he was a communist and courting Mami. He had always been devoted to his community. When he was nine, as old as I was then, he organized boxing matches, collected money from spectators, and, with his brothers, used those funds to build a community well. The coup d'état he led in his twenties came about because the land where his barrio was built was eroding—each month, a house tumbled down the mountain—and the mayor was criminally idle.

I sat with Papi, with my drink and my intuitive knowing of what it meant to be a woman. I waited until I knew he was in the place where the borders of what I was allowed to know of him and what he was allowed to know of himself became porous. Then I asked him again: *Papi, what was it like in prison?*

He developed a phobia of small places, he told me. He was unable to sleep. He came to know the terror of time that goes by too slowly, the cruelty of guards with too much power. But he found friendship in a man he played chess with in the courtyard. Before I could ask, Papi said: *I can't tell you who he is. He's the head of a guerrilla group now, strange to see him in the news all the time.*

A silence settled between us, and I made mental calculations. Papi had been held for thirty days. What could happen in that time to turn a communist man into a capitalist? *What did they do to you in there?*

Papi didn't answer, not even then.

Nothing ever goes away, he said once in response, but I was never sure whether he meant it as an answer to my question or as the beginning of a different story, which he was telling to shift my attention.

Nothing ever goes away. When I was a novice, the man who was the head engineer and responsible for the calculations of the drill made a mathematical mistake. Mine was the graveyard shift, and I always did it with a friend. One night, this friend told me he wanted coffee. So I went back to the trailers where all of us slept, to get us some. I was walking back, holding two cups, when the night flashed bright-orange. In a moment, I heard the sound of the explosion.

They could find nothing of the body. No skin, no bones, no teeth, nothing. He was gone. But nothing goes away all the way. Sometimes I think I can feel the heat of the cup of coffee he wanted still burning my hand.

Papi told me about his life when he was younger, before his family's farm was burned down by paramilitaries. In the Andes, he woke early to make a bonfire, heat water, and make coffee by filtering the grounds through a clean sock. He killed birds with a sling. After his family lost their land and moved to the city of Bucaramanga, Papi saw that education could be a way out of poverty. He tutored the wealthy. His family showed him affection only when he came home with cash. Their love felt conditional to him, something he had to earn. *I've never told this to anyone.*

In the morning, Papi did not remember a thing he'd said. This happened when people drank too much alcohol, he explained. You forgot whole swaths of time. It was known as a memory lagoon. What you lived became flooded. Land was memory. Water was forgetfulness. If he thought back to the night, all he saw was water.

The holiday season came and Mami, still cloaked in sadness, didn't feel like going to see her family in Cúcuta. We pleaded for Papi to bring us to his work, so we could see the oil he talked so much about. He said it was no place for children, but Ximena and I insisted until he gave in. All of us went: Mami and Ximena and Papi and I.

At Chitasuga, I was disappointed. The oil site didn't look at all like the holy place he had described. It looked like destruction. The land was razed to the horizon, and machines drilled into the earth in violent repetition, spewing out black smoke. We walked carefully around a man-made crater. It was a mile wide. I was afraid of falling in. After a long slip of earth, there was a pool of crude oil at the bottom. It wasn't all crude oil, Papi corrected. Beneath a top layer of oil, there was water, all of it runoff from the machines.

Here, at this site, I experienced my first memory lagoon.

Ximena and I asked to see the machines up close, and Mami said she'd wait by the trailers, where it was clean. Ximena and I walked behind Papi on a metal walkway into a forest of machinery. Steel hammerheads and thrusting pulleys loomed high above, engaged in hissing and repetitive choreographies, splashing the walkway with oil. At regular intervals, pipes released streams of crude oil into large rectangular vats. The oil was the blackest black I had ever seen. Beyond this, I have no further recollection.

Ximena says that Papi left us alone, that he went to check on something with a worker. In his absence, we played at jumping across the edges of the vats. We dipped our fingers into the sunless ooze. Ximena heard a splash. When she turned, I was inside the vat, gasping, struggling in the black mire. The walls of the vat were slanted and slick, and when I tried to climb out, I fell back in. The iridescent dark pulled me under. Ximena ran to get help.

Papi insists that the vats were not deep, and that he never left us unattended. In his memory, when I fell into the vat I was only waist deep in the crude oil, and there was never a danger of my drowning. What's more, as soon as I tumbled in, he fished me out.

I don't know whose memory to believe. I recall neither staring at nor jumping over the black sludge, neither nearly drowning nor being rescued.

I don't know if I remember sinking under the weighted liquid, or if I dreamt or imagined it—the discovery, in that instant, of time as a finite thing, only a minute more afloat and my muscles would give.

I know that I was brought to Mami by the man-made crater and the trailers, covered head to toe in crude oil, looking like a creature from a lagoon. I was stripped of my clothes in front of scores of men. The workers poured gasoline over my body to wash off the oil since it would not come off with water, and the fumes made me light-headed and sick.

Ximena said I was quiet for days after—that, no matter how many times I bathed, I still smelled like gasoline. She says that I didn't speak when spoken to, that my skin looked yellow at first and then green for two more days before it went back to normal.

What I can recall is that, some days after I fell into the crude oil, Mami and Papi, desperate for joy, made plans to go dancing. As always, Mami conjured up her ghosts to watch over us, and then left. I remember I was drinking water from a glass and that, just as I swallowed, I heard disembodied laughter. It was high-pitched and maniacal. I could feel the breath of it on my neck. I hid in the closet, where the sound of the thing that laughed paced on the other side of the door, and from where I could hear, in the close distance, maybe down the hall, the digital warble of Ximena playing video games. When Mami and Papi got home, Mami found me curled and hugging myself, on top of a pile of shoes.

Everything okay?

Uh-huh, I said, rising and ashamed. I didn't tell her what had visited me. I figured it was an isolated incident and I could keep it to myself.

Days later, I lay down and heard a violin. The melody crept into my ear, each note sustained until it bent and wavered into the next. I stood and reeled back, besieged by what was, and remains still, the most ethereal musical sequence I have ever heard. I rushed out of my room to be with my family, so we could experience the sweeping revelation of the violin together—played by some incredibly gifted neighbor, I assumed. But when I got to them, Papi and Ximena shook their heads in confusion, and Mami tilted her head to one side, observing me with attention. Nobody else could hear the violin, and in an instant it was gone.

The music had been so beautiful, I did not concern myself with its inexplicable arrival. But then, at the end of the week, when I was again alone, next to my ear I heard the quiet, insistent voice of a young boy describing with chilling detail the long tunnel of the barrel of a gun.

I covered my ears, but still I could hear the ever-darkening voice. I waited for it to go away. It only became louder. I ran to Mami, knelt before her in tears, admitted I was hearing things. I wanted her to make it stop. Mami placed her hands over my ears. This was something she could block for me. *You don't want it?*

I shook my head no.

Her palms created a quiet roar in my ears, what Papi said was the sound of my own blood circling my brain. I saw the whites of her eyes flare between her lashes. Color rose in her cheeks. I saw her lips moving. When she removed her palms, she kissed my forehead. *The second you hear anything again, you come to me.*

But the voice of the boy was gone, and I would never have to go to Mami again for such help: I didn't hear another disembodied sound. Whatever my fall had opened in me was now tightly shut.

That night, as if Mami were finally returning from a long-lasting, arduous journey, she told me a story. She told me for the first time of her falling down the well and how it had awoken in her new abilities to perceive. Falling could be the beginning of a mysterious journey. Some accidents were initiations. Hearing voices was a gift. But I didn't have to follow in her path if I didn't so choose.

When Papi overheard Mami, he made me sit in front of a science book and explained the chemistry of the brain. I'd had auditory hallucinations, not a psychic event. Papi tapped his finger over various sections of the brain diagram, naming parts of anatomy I did not know then nor do I now remember. Mami scoffed, grew incensed, reminded us that she had lost the power to hear ghosts when I was born. It wasn't my brain that was the problem, it was what I had inherited from her—which she could remove from me. We should be thankful that she still had enough power and knowledge to protect me from a destiny I did not want.

When school started again, everybody asked how come I wasn't at my fortune-telling spot beneath the trees. I couldn't say I had fallen into crude oil, I had heard disembodied sounds, I was heartbroken about my uncle.

At home, Mami announced she didn't want to tell fortunes anymore. Maybe it was the still-fresh heartbreak of tío Ariel's passing, my hearing things, the lingering effects of the born-again chorus that she was doing wrong. Whatever the cause, she folded up her cloth of stars, put away her incense and mirrors.

Following Mami's suit, I gave one last day of readings at school, and then I, too, closed my business. My last client was a girl who wanted to know about the architecture of hell. I didn't have to deal the cards to tell her, *I don't know if that's not already where we live.*

16

DOUBLES

For a little while after Mami shuttered her psychic business, it seemed like, if there had ever been a curse, we had slipped from its grasp. Just after I turned ten, Pablo Escobar was shot in December on a rooftop in Medellín, and it seemed like peace was just around the corner. Fireworks blazed the sky all that month, and in the streets people sporadically erupted into dance. We had money now and bought airplane tickets to Cúcuta, but as we crossed through security, I understood why we never flew. Papi had a homonym, a man who shared his full name (with both surnames, from father and mother) and place of birth.

The *other* Fernando Rojas Zapata, alias The Devil, was thirteen years younger and wanted for larceny. I had always known about Papi's homonym, but, just like the stories of Mami's appearing in two places at once, it sounded too incredible to be true. Yet, right after putting our bags through the X-ray, we were pulled aside. Papi gestured wildly. He shuffled through a sheaf of documents, explaining they proved he was the *other* Fernando Rojas Zapata. The security officer was so skeptical, he refused to glance at the letters and records. It was tense and quiet for so long, I finally asked: *So how long have you been looking for this other Fernando Rojas Zapata?*

Mami flicked her hand in front of my face. *No le pare bolas. Imagine my martyrdom—the girl wants to be a journalist.*

When I displease her, Mami refers to me as *the girl*, which I find hysterical. She also switches to *usted* pronouns, which we normally use to build polite distance with bosses and strangers, but which can be wielded against friends and lovers and family members to create an instant diss.

The customs officer snorted. *What about something safer, mi amor, like a teacher?*

I shrugged. *I'm going to be a journalist, I don't care if I die.*

See? Mami pushed me aside. *Más terca que una cabra, no me joda.*

De tal palo tal astilla, Ximena said under her breath.

The officer smiled at us.

Do you ever have to use your gun?

Papi glared at me. He was afraid of the authorities. He perpetually warned us that the state exerted violence and covered it up, that it happened all the time and could happen to us. Mami was not intimidated. She knew she could be downright hypnotizing if she wanted. Once, an officer pulled her over for running a red light, and it ended in Mami giving the man a palm reading and him handing *us* money.

Probably there've been no gunfights at the airport, Mami said to me, and then to the officer: *But what about exciting celebrity arrests?*

We were led to what might have been a waiting room, though I pretended it was an interrogation room, while a higher-up reviewed Papi's paperwork.

I had not yet had altercations with the authorities, and my excitement over our proximity to the illicit made me feel drunk. *Don't we all just want to go find this other Fernando Rojas Zapata, alias The Devil? What if he also shares Papi's face? What if it's Papi but younger, a Papi of a past Papi never lived? What if he also has a wife and two daughters, and what if these people are also our twins, except they've lived an opposite life?*

Ximena rubbed her temples. *How long is the flight again?*

All I know is thank God for earphones, Mami said.

Praise the Lord, Papi said.

Papi's new company had a program to help workers buy a home, and through this Papi and Mami got an apartment in Cúcuta, where they planned to retire. The company provided the money for the mortgage and a loan with low interest. For the first time, we had a place of our own, and we were determined to have a good vacation.

There had been an outcry from Mami's siblings when they heard of her plans. Many of them were still paying their mortgages, and if Mami had money to spare, she should help them. Mami explained that we didn't have new money, we were borrowing. Her siblings were resentful, but all Mami cared about was Nona, who gave her blessing, and who told her that we were welcome and had been sorely missed.

The newness of the apartment in Cúcuta startled us. The entrance to the building was still under construction, and the halls were half done. We gazed down the shaft where there was no elevator car, only a frightful drop, then took the stairs to find the apartment itself pristine and empty. The kitchen gleamed with new appliances. We had nowhere to sleep or sit, but we strolled down the block to the hardware store and bought a silver tinsel Christmas tree, then ordered pizza. Papi played music from a little handheld radio, the little battery-powered device that he kept on his person at all times like a talisman to battle his nerves and insomnia. He and Mami strung the balcony with lights, while Ximena and I stabbed the plastic branches into the center stem of the tree, unfurling the fluff of its metallic foliage. We slept on top of folded towels and blankets, overjoyed, never having dreamt we'd have a second home. The next day, Ximena and I draped ourselves all over the place, drinking cup after cup of coffee, sitting in front of the fans (also purchased at the hardware store), keeping to our weekend morning routines, discussing what made murderers murderers.

We went out looking for secondhand furniture, picking up cheap side tables, a living room set, pots and plates. When we returned, we found a tío napping in one of the rooms, a tía serving herself tea in the living room, cousins indulging in the view. One tía had helped with the practical details of buying the apartment, and she had a key. We inferred that copies had been made. Everything, it seemed, was multiplying without our consent. We didn't mind too much when it was tía Perla, tía Nahía, or tío Ángel and their kids in our apartment. But sometimes it was one of Mami's born-again siblings inside, standing erect and sanctimonious. They noted what we'd bought, hypothesized how much we'd spent, asked how we were, called Mami a witch and our new belongings the spoils of the devil's favor—then, as if it wasn't contradictory, asked for her medicine:

I'm in danger, Sojaila. Pronounce one of your protection spells. If you ever loved me, help me. Remember that we're blood.

Though they had insulted her, Mami thought of their children, her own nephews and nieces, and prepared water for her siblings to drink. Ximena and I watched from afar. Mami's born-again siblings pared apples for us, offered us candies, told us to draw close. But we were reticent before their confusing behavior. *Cría cuervos,* they called Mami. *Why don't your children obey their elders?* they harrumphed. *Wait until they come of age—it'll be an unwanted pregnancy, and that'll be that.*

I tried to understand Mami's born-again siblings. I thought they suffered from a jealousy that grew in proportion to their individual despairs. Some were in poor health and suffered job instability, were daily preoccupied with living in an unsafe neighborhood, lost sleep over the difficulty of feeding their children when they could not get out of paying the fees guerrillas demanded for *keeping the neighborhood safe.* And there we were, with a house in Bogotá, and a new home in Cúcuta. And even though Mami had been regularly wiring money to help her siblings, the dynamic only made things worse. Then, one day, we went for a walk by the river and came back to find our apartment walls covered in crosses drawn with oil. We didn't doubt that they had done this. They must have brought in a priest to perform a house exorcism of what they imagined were our satanic midnight rites. Then we found little voodoo dolls buried in the soil of our houseplants.

It was surprising, the degree to which our own blood did not love us—startling, even. Papi said, beneath it all, they objected to class disparity; but what surfaced was an unwavering fixation on Mami being a curandera. Back then, I didn't understand that their hate for us had historical dimensions, its colonialist bite. Now I know that we were a people over hundreds of years instructed to hate the brown part of ourselves. Mami was a seer, and to them, we lived at the edges of what was socially acceptable.

In colonial times, when the Europeans who arrived on the continent raped Native and Black women, they invented a caste catalogue—with pure white blood at the top and unmixed Black blood at the bottom—to classify the women's "impure" children.

In the main settlement of the viceroyalty of New Spain, what is Mexico today, a Spaniard and a Native produced a mestizo. A mestizo and a Native produced a coyote. A Spaniard and an African produced a mule. A mestizo and an African produced a wolf. And if the descendants of Native and Black lineage kept reproducing, the catalogue ceased to sound like a bestiary, and rang out instead in a series of rebukes. The caste name for a person who was half Spanish, a quarter Black, and a quarter Native was "Stop in Midair." Stop in Midair plus mulatto created a new caste—"I Don't Understand You." "I Don't Understand You" plus Native created yet another, called "Please Turn Back."

In the Americas, the closer to white you were, the less money you owed as tribute to the Crown, and the more rights you possessed. Many with mixed blood, wanting to escape bondage and tribute, focused on calculating whom they needed to marry and how many generations it would take to become as clean as possible of the trace of other races.

The whitest a person of color could be was a castizo, the child of a mestizo and a Spaniard. Unlike other castes, castizos had the right to become priests, had open access to education, and could become part of the aristocracy. But while Native blood could be whitened with each consecutive generation, Black blood could not. One drop of Black blood meant wealth would be inaccessible forever.

In Colombia, caste came up in marriage, inquisitorial trials, litigations to determine the tribute a person owed, and documents of lineage. Representatives of the Crown, when they visited the capital on census missions, often could not tell mestizos and Natives apart, as these two groups lived together and intermarried often. A person of Black and Indigenous lineage might be referred to as "Indian" in one document and "zambo" in the next. Mestizos were sometimes classified as "Indians" and mulattoes as "mestizos." If a person sought a Certificate of Blood Cleansing, their skin color and features as well as their behavior would be weighed to decide whether they could be classified as a race "above."

Across the Americas, we were taught that to be dark-skinned was to be lesser, and that one's worthlessness grew with the gradient. Even after the paintings were taken down and the catalogue fell into disuse, this oppression grew into an internalized hate, which was passed down by mothers who told their young to stay out of the sun lest they become darker, who instructed them to marry well, meaning to marry *light,* who slathered them in skin whitener and showed them how to bleach body hair in order to trick the eye, in order to appear whiter and therefore more beautiful. In elementary school, when we learned of the racial hierarchies in New Spain from our history books, the light-skinned called us names—*Mule, Wolf, Pig*—and professed that they had blue blood but we had descended from slaves. In school, the worst thing we could think to call one another was *I Don't Understand You.*

Now, I can only hope to be unintelligible, incalculable. To be spat out by a system of horrors as incomprehensible.

I don't know if Mami's born-again siblings realized they were only doing what the castizos before them had done—finding align-

ment with European churches, denying their brownness to purchase favor and privilege. We stared in disbelief at the oil marks
in the shape of crosses they left on our walls. Papi tsked. *All that
fuss over your mother. And all because of magic—which may not
even exist.* He shook his head in mock disappointment. *Where's
her power to mop? That's what I want to know.*

I wrung a laugh, then let my gaze fall again on the oil marks.

Maybe Mami's siblings were right—maybe we were cursed. But
not in the way they thought. We were a damned people, and not
by God but by white people.

Over the coming days, we tried to focus on our good fortune
and populated the apartment with the same furniture Mami and
I would one day encounter wrapped in fitted covers of white cloth
on our trip to disinter Nono. But our gaze kept straying to the oil
stains. At the highest points of each cross was a trail of four human
fingers that had pressed the shape on the wall. The smell of the oil
was subtle and indistinctive. Palm oil, we guessed. Finally, Mami
said, *It's the mean spirit with which this was done.*

We won't hate them, she continued, *but we will cut ties.*

Mami was generous, open—until the moment she was not, until
trust was betrayed and she saw no hope for a change in behavior.
We changed the locks to our doors. We refused the invitations
Mami's born-again siblings extended. We allowed their correspondence to pile up unopened. We donned party hats for New
Year's Eve. Tía Perla and her family came over. As did tía Nahía,
tío Ángel, their families, and Nona. The family who loved us best.
Nona only had one party dress. It was the same one she wore to
funerals, weddings, and airplane cabins. At our balcony, we ate
chicken from buckets, stayed up, turned off the lights, counted
down the seconds. Our noisemakers startled the sky, and we
grasped, making stray wishes for abundance and joy, not knowing, as we stood, plunged in a darkness that constantly renewed
itself after the neon glare of fireworks, that the opposite would be
true.

17

SORCERY

Back in Bogotá, Papi dreamt of a white man who pointed a finger at him. *A warning,* Papi said as he looped a yellow tie around the collar of his white shirt, getting dressed to go to work. We stared at him, perplexed. *I thought you didn't believe in that stuff.* Papi put on a jacket, one trembling arm at a time. *I don't.* It was after we heard his car start downstairs that Mami told us she'd had a dream too: Papi was dead, in a casket, wearing the same yellow tie he had just knotted around his throat.

Papi began to be visited by a recurring nightmare. In it, he had an aerial view of himself. He was at the oil site in Chitasuga, on the metal walkway, arguing with a worker. A large piece of machinery, high above, creaked with wind. Papi was standing just beneath. At always the same point in the dispute, Papi fixed his hands on his hips, and the piece of machinery tore loose, plummeted, crushed him under its weight.

The nightmares made Papi nervous. He departed for Chitasuga looking ashen, his hands worrying the steering wheel. Months went by; then, soon after he had forgotten about the nightmare, Papi found himself in Chitasuga arguing with the same worker as in his dream.

On the metal walkway, Papi placed his hands on his hips. The unpleasant familiarity of the gesture racked his body; he stepped back, his knees buckling. In a second, a heavy blast of wind blew back his hair. Before him, on the spot where he had been standing, a heavy chunk of steel machinery had fallen. It was denting the metal flooring, just as if it had amassed straight from his dreams.

One weekend, Papi did not come home. Surely he'd been delayed by an emergency, Mami said. Emergencies at the site were common, concerning gas and potential explosions. Mami called his oil site. It was a radiotelephone, and sometimes no one was in the booth. Her call rang and rang. This made Mami feel that it *was* an emergency. She imagined that everyone was away somewhere, working on the problem.

That night, one of Mami's old friends showed up at our door. He was a guerrilla member with whom she had gone to high school. His being a guerrillero had always seemed like a joke to Mami. *Imagine bearing arms for such an airy thing as politics,* she'd said.

Once, he had been a stocky, jovial man, then he'd become thinner and thinner. When he dropped in, Mami gave him whiskey and they laughed into the night. He would tell her about his life, and every once in a while, I'd overhear a bit of unsettling information—that there was a guerrilla presence everywhere, for example, normal people you didn't suspect, that the plan was to be ready at any time for a spontaneous attack.

Now, as Mami welcomed him in, his eyes roved wildly. He looked emaciated, smiling like someone at the crest of a roller coaster. He demanded to be fed. Mami pretended this was normal. She took his coat, served him whiskey, and pulled out a chair for him to sit at the dining table, where Ximena, Mami, and I had been spooning up soup. Mami's friend cupped the soup bowl Mami placed before him and drank, tipping back. She piled bread on a plate and he plucked some up and bit pieces off, staring at us as he chewed, all his muscles engaged. I wondered if his visit somehow had to do with Papi's absence. Mami's friend clutched his knife. His knuckles whitened.

Slowly, Mami blew on her spoon, making the liquid steam and rise toward the ceiling. She mused about the weather. *Just another cloudy day in Bogotá. What I wouldn't do for some sun.*

She set her spoon down, made her voice soft. *There was a time,* she said, *a long time ago, in Bogotá, when snow fell out of the sky.*

It was an old story, one that I loved to hear as a girl, though I have never found proof of it. I have pored over newspapers and historical weather databases and have come up empty-handed. Bogotá is three hundred miles from the equator. Snow would have been a magical occurrence. At the table, Mami described horses with snow-dusted hoofs, women in furs, children building snow-men, restaurant owners feeding log after log into fireplaces.

I continued spooning up soup, hardly tasting what was in my mouth at all, but understanding that this semblance of domesticity—my steady pulse, Mami's soft storytelling voice, Ximena's quiet presence—was the sorcery keeping the man's violence at bay.

The second Ximena and I had emptied our bowls, Mami told us to go upstairs. We took the stairs two at a time and locked ourselves in the bedroom we shared. But, anxious for Mami, I cracked the door open as quietly as I could and lay down by the stairs so I could overhear what was being said down below. I could hear a soft murmur, but nothing distinct. A long time passed, and I fell asleep.

Then Mami was standing over me, shaking me. When I asked if her friend was gone, she said he was. He had wanted our money. Mami had collected all the cash she could find and given it to him; all the while, to keep him from assaulting her, she described what she imagined snow to be like.

It must be light and cool to the touch, she told him. *Like flour. It must swirl in the air if you throw it up to the sky.*

She hadn't experienced snow back then.

Neither had he.

Neither had I.

Mami had also thought that her friend came to our house in connection to Papi, but when she asked him about it, he raised his brows in surprise. He asked her if she thought Papi had been kidnapped. Mami said she wasn't sure. He shared that some years ago he had seen Papi's name on a list of possible abductees. The guerrillas kept such lists in order to plan for meeting the cash quotas they owed to headquarters. Mami's friend had scratched Papi's name off, but there was always a chance somebody had added it again. Had we made any big purchases? Mami's friend had wanted to know. Anything like a car or an expensive vacation, something that would have landed us on the guerrillas' radar again? Mami shook her head, but at once she thought of the apartment in Cúcuta. Her friend promised to find out where Papi was, if he had been taken, and call us with news when he had it; then he bolted into the dark of the street. Mami called hospitals and the police, asking about highway accidents and unidentified bodies. There was still no answer at the oil site. There was nothing. Papi had disappeared without a trace.

I don't know how time passed that weekend, how the sun rose, how night fell. I know that Papi came home on Monday, a shell of himself. Something happens to people after they've gone through deep fright. Papi didn't look like himself. He seemed like someone else's father as he sat telling us that boys the same age as Ximena and me had held him at gunpoint and marched him off the oil site of Chitasuga and into the mountains. They bound him and locked him in a windowless shed. He thought he was going to die. When they finally took him to meet the head of the guerrilla group, Papi expected to hear how long they would keep him, how much they would extort in exchange for his life. Instead, there was a friendly slap on his back.

Fer! So nice to see you again! How's Sojaila? How are the girls?
Papi looked up. He beheld a man with whom, as a child, he had

played marbles. The guerrilla boss assured him he'd had no idea that it was Papi they had kidnapped, and ordered the rope binding his hands to be cut. Papi was escorted through the jungle by the same boys who'd captured him, and as they pushed him on with the muzzle of their rifles, past knotted trees and the retreating, flaming tails of macaws, he was sure they had orders to execute him. Once back in his car, he sped all the way to Bogotá.

A year later, our phone began to ring daily with threats, this time about Ximena and me. Mami tried to keep us from picking up and hearing what the voices said, though we could already guess. I answered once and received an accurate report of what I had done that day at school, a recommendation of how much money Mami should gather for my ransom, and then I was asked if I had pubic hair yet or if I was still bare. We suckled daily on fear.

It was easy, then, to believe in curses.

We knew people, poorer and richer, who had been abducted, some of whom had not returned. We stopped going outside. Our circle of trust included one another, our close friends, and a sixteen-year-old girl whose family had been displaced by paramilitaries, who had been with us for half a decade. When Mami had learned that the girl was the sole provider for her family, Mami offered a job doing chores in our house. Mami was in the habit of doing such things, helping girls who were stuck in impossible situations who reminded her of herself. I spent my afternoons with her, watching telenovelas, reading her horoscope. We took turns completing her daily tasks. But no care or deep friendship could change the fact that at some point in the day, I'd go off to do my homework and she'd stay to do more housework. We lived at opposite sides of a chasm, the privilege of our lives against the precarity of hers. We didn't know it at the time, but the guerrillas had threatened to kill her family if she did not comply with their plot.

In the end, Ximena and I were taken. At the handoff, while we were waiting for guerrillas to arrive, Ximena escaped. And the girl tightened her grip around my wrist. My fingers blued. I implored her to let me go. She paced. Her face hardened, then the hollow of her upper lip shook. I thought, *This is what happens when you weigh lives on a balance*, and then, I left my body.

I don't know why, in the end, she helped me, why she hailed a cab and cradled my hand gently as I got in, telling the driver my address.

Terror returned like blood slapping through my body when I saw Mami, standing right by where the cab pulled up. She opened my door, thrashed me back and forth by the hair, pulled me out of the cab and down a whole city block, struck me for not being fast enough, for failing to escape, for being an emotional fool.

These were the events that led to our leaving Colombia: a thunderclap of suffering. When we learned that the girl who had spared us was raped as punishment for letting us go, this was a torment that bore into my body. And when I saw her again, bruised and pregnant, all the details of the violence done to her alive on her skin, I dropped through many trapdoors of grief. I wished I had never asked for her pity. Regret was a searing that made breathing impossible. Then, a numbness took hold. My eyesight blurred and my hearing cocooned, and everything grayed out, peaceful as a grave.

We heard that when some of the born-again tías and tíos learned about how three of us were nearly kidnapped, they clapped. They'd always known we would be punished for our deviancy.

We lived three more years in Bogotá, our sentences morphing into exclamations, our trust narrowing. And when we were out and Mami was behind the wheel, she sped around corners and drove through red lights and didn't use her turning signals so as not to announce where she was headed, so that our whereabouts and destinations could remain mysterious at all times.

I kept hearing in my head tías and tíos as they had once asked, *What are the odds of all of this happening in one family?* Mami's siblings had by then wandered away from the Protestant church, but they continued to drift through this and that cult, after this and that charismatic leader, so that we continued to call them the born-agains, even when it was no longer factual.

After we left the country for Venezuela, in 1998, and in the subsequent years of our migrations around South America as we searched for safety, I saw that crossing a border, starting anew, was the sorcery through which we tried to forget what had happened. But where the mind forgets, the body remembers. The past returns, especially when it is suppressed, like a live wire.

So it was that, many years after, when I moved alone to the United States, I changed apartments every single year, as if there were something after me, something giving chase, something I could not outpace. Not wanting to disappoint my mother a second time, I rose every day, a feeling of gallop in me, and did my best to run.

18

FOUR WOMEN

(after Nina Simone)

We can call anything a curse—most of all, the things we seem to be unable to escape.

Mami was thirteen when Nono moved the family to live in Bucaramanga so he could grow his business. The house in Bucaramanga had an indoor courtyard, a rectangle full of sky, eight rooms, running water, a gas kitchen. Sex workers lived together down the street, girls not much older than Mami. When they came to the door, Nono fed them soup and cured their ailments. He never read their fortunes. The streets were lined with taverns, skittering lizards, and flowering guayacanes. Old men sat outside in plastic chairs, playing dominoes. This is where Mami grew into her big-breasted body. *Your beauty,* Nona told her, in case she didn't already know, *will be a curse to you.*

When Mami returned from school and got off the bus, men flicked their tongues at her, sucked their teeth, called out, *How much?* Sometimes, in anger, as if they were owed, they followed her. The sex workers kept vigil on the street. They stood in between Mami and the men when necessary, knowing she was the curandero's daughter.

Mami's body angered her brothers as well. They didn't care if she was a witch; they would kill her, they said, if she slept with any one of their friends.

Older men came to the house to offer Nono land in exchange for Mami. They brought bank statements, showed off their jewelry. I wish I could say that Nono was offended, that he told them

Mami was not for sale. Instead, he dissuaded Mami's admirers on the grounds that she was a bad investment. *She's more stubborn than a mule,* he began, listing off her flaws. *She won't cook, won't clean, does nobody's bidding. If I were you, I'd buy a flower vase; you'd be much happier.*

Mami liked boys. She sneaked out at night, and returned late on tiptoe. She climbed the walls to avoid going through the metal door, which creaked and would certainly wake someone. She pulled herself up over the wall, inventing and reciting prayers to make her father's sleep heavy, his tongue slow, his mind a fog. But Nono was always waiting for her, sitting in the courtyard having a drink, untouched by her spells. *Don't you know your magic doesn't work on me?* he'd ask. The spirits had told him where she was, he said, but not what she had been doing—so what had she been doing?

Mami was always dancing.

Mami longed for her spells to overwhelm Nono's perception. She experimented with bringing him a cup of coffee in the morning. Somedays she spit into it; other days she did not. She wanted him not to notice. When she brought him the unaltered coffee, Nono winked at her and sipped. But when she breathed her incantations, dropping her saliva into the hot drink, he refused to look in her direction. Mami brought him gifts all afternoon. *Papá, you know I didn't mean it. You say you're powerful; I just want to know how much.*

As I was growing into my woman's body, at fourteen years old, I sneaked out too. I met friends at midnight, and we climbed into the children's playhouse in the park where we lived in Venezuela. We smoked and drank. Mami did not wait up, but she would be cold the next day. *Throw your life away, be my guest.*

In that new land, when rain banged on the roof of our house, and water streaked our windows, I'd think back to the day Mami stopped the rain and doubt what I had seen. I'd go find Mami in order to state the obvious: *Mami, it's raining.* She would be making a map of the stars in a journal, or sitting in bed in her underwear, eating frozen red grapes.

Why don't you make it stop?

Mami doubled her attention on her food or her notebook pages, as if I hadn't spoken. She stared breathlessly into them, as if she were working out a complicated problem and couldn't let her attention stray for one moment.

I sighed. *You're right.* I sat on her bed. *Probably you can't do it.*

Mami threw notebooks at me, pens, pillows. She rubbed around her eyes. *Dios mío! Now I know how my father felt. Que desespero. I won't prove my magic to you—leave me alone.*

There was a gradual but constant rotation in Nono's long-term patients who lived in the house. Mami relished taking shifts to care for the select few Nono took on. One of them was a twelve-year-old girl who suffered from epilepsy. She and Mami devised a method. Whenever they were together, they carried with them a pillow and a wooden spoon. If the girl felt an attack coming, she threw herself across the pillow, and Mami stuffed the spoon in her mouth, and tried to hold her down while reciting the words for getting a spirit out. Epilepsy was spirit possession. The girl was on a treatment of herbs that Nono prepared fresh for her daily.

One woman suffered panicked episodes during which she tore at her own clothes until she was naked, and stared down the empty space before her, where, Mami gathered, stood an unseen assailant. Her name was Aura. Nono put Mami in charge of her, saying, *Sometimes only a woman understands a woman's pain.*

During her episodes, Aura repeated, *No, no,* and cried out for someone called Benicia.

Mami asked Aura when she was well, *Who is Benicia?*

Aura cast down her gaze. *She was a friend. Now she's dead.*

When Aura had her episodes, Mami wrapped her in a blanket, attempted to soothe her, told her she was Benicia: *I am here, I am here*. It seemed to help. Everything Aura said was a puzzle. The frogs bothered her—they were all over her body. The door had too many locks. Slowly, day after day, Mami pieced together what had happened. Her husband had tied her to the oven. At night, the mud kitchen filled with frogs. The frogs felt clammy on her skin. One day, he tied her to a bed. Another day, he tried to kill her. Mami sank into the realization—this was the man who had committed Aura to Nono's care.

The clearer Aura's narration became during her panicked states, the more she consciously remembered. Mami knew naming what has happened is strong medicine. As Aura remembered, her episodes grew further apart, then ceased. When her husband came for a visit, he left Aura's room brandishing a knife, looking for Mami, accusing her of implanting false memories in his wife's head.

Mami, who had been threatened by men all her life, laughed when he found her, noting that he was only waving the blade at her from four feet away. She waited expectantly, but as the seconds passed and he did not stir, she taunted him further: *Now we separate the boys from the men*. Inwardly, she was afraid Aura's husband would actually kill her, but she had learned from her brothers that men liked to inspire fear more than they liked getting in a fight. He didn't come closer to Mami, but he did carry Aura away, and Mami could do nothing but watch.

Once Nono came home from a day collecting herbs on the mountain, he and Mami prayed. They asked, on Aura's behalf, that she'd be able to escape, that her husband would let her go, that she'd be flooded with help. Nono knew they lived in a village in the mountains, but he hadn't asked where. He swallowed back a couple of shots of aguardiente and then lit a candle.

I have what Western doctors call an anxiety disorder. Mami calls it spiritual sickness. She says that the problem is stories that have not healed inside me. This is why I am sick. She's tried to cure me.

I have drunk her teas, bathed in her blessed waters, lain before her as she's beaten me tenderly with herbs. Nothing has worked. The complication is timing, Mami says. I am not ready to let the stories go.

When we experience trauma, it imprints a sensory map of what the body experienced at its unfolding. So, at times, I wake up in my life of relative peace seized by inscrutable fear. When in my current life the sensory map aligns with what I felt during moments of turmoil, I go on high alert. I can be in the middle of a peaceful nothing where I live now in California—a hike, a bath, washing the dishes, sweeping the floor—when something in me assures me that I am in danger, that I am back there, living out those childhood horrors.

It is easy to spiral into a panic attack.

My mind begins a loop, telling my body, *We cannot breathe*, and the body confirms it: *Actually, yes, we cannot.*

The experience is asphyxiation.

It seems like the hardest thing I have ever tried to do, to focus on the digital clock of my oven. I pace and gasp for air and try to read the neon numbers. The idea is to calculate how long I have left to endure—attacks last usually an hour—but I cannot read the clock. I am a turbulence. In this routine happening, I picture myself as a human-sized fish, out of water, heaving and wearing a silk slip. This makes me laugh, but it makes the suffocating worse.

I try to press the two buttons at the same time on my phone to take a picture of the screen, where the time appears. Sometimes I can read the clock this way. Often, I press the buttons at different times, I unlock my phone, or it tumbles out of my hands. When, finally, I succeed in taking a screenshot, I withstand the choking sensation for as long as I can. I am crying, I beg no one: *Please, enough.*

When I feel I cannot endure any longer, I struggle with my phone again until I take another shot of the home screen. My throat is a garroting, but I fight to stay with the task long enough to open the photo album. I swipe between the last two photos, grimly put myself to the task of decoding the numbers shown on one photo, trying to remember them, read the numbers in the next screen, subtract one from the other.

Please.

Please.

Most probably I am not forming words: my jaw is clenched tight, and I am sucking in air through my teeth because I cannot unclench my jaw. I've lost control of it. Likely, I sound inhuman.

When I am able to read the numbers, often only five minutes have elapsed, and then all I am is panic. I pace, now telling myself, *Just survive five minutes more. It will be over.* More inhuman sounds.

I know I am not really dying. I know I *believe* myself to be running out of air, and have come to believe it so strongly, I have convinced my body it is true. If a doctor were to take a reading of how much oxygen was in my bloodstream, it would be at 100 percent. This happened once at the emergency room, where I had checked in, thinking an attack was really going to kill me. I struggled to get the words out, but I managed to ask the doctor, *What if it doesn't stop?*

She was hooking me up to the drip. *You can transition into having a seizure,* she said, *but we have things to give you.*

And after?

The doctor was already standing, heading out. *I guess you could experience what will feel like you've received an electric shock. But we got you. Don't worry.*

Sometimes, when the suffering caused by the attack is too much, my mind leaves my body. I wake up to my own inhuman utterances in a room I don't remember entering, but I am thankful for my mind, because it has known to protect me by erasing time. It has created—at a moment's notice and in response to an overwhelm of pain—a memory lagoon. A place of no time, gray suspension, dissociation.

Each time, I am not sure how I survive the cycle, but I do. I fight the earthquake of my hands, take screenshots, weather asphyxiation, picture myself as a large fish, laugh, unlock the phone, beg no one, swipe between screens, do the math.

When it's over, I feel like I've been in a car crash. I want to go to sleep, and I cannot sleep. I want to be held, but I don't want to be touched. I will do anything not to have another panic attack. I call Mami the following day. I don't tell her I've had an attack, but sometimes I think she knows, because she'll say, out of nowhere and sounding disappointed, *If only you'd give your burdens to me, I could heal them in my body.*

We are quiet. *I can't,* I don't say.

There was a boy Mami knew, someone she hadn't slept with, but one day, he was there, taking up all the air in her living room, detailing to Nono how she had come to his house and offered herself. He didn't *want* to malign the family name, he told Nono, but if Mami were to marry him, there'd be nothing to fear.

Ask your spirits, Mami begged. *I didn't sleep with him.*

If Mami had not been in the habit of sneaking out, Nono said, she'd be free of the boy's threats. Now he couldn't protect her. If the community learned about what the boy had to say, Mami's sisters would not marry well, her brothers would not be able to find work, and the butchers might stop selling them meat.

Mami's family begged her to marry. What could she do? The choice was between her freedom and her family's well-being. She chose their well-being. She told the boy: *I'm going to start practicing crossing my toes inside my shoes—for when we're at the altar.*

She was sixteen. She wore a blue dress, and crossed the fingers of her right hand, as well as the toes of both her feet inside her satin shoes.

I don't know the name of the man she was forced to marry. I don't want to know. Mami doesn't mention him much.

After they married, he understood her body as his possession.

He decided that he wanted her pregnant.

Mami hid birth control pills under a ceiling tile, made herself barren.

She tried to leave him, and when he left her bruised and bleeding, she called tío Ariel. Ariel came in a matter of days. At gunpoint, he held the man back as Mami walked out the door. She rode the bus to Cúcuta with tío Ariel, her head on his shoulder and the gun in his lap. Mami cried for days, grateful for Ariel and angry with everyone else. Nono never forgave himself. He understood too late: women belonged to no one. He helped Mami get a divorce. In a few months, Mami would beg Nono to teach tío Ariel to move the clouds.

My sister has the spiritual sickness too. But Ximena doesn't have anxiety; she lives with an eating disorder. There was a time when we didn't know if Ximena would make it. A person has to choose to live. For a while it seemed she was choosing to go.

For a month in the winter of 2010, I slept on the floor of her apartment, which had been empty for many months, and Mami and Papi slept in her bed. Every day, we went to see Ximena at the inpatient program where she was staying. Ximena and I did not know what to say to each other. Girls died at the center. They became sitting skeletons, and one day they were gone.

We sat together and watched TV. My sister found CNN calming, I don't know why. That's what we watched. Because she might die, because there was nothing in the world I could do about it, I gave all of myself to those moments sitting next to her, as, week by week, her skin went through the process of shrink-wrapping against her bones. The television flared with a ribbon that alerted us only to what we already knew. The news was never new on CNN. But it made her calm. It made her life bearable. She fell asleep watching, and I observed the ridge of her ribs appearing and disappearing beneath her T-shirt. She looked like a child. Her eyes seemed bigger. The lids didn't close completely, and the slit of white at the bottom was screened over by the black of her lashes.

The inpatient program had provided an interpreter for Mami. The interpreter translated what the psychologists and therapists said with diligence and rigor to Spanish, but the words meant nothing to Mami. PTSD, trauma, disordered eating—these were all terminological pillars in a foreign system of medicine Mami had never engaged with and couldn't understand. Because the interpreter couldn't really translate for Mami, I took up the role. I translated for meaning, while also accounting for history, context, and colonialism, and tried to bridge the two cultural understandings of illness.

What they call PTSD, what you call the remains of a susto . . . What they call an eating disorder, what you call the spiritual sickness . . .

I hated some of the things I had to recite back to Mami in our tongue: *She can't walk for more than fifteen minutes or she'll have a heart attack.*

Mami looked as if I'd slapped her. *Why? What does that mean?*

She's put her heart through too much strain, I had to explain. *She's starving,* I added, barely able to hold it together myself.

From time to time, Mami and I joined my sister's therapy sessions. I went from interpreting, to participating in the conversation, to translating my own contributions after I was done speaking. Ximena and Mami cried. I did not cry. I let their words travel through my brain across languages, and then I talked about horizons.

She needs a new story, Mami told me. *That's what will help her.*

I was hungry for hope, but hope built in anticipation of my sister's future seemed dangerous, so I didn't ask Mami what she meant.

Mami prayed over glasses of water and asked Ximena to drink them.

Ximena and I fought about it in English. She didn't want to

touch them; she didn't believe in the water or Mami's healing. *You all are always trying to trap and fix me. I can't be fixed. Tell her I can't be fixed.*

It wasn't just at the inpatient center—I was always stuck in the middle between Mami and Ximena, mediating the language of their chosen realities. Ximena had always sided with Papi's skepticism, but over the years, as Papi's skepticism grew into belief, hers grew into disdain. Because she was older than I was when we lived through terror, she lived it to a more concentrated degree. She wants nothing to do with Colombia as a result, or any of our traditions. *Just do it,* I begged Ximena. *It's just water. It'll make her feel better and she'll leave you alone.*

Ximena drank begrudgingly, widened her eyes, set the empty glass of water down. *There. You happy?* She sat again before the television. To the blaring alarms and ominous jingles introducing each CNN news segment, she took up her knitting. Then, moments later, still not nourished enough to sustain wakefulness for more than a few hours at a time, she fell asleep.

I whispered to Mami in Spanish, *I hope it works.*

Mami could cast out the spirits possessing the bodies of her clients: bad airs, angry and starving ghosts, maleficios. She said that if my sister and I had shown up at her door in Bogotá, she would have diagnosed our ailments as belonging to the second order, troubles that could not be mended but that we had to adapt to and learn to live with.

But she was unfamiliar with the Western ghost that the doctors called an eating disorder. Because she wanted to understand what that ghost was like, Mami interrogated me about its origins, how it functioned, what fearsome tools it had at its disposal.

I could see where the two types of thinking, Mami's and my sister's doctors', met. The doctors defined trauma as the emotional shock that lingers after a stressful event. Mami said hauntings are what is no longer seen but still felt—the question mark, the unresolved—which on the strength of their ghost pierce our reality, filling up the air with terror.

I spent many hours doing this for my mother, translating Western medicine into a language of curanderismo. I'd had an eating disorder myself, so I knew what the experience was. If Ximena was starving herself to feel control over the undoing that had been our life in Colombia and the uncertain years since, then I could locate the time and place where the haunting had begun. *It's a ghost she picked up—I picked it up too—when we flew over the border. Maybe it's a ghost that thrives in places of transition.*

Good, Mami said. *What else.*

It can cast an impressive mirage, I told her, thinking about body dysmorphia, how my sister might look in a mirror and see healthy fat on her bones that simply was not there, or how I could take large gulps of air while believing I was asphyxiating. *Yes,* I continued. *That's how it gets you.*

Mami prepared water for Ximena and me based on this information, asking for what it takes to recognize a mirage as a mirage.

We were living in the intersection of different medicines, and neither worked. Mami would have liked to treat my sister's symptoms—the heart trouble, the peach fuzz coating her skin, which her body grew to keep itself warm since the scant calories she consumed weren't enough to generate body heat—but Mami didn't have the herbs available, and she didn't know what they were called, so I couldn't purchase them either. Mami knew herbs by sight, and none of the spritely bundles showered in mist on the refrigerated shelf at the market were what she was looking for. She honed her prayers into water we drank so we could have clarity in the face of what kept us hostage.

Ximena's therapists and doctors used recurrent phrases about recovery. That it wasn't linear. That relapse created strength. Beneath everything they said, there was an unexpressed yearning for a pure state, a return to the body and mind untouched, before anything had happened to them. Their words were plagued with binaries: bravery and fear, logic and senselessness, soundness and brokenness.

The pills my sister was given were meant to return her to a state of peace and wellness. But had we ever known a state of peace and wellness in the way Western medicine imagined it? We had grown up elsewhere, amid bombs and death. Yet this metric of okayness was held out before us, a pure state we had to achieve.

To Mami and Nono, purity never came into healing, because purity didn't exist. A person would always be visited by pain and grief. A person was an accretion, constantly growing in strangeness, becoming an accumulation. Healing was found in stretching toward abundance. It was not about leaving the past behind, dividing the self into good and bad, but about opening a path through ruins.

It doesn't matter how much violence my family experienced, together and separately, or what names we give it. I can say, *There was desperation and war,* but that never feels sufficient. I no longer try to explain the aftermath. Now I simply say: Is this not what comes from war and migration?

Once, Mami gave me an aloe plant for protection. After the worst panic attack I've ever had, the plant shriveled up and died. Root rot.

Many remedies do not take, Mami tells me, explaining why she hasn't been able to disentangle all that ails me. *The body has to be ready to receive the medicine. You have to allow it.*

I think about allowing medicine in. I tell everyone what is wrong with me, saying, *I don't know what is wrong with me.*

Call it suffering, call it a curse.

Mami has been trying to teach me my whole life: there is no such thing as a curse. Crisis is routine. Anything can be called a curse, just as anything can be called a gift.

Mami doesn't say, but I know: the space between a curse and a gift is the end of the story.

There is surviving, and then there is surviving the surviving. There is a version of the story in which a survivor doesn't make it; and a version in which a survivor is remade.

I can locate in the dictionaries, in Spanish, in English, the agreed-upon term for the self-punishment that comes after one survives at the expense of others. *Síndrome de supervivencia. Survivor guilt.* But no term feels like it can hold the lived experience.

Your dreams say more than anything you can tell me, Mami says.

I dreamt of living in a burning house. I walked through flames to the kitchen to brew myself a cup of coffee.

Yes, but did you burn? Mami asks. *Were you on fire?*

I dreamt of living in a freezing house; my pet a polar bear to whom I fed everything in the fridge, and then the furniture. The polar bear was destroying my home, so my only option was to walk out with it into the white, into the snowdrift.

Your only option, Mami repeats for my benefit, so I can hear myself.

I dream often of the same building. There are seven floors. I am captive in its architecture, a labyrinth I can never figure out. I take stairs up and they lead me to the basement. I go through a door and suddenly I am trapped in an elevator. The way out is through a skylight. Once, I reached for its blue but was immediately pulled down, to the basement again. There is a minotaur on my trail. I don't know what the minotaur looks like. I've never actually seen it.

Tell me about each floor, Mami says.

When I was younger, I tried cutting.

In my twenties, I prepared myself lavish plates piled with food. I sat before them, forking imaginary bites to my lips. I finished my meals in the theater of my mind, then walked the untouched plates to the garbage.

I wanted to be destroyed. I courted dangerous men. Once, I lay beneath a man. He forced himself.

I can't talk about that time, Papi says, when I ask him anything about Colombia. *If I look back, I'll sink.*

I think there are things you don't remember, Ximena tells me. *I remember, because I was older. I can see they affect you, even if you can't see that.*

Every floor leads to the basement.

Once I lay beneath a man. I fought at first, then stopped, deciding I deserved it, for surviving.

Nobody wants the truth, but everyone wants a story, Mami said.

Tell yourself a different story, Mami now tells me.

My whole life, Mami has been trying to teach me: there is no such thing as a curse.

More and more, I understand what she means.

Everyone suffers.

To believe in a curse is to believe oneself above suffering.

No one is above suffering.

You can only believe in a curse if you believe in being spared.

19

HUNGER

Mami says that what ghosts miss most is hunger. Want. The pangs of a lack. The orbits of desire. Satiety.

Why doesn't she just eat? Mami asked about my sister.

We constantly went over what afflicted her, and Mami routinely forgot all I told her, possibly because it was too much to hold. She could do nothing but watch her elder daughter wane. Papi had returned to Mexico City, and I to San Francisco. Mami stayed in Minneapolis to keep Ximena company. It was 2011, and Mami called me every day as she made the trek to the inpatient center. Mami, who doesn't know English, rode public transit, figured out the foreign currency, and communicated with people about her destination through gestures of her hands and face. Because Mami was so focused on trying to help my sister, and to my eyes, failing, Nono was foremost in my mind. What would he have done?

It's not about hunger, I kept telling Mami.

Half a year had passed, and, still, I couldn't bring myself to explain that turning to starvation was a self-inflicted agony that displaced a worse emotional distress. There was a feeling of triumph that came from subduing hunger. How to tell Mami that it felt *good*—perhaps for Ximena too—to make the mind into a throne from which to observe the body wither. In which language would it spare Mami's feelings to hear me say that it felt *powerful,* that at the other shore of hunger, after one withstood the worst pangs of it, there was an addictive, clean, almost spiritual, feeling?

It's a mocking ghost, I tried, which was as close to the truth as I dared to come. *It wants to drag you to the other side, and so it gets you to starve. The more you starve, the better it makes you feel, and the better you feel, the closer you inch toward dying.*

Mami was satisfied with this, but forgot it in a day. *Why don't you write down what you tell me? I can't hold it in my head.*

You write it down, Mami.

Neither of us wrote anything down, I imagine, not wanting to have a truth spelled out in a language we could not ignore or take back.

When I tired of translating what I knew of the experience into her language, I gave Mami what Western psychiatrists repeated to me about eating disorders: *It's not about hunger; it's about control.* This was a language Mami was not fluent in, and yet, week after week, no longer able to risk myself by wandering into a grammar that revealed as much about me as it did my sister, it's what I offered her: *If life is too chaotic, then people turn inward and control what they can—which sometimes is hunger.*

Who denies themselves their own hunger? Mami asked.

Ghosts craved hunger because, no longer having bodies, they remembered with nostalgia what it felt like to be parched, to cave internally under the tick of an urge. They yearned for hunger as a land of exile.

I had always wanted to see a ghost.

Before our phone rang with threats to Ximena and me, before we turned to starvation for comfort, when I was twelve and we still lived in Colombia, I said to great-tía Carmen in Ocaña that I would give anything to see a ghost, I didn't care if it meant I'd be haunted for the rest of my life.

We were sitting in a circle on great-tía Carmen's back patio, which in Mami's time had been great-grandmother Mamaria's patio, where Nona had once stood telling Nono through the wall, *I am still shaking from your kiss.* Somewhere up the hill was the well down which Mami fell. We were surrounded by our family from Ocaña, cousins on the floor and elders in plastic chairs. The sky was glowing indigo. Great-tía Carmen clapped the air to shoo away my words. *Be quiet, be careful! Here there are ghosts who can hear.* Great-tía Carmen said she didn't know how things worked in the city, but ghosts were nothing to wish on oneself. Then she told us a story.

Once, there was a girl orphaned by war. The girl couldn't hear or speak; she was in shock. She showed up at great-tía Carmen's doorstep, and Carmen took her in. One day, there was an earthquake. The girl remained rooted, frozen in the courtyard, as the family took refuge under a door frame and pleaded for her to find shelter. The courtyard wall fell. Great-tía Carmen feared the girl had been buried beneath the rubble. But when the dust settled, the girl was untouched. There had been a window, a carved-out space in the adobe. As the wall fell, the window opening slipped over the girl's head like a dress. There was a tight square of grass around her feet; then, a few centimeters out, the ruins of the crumbled wall expanded into an imperfect rectangle.

When the wall fell, it revealed a second wall. A hiding wall, great-tía Carmen called it, an original wall, which someone had taken pains to wall in. Buried into a crack in the brick was a silver necklace. It was good silver. Great-tía Carmen knew it was meant for the girl, so she sold it and gave her the money. The next morning, the girl was gone, and great-tía Carmen was still not sure if she had been a girl or a ghost.

Ghost, voted the cousins.

Girl, voted Mami.

I did not know how to vote. I thought about what it would be like to spend a lifetime unsure of whether a person living in close proximity to you was living or dead.

As we sang together into the night, I thought of a worse thing. Maybe the girl herself was uncertain of what she was. I looked around, wondering, how many people, including ourselves, might actually be ghosts.

————

After surviving our years of terror, Ximena and I had a hard time making sense of who or what we were. Papi had professional connections, and he was able to find work that lasted a few months or a year in countries neighboring Colombia. We moved from place to place, grateful, physically unharmed. We promised to start anew, then drifted into ascetic tendencies.

I cut into my arm, and, like a magic trick, the lingering trauma of being followed and taken, and the guilt of surviving, dissipated, then was gone. A manic tranquility surfaced in its stead. At the time, I likened it to the exorcisms Mami facilitated for other people, an act through which I rid myself of poisons, but I can see now that I was only bonding with my ghosts.

Before moving to the United States, I had assumed that everyone had in their family a real or pretend curandero, that everyone pored over dreams, received prophecies—or, if not, that at least this kind of thing was not uncommon. In Chicago, where I went to college and lived alone, I discovered this was not the case. No one I met in that city had even seen a ghost, nor did they care about their dreams. Ghost stories were spoken of with derision, catalogued as legends and *old wives' tales,* an idiom that told me everything I needed to know. The whole continent enfolded what it wanted to devalue with women.

White people in the United States held on to a hard line between fact and fiction, between what was possible and what was not. This made sense to me. U.S. Americans flew the Confederate flag, then insisted racism didn't exist. They told me theirs was a country founded on ideals, then got upset when I brought up the genocide of Indigenous peoples or slavery, which were clear indications to me that the country was founded on something else.

To believe in ghosts was to know that remnants of a past violence return.

A country that doesn't even believe in its own history cannot believe in ghosts.

This was why, in Colombia, we felt haunted by the ghost gold fever. We knew what had ravaged the country and feared it, watched for how it might possess us, work its way through us, make us ravage ourselves.

In my second year in Chicago, Mami telephoned to tell me that in Venezuela, where she and Papi then lived, a woman had called her house and told her that she had been given her telephone number in a dream, and that she had dialed because she was looking for someone to help her make a connection to the world of the dead. The next day, as I was unlocking my bike from in front of the journalism school where I was studying, a wiry man approached and told me he had access to dead bodies. *I was told in a dream to look for you at this intersection at this time. I practice necromancy—do you know what that is?*

Mami and I made jokes at the time about dream-world Do Not Call lists and how to get on them. I didn't tell anybody except Mami about the necromancer, because who else would understand? I carried unlike worlds inside me, one excommunicated from the other. It was easier than having to educate people. Where could I even begin? When you see a lot of death, you begin to live inside the unexplained, you conjure a porous communication with the past. But I had no language for this kind of thing, didn't even know the term "code switch." I walked around distending, an impassable hair's breadth between the woman I was and the one I had to become.

I started denying myself my own hunger when I first arrived in the United States. I grew acquainted with the hard curves of my skeleton, probed the dips between my bones, established that they led to a terrifying nothingness. I sucked on ice cubes and filled pages with words. If I went out with friends, I drank absurd amounts, woke up bruised on couches or in beds I did not remember falling into.

But something stopped me from spiraling further. That summer, I went to Virginia with two friends, and we went to swim in a lake. The sky was clear and bright. We had calculated it would be an easy ten-minute swim to the small island in the middle of the dark water. My muscles braced against the cool lake as I dove. I was surprised to find myself fatigued a few minutes in, then remembered I was weak from not eating. I was used to having my mind subdue the pains and needs of my body, so I continued, expecting it would be like enduring hunger, that at some point there would be a daybreak of good feeling. I flutter-kicked my legs, spiked each arm into the water, propelled myself under the surface. A tingling spread over my limbs. Halfway to the island, I tried to raise my arm and could not. The muscle spasmed, hamstrung into stillness, and my legs too. There was no fat on my body, nothing left to turn into fuel. I was shocked at my body's betrayal, then understood my own part: I had starved it. The surface of the water, the glittering play of light dappling the top, receded, and I dropped into the green murk.

I would have died, except that one of the girls I was with worked summers as a lifeguard. She dove me up, embraced me in the hold in which the drowning are held. Her forearm clutched around my chest, her legs scissored beneath me, and stroke by stroke, we neared the island. I stared back at the shore, watched my two feet drag a wake in the water behind us. At the island, I said I was a worse swimmer than I knew, and we pretended nothing had happened; she swam me back to the shore.

On the sand, I was dizzy and outside of my body. The girls sucked on a shared joint, making its tip flare, and I stared at the sky, and we talked about abortions. I shared that my childhood best friend got pregnant from a rape. She couldn't tell her parents, so, to hide the cause of her growing stomach, we ate chocolate together. We gained weight quickly and as a unit, until she was able to get an abortion. While I spoke of wandering with my body into the pain of another's, I showed off the white stripes on my thighs that were a mark of the love and care I was capable of.

I wondered then how many women, beset by burdens, had

drowned in lagoons, and if there were many, and if this was why in Colombia we spoke of hungry lagoon spirits.

Maybe all water is haunted. Maybe all water carries the incantatory chorus of the dead, has a woman standing at the middle of it, a hungry mouth calling for a drowning.

I knew that by denying my own hunger, I had wanted to drain myself of vulnerability, as if there were a prize at the center of myself I could extract. I shuddered, remembering the feeling of sinking of a few moments ago, and finally, I bent toward surrender.

The image of a woman standing at the middle of a lagoon is all over these stories, I realize as I am writing this. I don't mean to write her in. She just emerges—in the middle of a forest, at the center of a skirt of black silk, surrounded by crude oil, lying at the bottom of a well, standing amid the ruins of a wall—bidding me to look.

I suppose a woman entering into water is always half vanishing. To vanish into water is to become half nothing—the you that is there, and the you that is gone. The ghost must be in the reflection, the upper half rippling on the water.

To starve oneself is to will oneself to vanish too.

From the oldest memories surviving in our land till now, the stories the men told made us believe our hunger was wrong. Their stories are plagued by women with ravaging appetites, ambitions, and desires, who, because of their hunger, suffer terrible and ignoble fates.

As ever, those men were wrong.

There is nothing wrong with hunger.

Hunger shapes us into a wisdom we cannot yet know.

I never got as far into an eating disorder as my sister did. My near drowning had forced a recognition: the power offered me through denying my hunger was an illusion.

As I began to eat again, my anxiety and panic attacks, embodiments of memories that I wanted to repress, returned. I let the un-dealt-with fears of the past pass through me in a flash and a ravage. Many things we are come wrapped in barbed wire. Now I know to reach for the sting, so I can get to the good.

But you're okay now, Mami will say to me, exasperated, when I tell her about the visitations of fear I experience. *You have housing, income, food. You survived. Why be fearful in the face of plenty?*

How do you convince the body, which has decided to be afraid? Fear once taught the body survival. Teachings leave their echoes.

It's a ghost, Mami, I say to her when I want her to understand.

You just don't get it, I say when I don't want her to get it.

There's surviving, and then there's surviving the surviving, I never say but always think.

Mami says she can't take my panic attacks away. Some ghosts need to be faced, and I must face them. Over the phone, she prays over water for me so I may learn what the ghost wants. Mami says ghosts have their own language, articulation. It is up to me to listen.

Two thousand eleven was the year when my sister's symptoms peaked, and the year when my panic attacks and middle-of-the-night episodes became more frequent.

In the daytime, I did my best to keep my panic attacks under control, but twice a week, at night, I went from ghost to revivified body. I did my best to be a good audience. I never knew when, exactly, the nighttime amnesia would occur. I tensed in anticipation of the horror I would feel when I sat up in bed without recognizing my surroundings. I knew I would scan the room and feel an abundant emptying, isolation, translucence. I was a ghost. But once I observed I had a body, I would, as always, remember wrong—arrive at the conclusion that I had slept with my brother, or that my body was a prison. Then I'd experience a despair so large it seemed to crater the spot in the mattress on which I sat.

Mami knew a lot about ghosts. *The ones who don't have self-knowledge are the worst,* she shared. *They're stranded in one moment in the past, which they relive for eternity.*

How do you get rid of that type of ghost? I asked, thinking about my nightly episodes with amnesia.

You know, Mami said, then was quiet. *I always passed up those jobs.*

How come?

Ghosts hunger for hunger. The kind of ghost that is stuck reliving a moment has the worst unmet hunger. They walk an addictive circle, always after something they can never entirely get. You'd have to break their reality in order to free them of what's keeping them enacting the same scene. It can take so much time. Hardly worth the money.

I considered what Mami had once said about me, that I'd rather die than ask for help. It was true that it would be much simpler to just ask for her medicine. Instead, I posed inscrutable questions and searched her words for how I might help myself.

Maybe I was addicted to the memory of being a blank slate, but as I came around to discovering that I was only a human forgetful of her burdens, inevitably, the experience blighted into a nightmare. If I wanted to break the cycle of recurring amnesia, I'd have to excise the idea that being a blank slate was better than being an accumulation. I'd have to practice surrender.

There were many things the accident in Chicago changed in me, though a lot of it went unnoticed as I focused on outliving the fear that memory incited in me. I didn't notice at first that when I entered stores that had a single exit, after going down an aisle, I could no longer find my way out. It took a while for it to dawn on me that I was encountering difficulties remembering where the grocery store was, even though I went there consistently and it was only a block away. Then, one day when I was driving a friend's car and he asked me to go around the block, I turned once but could not work out which way to turn next. Walking from place to place, if I gazed at maps, I had to sit down, sweating, no longer able to translate the information they held.

By 2011, I knew that the neurological condition was a consequence of brain damage, and it had a name, *topographical disorientation*. This meant that my brain could no longer make maps. It's different from what we colloquially refer to as having a good or a bad sense of direction, a concept that alludes to a spectrum of how easy it is for the brain to make a cognitive map. Most people can form a mental map once they've traveled a space once, twice, or twenty times, but in topographical disorientation the map is not created at all. To have this condition is to be permanently lost. Even when I am reading at home and stationary, if I am introspective, if I am looking down at my hands, into the ice cubes in my drink, I am lost. I look through a window to a sight I've seen a thousand times, expecting a different street to be there.

Before, I invested a lot of time trying to rebuild what was gone. I walked away from home, then gave myself the task of navigating back. For hours, I'd stare at the map on my phone and the circle that represented my body. I'd be only six blocks south and two east from my apartment in San Francisco. I could intellectually understand the layout of space on the surface of my screen, could count how many blocks there were, could grasp the route I'd need to follow. But the moment I looked up, I couldn't work out which way to go. I watched the dot move toward the left of my screen as I moved forward. *Okay, so . . .*

The little dot advanced some more. *Okay, so . . .*

Trying to carry the spatial information from my phone to my brain so that I could apply it to the landscape around me felt like having sand sift through my hands. I got vertigo, doubled over, feared I would puke. I turned on my phone's voice directions and, following the simple instructions given to me at the appropriate times, I made it back.

By 2011, I had embraced space as an ever-changing sea, in

which streets were subsumed and reappeared with no rhyme or reason, and I reconsidered what navigation might mean to me.

Navigation is simply the ability to pinpoint the self to a meaningful crosshair. Therefore, anything can be a meaningful crosshair. I learned to plot my regular routes through language.

When it is the library I am going to, I step out the door of my building and search the awnings and marquees visible from my doorstep up and down the street until I see the word "Odd," and I walk toward it. Along the way, I've chosen other words at crucial junctures, which act as breadcrumbs guiding me to turn left or right or go straight. The phrase that forms a map that leads me to the library is *Odd temple American warfield.* To go to the grocery store, it is *Except longitude no warning.* To me, the world remains insurgent, undiscovered, untamed. There is a small wildness in it. I live beyond the politics of the map, through which much of the world has been seized.

But what space could I open in the face of panic and midnight episodes of amnesia? I had to make a home with distress. Surrender means to answer to what shapes us, the layers that we are. Many things don't have to be overcome, only outlived, and then lived with.

To get rid of a circle, you externalize it, Mami says. *You tell a story.* I needed a new story too.

In 2011, as can happen with recovery, Ximena got better, then worse. She was released from the inpatient center, then re-admitted. Everything hinged on her honesty—her ability to tell us whether she was eating or not, and whether she was lying about eating or not. Mami doubted her own ability to heal her, but Ximena was not cooperating. *If she dies,* we said to each other, then stopped.

That December, we spent the holidays in Minnesota, eating the same things Ximena ate, so as not to trigger her into a bout of restriction. We followed the strict dietary plan her nutritionist and psychologist had designed for her. Mami and I felt stuffed all the time, but we didn't let on. Every meal had a dessert, more sweets than we were used to.

It might have been right after our second daily slice of chocolate cake that Ximena announced, *I think I want a baby.*

I remember that I lunged for her, hugged her, that we raised a glass to celebrate how she was taking a step toward her own life. My happiness lasted an hour, until I realized that if Ximena got pregnant she would have to witness her own stomach grow. What if her dysmorphia got worse? If it did, she could begin to starve herself and therefore also the baby. I kept this horrific worry to myself until nighttime, when I shared it with Mami. Mami was angry and impatient with me. *Pay attention,* she said. *This is the new story.*

Papi and I had to work, so we went back to our respective homes. We kept filing for extensions for Mami's visa. We needed someone to care for Ximena. Mami and Ximena lived together, and did not get along. Mami called me every day to tell me about how she was fine-tuning her prayer, just as she had once done for Papi after he lost his job and became depressed. She prepared water for Ximena to cast out illusion, then to cast out the so-called Eating Disorder Ghost. Ximena struggled to stay on her dietary plan. Mami kept trying to slip her exorcism water, but Ximena always figured it out. One called me to complain about the other.

Just give the water to your plants, I told Ximena.

Just give the water to the dog, I told Mami.

Ximena called a few days later, spooked. *I don't know how to explain this—but, like. A shadow came out of my dog.*

I was quiet, processing what she'd said, but Ximena continued: *Like, a real black shadow came out of my dog, and then the dog yelped—like he had* also *experienced a shadow coming out of him—and now the dog is hiding in his crate.*

So . . .

All I'm going to say is that it was strange.

So. Well. Okay. I told Mami to give your dog exorcism water.

Ximena sighed. *Now, why would you do that?*

I don't know. I scratched at nonexistent stains on my pants. *I'm always in the middle.*

When Mami's visa ran out, we worried about what would happen. We had done all we could. Ximena had to choose to live.

We cried when we got news of the pregnancy. Mami was back in Mexico City with Papi, and I was still in California. We were happy for four months; then another call. The doctors had done an ultrasound, and there was no heartbeat. I was charged with telling Papi and Mami, but Mami scoffed at me over the phone. *The baby is fine.*

No, Mami, you don't understand. And then like an idiot, I explained to my mother what an ultrasound scan was, as if she had not gotten multiple scans when she was pregnant with us.

I don't care what the doctors say. Mami repeated: *The baby is fine.*

Ximena had the option of going to the hospital, where they would vacuum the dead tissue out of her, or of waiting until her own body expelled it. Over the phone, we talked about the advantages of the operation, the advantages of waiting. It seemed we had just hung up when Ximena called me again, crying: *Why is our mom being so crazy? The baby is dead—doesn't she know how much it hurts me to hear her say that it is not?*

I am so sorry, I am so sorry, I said, then dialed Mami again. *You have to stop telling Ximena you think her baby is alive.*

But it is! she protested.

Well, but stop telling her!

Of course, Mami did not listen. Like many before me, I found that, once she had made up her mind, there was absolutely no way for me to get her to do as I wished. Nothing I said to Mami had any effect: *What if you're wrong? What if you make her relapse? Leave her alone, she's just lost a baby.* I begged Ximena too: *Don't answer her calls. Just, please, block her number.*

Mami continued to call Ximena to warn her not to have the operation, telling her that if she went through with it, it would kill the baby the doctors were sure was dead but which Mami knew to be alive. Ximena continued to pick up. I sat by my phone in turn, hour by hour, expecting the worst. In the end, Ximena decided to wait—but not because of Mami. She just couldn't bring herself to get dressed and drive to the hospital. I exhaled, then slept for many hours. I checked in often with Ximena, but days became nights, and Ximena still had not bled, as her doctors said she would.

After a checkup appointment, she called: *So . . . the baby is alive.*

What? I remember I was boiling water for tea, and immediately turned off the stove and sat down on the black tiles of my kitchen floor.

The baby is alive, she repeated.

Wait—you mean Mami was right?

Technically, she was half *right,* Ximena said. *They think there were twins and one of them died and the other lived.*

So . . . your baby inside your belly has a ghost sibling?

Worse. The living fetus absorbed the dead fetus.

What—in the actual fuck.

I know, Ximena said, an excess of joy in her voice. I could hear her starting her car. *Life is weird.*

As she pulled out of the hospital parking lot, and Ximena told me with excitement that her baby had been the size of a poppy seed, a peppercorn, a pomegranate seed, and soon it would be a peach, a mango, and, last, a watermelon, I remembered that Ximena had always been this way, unfazed by strangeness.

I kept expecting that it would be hard for Ximena to witness the changes in her body, but if it was, she never let on. Instead, she had a new respect for it, couldn't recount to me without wonder the fact that she consumed food and her body turned it into bone, milk, tissue.

See? Mami asked me continually, in a way that was annoying, each time Ximena's recovery came up. *I told you she needed a new story.*

Mami couldn't forgive that, when it mattered, I had believed the doctors over her. *I don't know why everyone in this family always doubts me—after all the things I've done, what more proof could you need?*

20

MEMORY

All stories begin and end with memory. Personal memory that goes with the crack of a skull on rock, on pavement. Cultural memory oppressed and re-dressed in the foreign clothes of Catholicism. Ancestral memory hidden for centuries from occupying powers—and in secrecy becoming something new, a bifurcated thing.

One function of amnesia is survival.

The Spanish called the brutal invasion and overtaking of the continent and her people The Conquest. In the aftermath of genocide, many mestizos focused on becoming as white as it is possible to disappear. In others, memory was resilient. Under the cover of secrecy, after generations of war and against the erosion of time, we passed down our stories and medicine knowledge, and these were our own map for who we were and where we came from. The stories we loved made us indigestible to the pressures of assimilation and erasure.

When Mami and I lost our memories in our accidents, the function of amnesia was patterning. By losing our past and watching it reassemble, we found a way of belonging to each other and ourselves and a larger story. In my family, destiny is a force that chooses, that passes over some and not others, and stories seem to repeat across generations, diverging only in their particulars. After Nono made love to Nona in a dream the night he died, she woke up and saw clumps of earth on her sheets. The morning Papi sought a kiss from Mami's apparition, he found out it was like kissing the air. There was the dark circumference of the bottom of the well in which Mami lay unconscious, and the black skirt of the gown I rearranged around myself when I was all oblivion.

Ximena and I learned that forgetting was a path to subsistence. We are engineered this way, made to abandon what is too heavy to hold. But the body is a document. It keeps a memory of its own. We are made of loops and loops of time.

For example: When I walk around in the street and become afraid, clenching my jaw, my vagina clenches too. I am told this is common in women who have been assaulted. The body makes its own associations.

The gift of amnesia was bewilderment. After my accident, in the throes of memory loss, I was a person to whom nothing had yet occurred. I was a process constantly bridging to a cusp. I belonged to the perpetual second. And the perpetual second was an unknowable, deep delight.

The gift of remembering was the anger that allowed me to parse how I was made. The things passed down to me had made me into a battleground. Our Indigenousness was mocked, and our assimilation to whiteness praised. As I received the knowledge about these pieces of myself and dreamt of the seafloor that the departed ocean revealed, as I climbed down the crisp, hardened mounds of what had once been lava, running my hands along the black wrinkles in the rock, I knew that here was a second chance at becoming.

There is a difference between keeping secrets, the things I am not allowed to say and will never tell, and *keeping life a secret*. We are not meant to live in halves.

The pliable texture of memory has its use. It leaves breathing room for the ghosts.

Mami and I claim our memory, as we do our hunger, as we do our ghosts.

And still. If we are honest, we must admit we liked our lives best when we were more there than here, when we were more ghosts than flesh.

From time to time, Mami and I call each other to ask, *Remember what it was like to not remember anything?*

Yes, we say, with the wistfulness of a lover. *Yes.*

21

RECORDS

Some stories return, and it's almost like they're half told by ghosts. Just before Mami and I flew from Cúcuta to Bucaramanga to disinter Nono, we went to Ocaña. I had told Mami it was essential that we go, so I could dig up genealogical records and gather facts. She rolled her eyes at the word "facts," and in the back seat of the cab of Mami's cousin José, great-tía Carmen's son, whose help Mami had enlisted to get us to Ocaña, she pointed at me and said: *Can you believe the girl is going to Ocaña to look for facts? To Ocaña! In a family like ours? With the quality of our stories?*

José, broad-chested and dark, leaned forward and grinned at our private bickering in his rearview mirror, lightly touching his tongue to the back of his teeth. *You don't say.*

The seats were crushed velvet and yellow, and our windows were open. Fuzzy white dice hung from the rearview mirror, tumbling in the foreground of the foggy mountain we were driving through so early in the morning. I began to say that facts made stories flesh and blood, but Mami interrupted. *Do you remember the skull? The one the dentist gave Nono for ambience?*

A short laugh escaped my lips. I was unsure why she was bringing the skull up at this precise moment. *Why?*

Tell her, José—once, it rode in this cab, and right here, where we are sitting.

———

The skull had disappeared during Nono's wake, but after tío Ariel's death it reemerged. Mariana discovered it in her late husband's curandero office, on the floor by a cabinet, where he must have set it down while reorganizing his consulting room just before dying. Mariana wrapped it in a white bedsheet and left her house, then rode a bus for four hours to Ocaña with it on her lap. She wanted to be rid of the endless drama of our family, with our skulls and curanderos and secrets and gifts, and now that Ariel was dead, even more so.

When Mariana reached Cristo Rey, great-tía Carmen welcomed her into the kitchen, where the family was having breakfast, offered her coffee and a chair, and asked if she had slept well the night before, as though Mariana lived around the corner and was in the habit of dropping by all the time. Without taking either chair or coffee, Mariana set down the white bundle in the center of the table. She peeled back each corner of the sheet, letting it shroud the plates full of arepas, the bowls of fruit and cheese, and the cups of coffee the family had been about to enjoy. *Here,* Mariana said, exposing the skull, *is Papá Luciano.* Great-tía Carmen braced herself against the wall.

After Nono died, tío Ariel had pilfered the skull. Apparently, tío Ariel had been under the impression that the skull on Nono's altar had belonged to Nona's father, whom the family called Papá Luciano. Evidently, Nono had started this rumor himself. No one can imagine why, except maybe for the chance to posthumously direct a Shakespearean comedy and mess with tío Ariel and Nona from beyond the grave.

To begin with, Papá Luciano was not a curandero, was not even supernaturally inclined; he sold shoes that he carefully crafted from foraged car tires. Still, tío Ariel had confided in his wife, Mariana, telling her the skull was Papá Luciano's, and that this was the real source of Nono's powers, and once he had it in his own possession, tío Ariel's powers would equal Nono's. He built his own altar in a close imitation of Nono's. But, unlike Nono, he asked the skull in earnest for answers to the problems his clients brought.

At great-tía Carmen's, when Mariana set the skull down on the table, José remained immobile, staring into its hollowed eyes. Mariana was saying that Nono and tío Ariel had used Papá Luciano's skull as a bridge to the world of the dead, and now that they were both gone, the skull had been tormenting her, not letting her sleep a wink, and she couldn't bear to be in its presence any longer. With that, she left.

Great-tía Carmen put the skull in a corner of the kitchen, started to recite a long rosary, and sent word to Nona, asking what she wanted done with the skull of her father, now returned. Nona was outraged. She had known Nono to be a callous man, but so cruel as to steal her own father's skull? And, Nono was dead—how could he still be hurting her? She called our house and left an outraged message on our answering machine: the skull of her father had turned up alone, *without the rest of its skeleton,* in Ocaña—what did Mami know about such blatant and utter disrespect?

Mami laughed hysterically for half an hour when she found out what Nono had told Ariel. She had to go into another room so we wouldn't make her laugh as she called tía Carmen's—where they were in the process of lifting the tiles in their patio to give the skull a resting place—to urge them to stop. The skull was not Papá Luciano's; it belonged to some anonymous person who had been bequeathed to Nono by a dentist many years ago for the sake of ambience.

Quickly, whatever remorse, heartbreak, and trepidation had weighed on tía Carmen's family as they looked at the skull now morphed into the singular desire of being rid of it. Guille, José's father, had run through many scenarios in which he walked into the cemetery and explained to the groundskeeper that the skull was an ancestor who had been aiding the curanderos in the family, and now that they were dead, he was returning the holy skull to rest—but all the scenarios ended with the groundskeeper suspecting him of murder and calling the police.

So, instead, at midnight, Guille and José hopped into José's cab. The skull, wrapped in the same white sheet Mariana had brought, sat alone in the back seat. José and Guille feared being found by the authorities in possession of the skull, but they also feared offending the stranger to whom the skull belonged, provoking his haunting. For this reason, even if it was suspicious, they drove slowly in circles around the cemetery, trying to figure out the best way to creep inside.

Let's leave the skull at the gate, José proposed.

Are you out of your mind? Do you want to be haunted for the rest of your life?

They glanced at the skull, the white bundle in the back seat.

Guille whispered his plan to José: they could lob the skull over the graveyard wall. *If we say a Padre Nuestro and pitch it as delicately as we can, and it lands, you know, on holy ground, I bet we won't be haunted.*

First José, then Guille took turns getting out and intoning the prayer, but as soon as they were ready to toss the skull, they heard someone approach. Like men on the run, they dove back into the cab and sped off. They kept circling the graveyard until about two in the morning. That's when Guille got up enough nerve. He stomped his foot, breathed out a quick Padre Nuestro, hurled the skull, leapt into the back seat, and yelled, *Go, go, go!*, and all before, according to him, the skull even had occasion to land.

In the morning, José's family dressed up to go to the cemetery. If asked, they would say that they were there to pay respects to their dearly departed. At the cemetery, they weaved in between the graves looking for the skull.

Finally, they ran into the groundskeeper.

Oh! Hello!

They asked after the groundskeeper's health, whether he had family nearby, whether they were from Ocaña, inquired about how he had gotten into cemetery work. After they could think of nothing else to say, great-tía Carmen expressed interest in knowing whether anything strange had happened in the cemetery as of late.

Funny you should ask.

The groundskeeper told them that people left behind bones all the time, who knew why, and it had happened the night before. He pointed to a little arch carved out in the wall of the cemetery, which was piled with random bones. *I put them in a corner with the rest and say a prayer. What else can I do?*

You don't say, great-tía Carmen mused. She was impassive, but only because she could discern, even from a distance, with unnerving familiarity, which one had been, for a little while, their skull.

Having reassured themselves that nobody would be dusting the skull for fingerprints, and that they were not in danger of being questioned by the authorities about its provenance, great-tía Carmen and her family went to check on the family crypt so they could ease Nona's mind. Behind chicken wire was a group of small funerary urns collected atop two aboveground crypts, everything undisturbed.

In José's cab, we laughed for hours about the skull. Then, as we neared Ocaña, we remembered to be afraid. This felt very Colombian—to laugh about death one second, and grow deathly afraid the next. José told us that we now had to cross guerrilla territory. Ocaña is in the choicest drug-producing region in the northeast of Colombia: Catatumbo. It's incredibly fertile ground. Guerrillas, paramilitaries, neo-paramilitaries, and the army fight for control over it. FARC hadn't demobilized back then, and were still years away from striking a deal with the government in exchange for peace. But Mami's intuition said it was safe. My intuition was I didn't care. I wanted to touch my feet to our land. We rode in silence until we got out at a farm stand heaped with glowing mandarin oranges to ask about the Situation. The women selling the produce told us that, last they'd heard, FARC had packed up their camp and gone higher into the mountains; we should be okay to drive through.

There was nothing but breathtaking landscape for almost all the rest of the way—and then we saw them: standing at the side of the road, a bonfire smoking at their feet. Three of them, in camouflage and FARC armbands, machine guns propped against a tree. They had their backs to us, and they were hugging, one of them pointing up at the sky. They must have been admiring, as I had been a second ago, beams of sunlight piercing the fog, setting the treetops aglow. José accelerated.

It wasn't FARC we feared per se, but the individual men. We know, have lived, have heard stories of what happens when bored, sullen men who enjoy regular impunity see something they want.

In Ocaña, I got us a cheap motel. Mami and I shared a room. After, José drove us to see the village, to see what had changed since I had last visited, when I was thirteen. I didn't remember the village well, so everything seemed new. The air was warm and humid, making my clothes cling, and the horizon was full of tree copses and terra-cotta tiles and metal roofing; and here and there vendors pushed carts full of fresh fruit.

Echoes of violence followed us everywhere we went in Ocaña. One woman told me about her pretty daughter, how she had been making her way through the village square when she responded to a catcall by cursing; and later, the man she cursed entrapped her with four other men, all of them, it turned out, paramilitaries. The woman assumed her daughter had been raped, but what she knew for sure was that they had dumped her body in the wet foundation of a road and over her body poured cold cement, and this woman told me all of this in passing, as I was asking where she thought I might buy a city map. We were in the waiting room at the city records office. Maps were something I collected, objects I liked to stare at, most of all because I could not decipher their coded information. The woman told me she was still trying to find out where the body was dumped so she could go dig it out, and then, remembering why I was standing before her in the first place, she said, *I don't know where you can get a map—maybe a bookstore—but I'm still trying to get information on where my daughter's body is so I can get her back.*

Is anybody helping you? I asked.

A journalist, she said, opening, then closing a drawer. *He's talking to paramilitaries in jail. Maybe they saw. Maybe they participated.*

I held her hand, then let go. Everyone had lost so much, and justice was always out of reach.

Part of the building of the government palace, where the city records office is located, used to be a prison. It's a Spanish Mission building, with squared windows and balconies, a tower, and a tiled roof. Now the mayor had his office on the second floor, and the first floor was reserved for all manner of city services. I was there to speak to the archivists. The archival office was past the indoor courtyard, after the palm trees and manicured lawn, at the end of a corridor and out of the way. Each of the four archivists had a desk at a corner of the room, and they all faced the middle. I stood in the center, and rotated as I spoke to address all of them, like I was greeting the cardinal directions: *I am looking for the names of the victims of the Spanish Inquisition.* I didn't think I was related to any of the victims—or, rather, I didn't know—but what I wanted was to find out what the city had done and against whom.

There was a breeze in the room whose source I could not pinpoint. Without answering my question, the archivists informed me that I was shivering because the room we were in was haunted.

Some time ago, they heard footsteps coming from the ceiling. A couple of times, they went outside to check whether someone was on the roof, but no one was there. Eventually, they took a hammer to the ceiling and bored a hole in the plaster. They discovered a sealed alcove filled with dust and old city identification cards, surely what was drawing the ghosts. I gazed up. *Are the IDs still up there?*

The archivist to my left brightened. *No.* He pulled out a little ruled notebook from his bag. *I sell them.* He fanned the pages, and I saw that taped in a neat grid were the sepia-colored photographs from the IDs, which he had peeled off. He wrote beneath each portrait the name and date of birth of the person. I wasn't sure why he had gone through that laborious process, but I longed to see the photos.

Shouldn't these be in the city archive? I asked, amused.

These are haunted and black-market, reina. People are always seeking their dead; sometimes they're here. I smirked as I took the notebook and turned pages. Then I froze, stunned to come across a familiar photo. It was Papá Luciano, Nona's father, whose name had been on our lips for hours on our way to Ocaña a few days ago. The record keeper rose from his chair and came around me to glance over my shoulder.

That one yours?

I laughed, nodded.

That'll be five thousand pesos.

I parted with the bills and watched the archivist peel off the tape holding the passport-sized photo to the notebook with care. He handed it to me, unblemished. As I was tucking Papá Luciano inside a book on the history of Ocaña I'd just bought, the city archivist sat back down and told me he thought he remembered hearing that there *was* a list of the victims of the Inquisition, a document with stamps and signatures, but that the city had buried it beneath the cement foundation on which rests the statue of Christ at the top of Cristo Rey.

He said, angling back, that the statue of Cristo Rey was heaved up the mountain because of hauntings in the first place too. *People who died at the mount didn't get justice. People who walked by that place got their hair pulled, heard whisperings in their ear, saw things. So the city tried to give ghosts a proper burial; there was a priest and everything.* I stared at the ceiling again, wondering if the same logic was behind the sealed alcove, or if somebody simply forgot what was up there.

I wanted to believe, as much as the city archivist did, in a list we could dig up, whose names we could learn and speak. But later, I'd find out that colonial-era executions at the mount were extrajudicial, and being extrajudicial, they don't exist in any record. All we have is our oral history.

Or maybe it wasn't only the hauntings, I said. *Maybe the city wanted to bury inconvenient history.* The four archivists assented.

When I was done at the government palace, José drove us ten minutes up the mountain to Cristo Rey, as far as it was possible to go, and then we walked. After five minutes, the statue loomed at the center of what was a neighborhood plaza—Jesus opening his arms. There was a little church on the side, and a gated balcony overlooking the drop. When I looked back from where we'd come, the Andes rose at the horizon. The distant, blue-gray mountains rose above a jungled canopy, and closer, the cluster of adobe buildings that people called downtown Ocaña were hemmed in by wild greenery: the plaza where once Nono and the family had strolled at sundown to meet their neighbors and receive the witches' mail, and the city government palace where we had just been.

When Mami was a girl, she'd hike up to the peak of Cristo Rey from her house. She liked to nap on the grass that people said was frequented by ghosts because nobody bothered her there, though from time to time the ghosts did yank her hair.

As Mami sat down to talk with José, I went to greet some locals, young men standing around enjoying the sun, and asked if they happened to know stories about the executions. They shrugged. *Only what the abuelos say. That there were hangings and burnings. That you could smell the burning bodies for days. And that's why there are hauntings.*

Others got curious about me, my city accent, and what I might be doing among them. I mentioned my grandfather, and an old man broke into a smile. *I can see him in your eyes.* He called some others, and suddenly I was surrounded by abuelos and abuelas who peered into my eyes and argued with one another over where exactly my grandfather lived on my face. I felt surrounded by gen-

Papá Luciano's black-market photograph. San Francisco,
2021

tleness, and I tried not to cry in front of them, but I did. I wiped my cheeks and explained I lived far away and it had been some years since I'd been back. One abuela rubbed my back, another whispered, *Bienvenida*. Mami walked over to see why I was surrounded, and soon the abuelos and abuelas turned their attention to her and fawned over her face as they had mine. I slinked away to walk around the statue, toward haunted ground and the ghosts of those who had disappeared.

The statue of Cristo Rey, at the site of colonial-era executions, according to our oral histories. Ocaña, 2012

22

THE BOOK THAT SELF-COMBUSTS

I n Ocaña, Mami and I trod along the middle of the dirt road that snaked down the mountain, tracing what had been her usual peregrinations in Cristo Rey. Mami perused the plants bobbing along the road. *These are good for nerves,* she said of yellow wild rue flowers. *The leaves are good for protection.* I was taking in their orange scent when Mami pointed out the houses with thatched palm roofs and adobe walls climbing the steep, and told me that Nono had built them.

Nono built houses? In my family, it is the quotidian that shocks.

Once, while socializing in the plaza, Nono had been introduced to the mayor, who mentioned, in passing, that he wanted to arrange for new housing in Cristo Rey. Nono replied: *What a coincidence, I happen to be an architect!* Nono had taken pains in raising himself a house before, but only as his forefathers had done, after the manner of Indigenous huts. He wasn't *completely* lying. But he was lying nonetheless. He paid for a forged diploma, hired a real architect to draw up a sketch, and had Mami proofread both since he could not read. When Mami approved them, they were delivered to the mayor in a manila envelope. Within days, Nono nudged close to people who needed housing, and in low whispers confided a building crew was the usual for this kind of thing, but he could also help them build and pay them and himself a salary from the city's coffers. He also arranged that the prospective owners could buy the houses for a price they could afford. Many of the houses Nono built were still standing. I found them to be quite beautiful. Inside, you could look up and feel like you were in the forest.

When we had walked down the mountain about a quarter of the way, Mami said we were near where the well once stood, the one she had fallen into. She stopped. She pointed to a yellow adobe house topped with dried palm fronds and told me it was Nil's house.

Nil who?

Nil as in your tío Nil, Mami clarified. *Son of your great-tío Nil. Your great-tío Nil was Nono's brother, the one who relaxed Nono's hands in the casket the day of his burial.*

Oh! But also the one who got the ghost gold fever and heard disembodied coins falling everywhere?

I hastened after Mami, who had walked up to the door of the house she had pointed out and was knocking. *The one and the same!*

When tío Nil opened the door, he gasped: *Uy!*

We hadn't told anyone save great-tía Carmen and José that we were coming, and now we watched tío Nil look from Mami to me, his eyes roving over each of our faces. Like all our family in Ocaña, he remarked on my resemblance to Mami when she was my age. *What'd you do, ask for a scanner?*

She is a better copy of me, Mami replied. *Smarter, more beautiful; she's just brimming with qualities I never had.*

Mami was in a good mood because I'd done an exemplary job taking care of her needs that morning—brought her coffee (with a splash of soy milk) and a plate of fruit and arepas, and I had asked about her dreams while she stayed warm and cozy in bed. When I wasn't so attentive, Mami responded to similar remarks by looking at me with boredom: *I don't know why such things happen: you think you're having a daughter and instead you give birth to a mirror.*

Inside tío Nil's house, the ceiling was high, the air cool. This

One of the houses Nono built. Ocaña, 2012

was a house Nono had built. A thin but beautiful curtain hid a bed. Tío Nil collected hard-backed chairs from different corners and placed them in a triangle. We sat down. He had just been thinking about Europe, he said. He told us about visiting Paris, going to museums, drinking in the cafés.

The world is so big, he concluded. *Conversely, it's never big enough, not if you're trying to forget a woman.*

I laughed. *And what did this particular woman do to you?*

Tío Nil held up his hands. *Women don't do anything! Ever! They just worm themselves inside your brain like parasites and refuse to leave.* He crossed his arms, nodding, agreeing with himself. *Yes, that's what they do.*

I wondered if tío Nil was someone who liked hunting for guacas, or if, because of what had happened to his father, he steered clear of them. Not knowing whether this was a sensitive subject, I settled on asking if he knew any guaqueros.

He leaned back, aghast, his hands alighting on his chest. *Me,* he said. *Me.*

He was scandalized that I didn't know. He regularly went into the mountains to look for glowing ground. He used his father's divining tool, a three-pronged iron pendant. He retrieved it from somewhere in the back of the house and showed it to us; we watched it swing over the cemented floor. I had never seen a treasure-divining tool before. Tío Nil said the instrument was blessed and had been made in such a way that it pulled in the direction of wherever a guaca lay in hiding. Unfortunately, he had never come across glowing ground. He went hunting for guacas year-round, on the chance that a ghost might choose to give him its treasure.

I already knew about this, but in case he might tell me something I hadn't known, I didn't interrupt as tío Nil explained that guacas are revealed during Holy Week, and the rest of the year they choose whom they appear to. If a ghost picked you for its treasure, it wouldn't stop until it got you to dig, tío Nil shared. Many people, including his father, made the mistake of digging

Nono's brother great-tío Nil's divining tool for haunted treasure.
Ocaña, 2012

where the ground glowed, but this only triggered the treasure's curse. To avoid the curse, you had to wait for the ghost to material-ize. The ghost could be terrifying or serene: A man hanging from a tree. A woman trailing the tail of her wedding dress over the jungle. Wherever the ghost disappeared, *that* was where the hole should be dug.

When a ghost didn't want to give up a treasure, or if the pro-cedures for unearthing a guaca were not heeded, a haunting was the result. There were other secrets for unearthing treasure, pro-cedures that made it possible to excavate a guaca safely, but tío Nil said this was all I was allowed to know.

I did know one more thing, and I told him: one should hunt for treasure in a group that was odd in number; it was important that the number be odd. Tío Nil laughed.

As I sat smiling at him, something about the easy creases at the corner of his eyes and lips made me suddenly remember that I had met his father, great-tío Nil, a long time ago.

It was the year I was twelve and great-tía Carmen had told her story about the girl who was either a girl or a ghost. Nono's side of the family was secretive, hard to reach, so when Mami heard that great-tío Nil was in town, she made sure I could spend some time with him. Ximena was invited to come, but she opted out of any-thing that had to do with magic, much preferring the company of her Game Boy, which she thumbed with enthusiasm.

Great-tío Nil, Mami, and I climbed the winding road of Cristo Rey together. Great-tío Nil was serious, soft-spoken. Dust gath-ered on my ankles and dyed my socks orange. But great-tío Nil's white linen pants remained unsoiled.

Mami told him her dreams, and then I told him mine. This was the proper introduction. Dreams indicated the true state of our lives. I wish I could remember what my dreams were at the time. I know great-tío Nil listened with attention. When I stopped speak-ing, he looked uphill, where the houses nestled, retreating into the mountainside like sudden alcoves, all around them oases of green palms and jacaranda trees.

I wanted to ask what he had done to make Nono's hands relax in the casket, but I knew it was not my place. Instead, unaware of how he'd once been devastated by the ghost gold fever, I asked if he liked treasure hunting.

After a moment's silence, he said: *I'm leaving this world soon. I can feel I don't have much time.*

I understood that my question had been stupid. I looked down, then back up. Mami nodded. *Are you ready?*

His eyes turned under sunlight, caramel when he looked at Mami, honey when he glanced at me. *Already I am more there than here.*

Will you look after my daughter from over there?

We were standing at the middle of the dirt path. Great-tío Nil sought my gaze with such inordinate care I felt uncomfortable, but not unsafe. My question about treasure hunting had hurt him somehow. I didn't feel I deserved his protection. He tilted his head to the side.

Grasshoppers in the bushes surrounding us filled the air with a rising stridulation. A breeze blew between us.

He looked up at the sky, then at me. He smiled. *I will.* He nodded at the ground. *I will.*

After saying our goodbyes and leaving great-tío Nil's son's house, Mami and I continued to hike, now heading for the spot where the well used to be. Some five minutes down the dirt road, we veered onto a footpath through the forest. The sloping soil of the hill gave easily under our step, and from time to time we slipped. The sun was high, and we were sweating, walking slow. Thorned bushes framed the path, and then we came to a clearing.

This is where the well used to be, Mami said.

I walked over the patch of soil, now covered with a sparse blanket of grass. *Are you sure?*

Mami nodded. In just one hour, we'd arrive at great-tía Carmen's, where arepas and cheese awaited us. But now, for what felt like an interminable, infinite time, at the clearing with my mother, I crouched and pressed my palm on the ground, trying to feel the ghost of the tunnel into which my mother fell, through which everything changed.

Over the coming days, I was introduced to many family members whom I hadn't met on previous trips. Some were distant relatives, others were related to us so many generations ago that they weren't technically family anymore. Somehow everyone kept track. There were a multitude of Nils, Luises, Alicias, and great-tíos introduced me to their cousins, and to their friends, telling me things like *This is the son of a cousin of your great-great-tía Alicia.* Most people just looked at my brows and canela skin and declared that we shared blood.

I wandered around Cristo Rey by Mami's side, and on every block we were invited into a new home. By noon, I'd tired of trying to keep a grasp on the genealogy everyone else seemed to have a natural handle on and settled on calling everyone uncle and auntie, and had had my fill of hot chocolate and salty cheese, but I didn't dream of declining. Some tías told me we were potentially family, depending on whether I understood children outside of wedlock to be family, and whether the children of those children counted as relations. *Of course we're family,* I said. A tía looked away, wiped under her eyes, and gave a quick smile. *You'd be surprised how many people here refuse to talk to you for something your father did.*

Being ushered into house after house is how I ended up at tía Alba's, who was distantly kin to us through Nono's side. The three preferred subjects in Ocaña, as far as I could tell, were infidelity, runaways, and ghosts, and with tía Alba it was ghosts. She had been haunted by the ghost of a Spanish colonizer since she was a little girl. He always appeared wearing the same thing—a frilly shirt, riding pants, tall boots. He beckoned her to come with his finger, and was always standing in the same spot. Tía Alba walked by the spot often—it was on the way to the main dirt road, and whenever she did the sound of coins falling reverberated in her ears.

Here in Ocaña all of the land is infected with the ghost gold fever.

When I was at a restaurant with Mami, a waiter whom we were not related to told us his uncle heard the coins, too, after a failed treasure hunt. He hacked holes into the adobe walls of their house. One day, the family woke to find that a deer had sneaked through a hole in the night and was sleeping soundly by the heat stove. Another day, they found an anaconda curled up on the middle cushion of their living room couch. *We had to tie my uncle with rope,* he told us, then repeated: *In the end, we had to tie him up. There was nothing we could do. He had lost his mind.*

Knowing the stories, tía Alba wanted nothing to do with a treasure that could make her mad.

Do you think you have the fever? I asked.

As if she hadn't heard my question, tía Alba told me of another ghost: a woman screaming in the middle of the night. The ghost's screams bespoke a deep horror, a woman in danger. But the ghost should not be helped.

If you hear her, tía Alba said, *never open the door.*

Why, what would happen? I asked.

You'll be gone, too, then. You'll be the woman who screams in the night.

I told Mami I was planning to find genealogical records for Nono's family through baptismal records and she laughed in my face. First of all, she told me, people in Ocaña didn't heed the imported Western systems of record keeping as they did in other places, such as Bogotá. A perfect example of the attitude here was the city archivist selling me black-market history during his working

The exact spot where tía Alba heard the disembodied sound of coins falling. Ocaña, 2012

hours—*while in the government palace,* she emphasized. *Second of all,* she added, *who do you think we are? You think we're the type of people to be in the public record?*

In Ocaña, Mami tells me, there were the other Contrerases, the white ones. I would find *them* in the records for sure. The name Contreras is all over Ocaña. Some are the true relations of the European who founded the village, but others hold the last name because it was what was given to Indigenous people whose naming traditions didn't correspond to the Europeans'. One of Nono's great-grandmothers married a Contreras—a true relation, as far as I can tell. This great-grandmother was a campesina, brown and poor, and the Contrerases never accepted her as part of the family. So she lived in the mountains with her people and her white husband.

The white Contrerases owned a great house, filled with antiques from Spain, and a corner store. They had photo albums that went back several generations. Mami says they were the type of family who kept a carefully labeled family tree, documents, reports that proved their Spanish heritage.

Our side of the family, by comparison, Mami noted, would be impossible to trace. We don't have family albums. Our foremothers gave birth at home, so there would be no birth records. There would be no census documents, because censuses were halted by civil war. And there would be no land-ownership documents: we owned nothing.

Because I am stubborn, and because I always think I know more than Mami, I spent many hours at the baptismal registry annexed to the white Chapel of Santa Rita in downtown Ocaña, trying to prove her wrong. Getting baptized was a cultural prerequisite to having good social standing, and I was sure I could trace the family this way. The Chapel of Santa Rita, as it happened, was once the headquarters for the officials of the Inquisition. Not much is known about this history—except that a dungeon, with shackles and human remains, was eventually discovered.

I left Mami at the nearby hotel first thing in the morning,

followed my phone's instructions to the chapel, and, as I would do each day, looked for names at the registry office. The baptismal registry is a direct opposite of the stuccoed, high-ceilinged chapel—the little office was hot and filled with people, and it was a woman (not a priest) who saw to the community's needs, which were applications to get babies baptized, requests for copies of baptismal records to report a marriage, a death, a divorce. My petition to look through the registries struck the woman as odd, so she had me stand to one side and out of the way. I spent many afternoons standing there, shifting my weight from one foot to the other, using the counter as a table.

It was easy to locate the book that contained Mami's record, easy to find the book that contained Nona's and Nono's, difficult but not impossible to find her two sets of grandparents. But then, on both sides of Mami's lineage, I came upon a complete blank. On Nona's side, I got stuck at her father, Papá Luciano. Papá Luciano was illegitimate. He took his mother's last name, and the system is devised to keep track of men. Without the father's name, I could not work my way back. I had no luck with Mamaria, either. Day after day I returned, asking for books from 1870, 1860, 1850, 1840, turning the dusty pages, looking for the baptismal record of Papá Luciano's or Mamaria's parents, but it was no use. Nono's grandparents proved to be just as elusive. I couldn't find them in the records at all.

I found something else instead—a note from the priest in charge, penned into the registry in 1877, explaining that the records from the year before had been lost, and many baptisms since had not been recorded because of war; and like many Colombians then and since, he proceeded to describe the plot of violence as it led from one conflict to the next.

The current priest at the church, who grew accustomed to seeing me standing at the counter inhaling the dust of books, heard me exclaim at how many children were labeled as illegitimate. I was staring at one page dedicated to one man, and the sixteen women who bore his children to whom he gave his last name, but whom he would not recognize as legitimate.

The priest brushed his hands on his black cassock, leaned over the counter, and told me that "illegitimate" often meant that the father was white, married, and with a family, and the mother had been brown or Black. Otherwise, it meant the father was one of those irresponsible hummingbird men, as he assumed of the man in question. I nodded, continued turning pages. He told me that, in his opinion, if my grandfather had descended from a lineage of curanderos, probably they never came down to the village to be baptized, and maybe this was why I couldn't find them.

I smiled and offered that he was probably right, but, still, I had to look.

You should wear a mask, anyway, he said. *You may get sick from the dust.*

I thanked him. Just as he disappeared through the little side door that led to the chapel, I opened the dark flap of an especially old book.

I gasped, admiring the calligraphy. The pages had yellowed, but the ink detailing baptisms was still jet black, and the notes on the margin scarlet. Slanted titles bore the names of the baptized, but the calligraphy was so decorative it was hard to read.

I was admiring the plunging curve of a serif when I shifted my arm beneath the thick, leathered book and caused the block of bound pages, untethered from the cover, to slide. *They will have to be resewn,* I thought, then watched in horror as the paper, like a fissuring earth, broke into uneven caesuras. In the seconds it took me to gasp, to react, to invoke the motions for setting the book down, the fissured paper glided along the angle which I had created; it snagged on itself and snagged again, cascading, pulverizing, rolling, pulverizing, like the book itself had decided to self-combust. I inhaled then covered my mouth. The book was dust wheeling in the air. The book was dust piling atop a few surviving pages unbound from the leather cover. *All those names lost forever.*

The woman overseeing the records drifted to the counter and took what was left of the book from me, not at all concerned or surprised by what had happened. She replaced it flat into its place in the row where it belonged. *It's an old book, what do you expect?*

I sat on the curb outside and cried. Mami had to come and get me. *It's just a book,* she said.

I wiped my nose with my shirtsleeve. It's inevitable, for some of us, that our inheritance will look like nothing. That war, poverty, violence, the politics of the archive will erase the palpable trace of our past. I didn't know how to explain that I had held a book I thought was solid, but it was always sand in a guise, just me fooled by the illusion. *It's like I watched history erase itself,* I said.

She stared at me. *And what do you think happens second by second?*

I think I may be full of the dead, I didn't tell her. *I inhaled the names,* I didn't say. I knew Mami would give me exorcism water. But I thought about guacas choosing the person, and decided I didn't want to be rid of the dead just yet.

Once, Mami told me, she had the opportunity to meet the white Contrerases. It happened when she was about six, and Nono had to travel to Venezuela for a job. In that time, while Nona was often all alone with her children, the other Contrerases allowed her to live rent-free in the servant quarters connected to their house.

Mami was little, but she remembers waiting in the servant quarters until there was no sound coming from the great house. She and her siblings were expressly forbidden to do so, but once the coast was clear, they opened the French doors that led to the house and investigated the fine rugs, the lace curtains, the leathered chests, the paintings, and a surplus of objects that belonged to an order of opulence they had not known could exist. They opened small lacquered boxes displayed on side tables, which were always infuriatingly empty. There were beds with posts of solid wood from which hung soft white cotton.

The other Contrerases may have had wealth, Mami says. *But we, we were always rich in our stories.*

After Mami and I returned to Cúcuta, long after I stopped looking for further evidence of Nono's family, I found what I was looking for—which wasn't what I had expected. There were court documents in tía Perla's possession, detailing debt, measly inheritances, gravesites given out on loan. On all the documents, all of Nono's brothers and sisters signed their names *X*.

There is not a lot you can tell from an X, two lines simply etched, crossed at the middle. X's are shut doors. Refusals. But X's also mark the spot.

Nono is the only one who has a signature in the documents.

Mami told me he got someone to write his name in cursive and learned to mimic the drawing of the words. He spent so much time pretending to be literate—signing his name, drawing up contracts, passing out business cards—not out of shame, Mami says, but so that he could steal a wealth that was meant to be held beyond his reach. Nono knew that nothing is truly inaccessible, that creativity in the face of a limitation is also intelligence, and that, when power is used to oppress, it always deserves to be mocked.

That night in Ocaña, after the book disintegrated at the records office, once Mami fell asleep, I recited my incantations against amnesia: *The woman next to you is your mother, the woman next to you is your mother.* For, as much as I had, as a young girl, wanted to see a ghost, after I witnessed Mami's clone reading her own tarot cards in our living room in Bogotá I dreaded it happening again. Seeing Mami's clone now sounded chaotic and terrifying. But it happened anyway. Mami's breathing was deep next to me in bed, and at the same time, I saw her walk past the door to the bathroom. I saw her for only a few seconds, but clearly it was her. She was lit by the yellowed streetlight coming through the hotel window, and was wearing the day's clothes, which were folded to my left by her suitcase. Her black hair fell to one side, and she was brushing it, sweeping it into a gleam.

I was not scared, as I'd imagined I would be.

I did not need to fear ghost women—not the kind that floated in lagoons or shrieked at front doors, and not my mother, who doubled during fevers and profound sleep. It didn't matter whether what was happening was inside or outside of my brain. To question the nature of the doubling was to miss this particular story. I didn't need to go check and see what was in the bathroom. I didn't need to prove whether I saw or didn't see something. Instead, I turned on my side to face Mami, who looked so soft in sleep. I understood what Papi said, that seeing Mami's double was a comfort. I closed my eyes and addressed Papi in my mind as though he could hear me: *It feels like she's taking care of me.*

THE MIRROR

let's return to the sea.
those who don't know how to leave their loot on the sand
will drown in the air.

—RAQUEL SALAS RIVERA

there is room in the language for being
without language.

—KAVEH AKBAR

THE MIRROR

When Europeans settled on the continent, they parceled out the land, forcing grids and edges onto an unfathomable thing. To better understand what they had taken, through the centuries, they bordered the territory. They bordered our thinking too. They told us what was real and not, what history and what legend, what oral history and what folklore, what religion and what superstition. They gave us a road map for how to disappear. All my life, I've fallen into the traps set by this colonization.

There are many ways to erase the past. In the 1990s, in Bogotá, my secondary school thought it important that students learn English. They welcomed young teachers who came from England, and later from the United States, twenty-year-olds who wanted to spend an exotic year abroad. The British made us pronounce English words with their accent, and then the teachers from the United States corrected that accent, told us that wasn't *English*. Both strove to tutor us on assimilation, even though this was our land they were on.

In their classrooms, we spent inordinate amounts of time poring over the histories and literature written by the white men of their lands. They lectured us on the things that were hard for us to grasp. For example: that realistic fiction was Jane Austen, and fantasy fiction was Gabriel García Márquez. Magical realism was just *realism* to us, and Jane Austen was not any life that was possible in our land. Still, they renewed their efforts to teach us clear boundaries, strict differentiations. There were names for what some of us lived, saw, and believed—legends, superstitions, fictions.

The histories and stories of a people are a mirror—they tell how and when and where and why a people lived. No matter the year or the hour, empire will always seek to destroy the mirrors in which it does not see itself. This is why the colonizing culture does not consider our stories passed down through memory to be a valid document; why they are deemed to be more dreams than history, just as our perceived realities are deemed to be fiction.

This is the language in power. It has never been able to imagine anything outside itself.

But where their thinking ends, ours begins.

The world over, the oldest mirrors might have been another's pupil, water during moonlit nights. We filled dark bowls with water, inventing portable mirrors we could own.

In the state of Santander, one of the main rivers that flow through the land was named by the Guane as Chicamocha—silver thread in the mountain on a full moon's night—so it must have been that, long ago, in the dusking forest, the Chicamocha unrolled its silver waters and drew the Guane to its floating mirrors. The Guane were master weavers whose preferred weapon was the poisoned arrow. The Spanish feared them, especially the grandmothers, since they needed no maps and could foretell where the Spanish would tra-verse. Without being present, they felled whole platoons simply by burying venom-tipped spikes along the footpath. They lived in the canyon, overlooking the Chicamocha from great heights.

Who knows exactly when it was that we turned to the material that land spat out in order to birth itself anew, and noticed how lava, rich in feldspar and quartz, cooled into obsidian, that natu-rally occurring volcanic glass?

The oldest surviving man-made mirror to be found is obsidian and was buried in a grave in Turkey eight thousand years ago. It is slightly convex, and polished, its sharp edges smoothed so it can be held in the palm of the hand, its reflections all shadowed gleam.

Similar mirrors could be found in Mesoamerica, where obsidian is plentiful, but down the continent, at the Caribbean, people buffed chunks of pyrite and wore them as pendants suspended from their necks. Farther down, in Colombia, our mirrors were sometimes pyrite and sometimes gold. We had a lot of gold.

Humans have always seemed to know that a mirror is an eye, and that to look into a mirror is to see, but also to be seen by what sees.

In Egypt, copper and bronze were polished into mirrors and socketed to represent the eye of the god Horus, or sometimes the moon, which in the sky was also the eye of Horus. Mirrors were piled at the feet of the gods. To offer a mirror was to offer light.

It was the French, in the Middle Ages, who worked out that if clear glass was coated with a mixture of tin and mercury it produced an immaculate doubling.

But such mirrors were hard to make.

The French formula for glass was two parts beech-tree ashes to one part sand. The mixture was heated, and then a master blower exhaled into his stem while rotating it evenly, making the orb of a glass balloon. An assistant then pierced it, and the heated glass flared out and settled onto a tray. It was a delicate process, in which the glass would often break. If it survived, it was brushed with tin and mercury. The biggest mirror they could make was no larger than a dinner plate.

Mirror makers were handsomely paid, and mirrors were prohibitively expensive. Royalty could afford them, and the aristocracy. Ordinary people made do with tin mirrors, in which they saw themselves blurrily cast.

Perfect reflection was a privilege.

Perfect reflection has always been a privilege.

I was in my twenties, a few years after migrating to the United States, when I caved.

I wrote from real life, and when Northerners advised me it was fiction, I conceded that maybe it was. What did I know—an immigrant, writing in her second tongue? Maybe my life *was* a fiction.

But what I wrote under that guise came out repulsive, in a language I didn't want to touch. The words stopped coming. Meanwhile, the same Northerners who'd classified my reality now told me they'd become *magical realists*—a term that filled up their mouths, and which they enunciated with relish. It amounted to a narrative tone, they explained, and was just another tool in the writer's toolbox, in which the magical was delivered as if matter-of-fact.

Whiteness has a circular logic, a tautological theft.

The lessons I had received all my life told me I was of worth only when I was digestible—only, therefore, when I was make-believe.

When I lost my memory, I did not remember any of this. All I had was the stories from which I came. Immaculate mirrors.

If I look into the mirror my mother gave me—not the same shaving mirror that Nono placed beneath her pillow so she could remember, but one he gave her a few years later—I see my face broken up by a pattern of scales, which are the places where the silvering of the mirror has scratched and revealed the slate gray of the metal beneath. The coating has worn off through the years of rubbing and attrition, of our tossing heads as we shifted on the pillow with it beneath. This mirror must have its own memory of our looking—Mami, age fourteen to fifty-one, as old as she was when she gave it to me, and me, age twenty-three to now.

Because I had amnesia I know:

In the beginning there was us. Then there was the mirror.

When Mami lost her memory, she hungered for a mirror the moment she experienced others gazing at her with repulsion, but when I lost mine, I did not remember what mirrors were.

I know what it's like to exist without knowing what one is.

I know that the meat of the body imagines itself to be air.

That wind passes through us, sunlight delivers us to the blood, and the blood, unceasingly, chants maps into being.

Once, I knew exactly everything there was to know about existing.

Then I lost it all on my reflection in a dark window in Chicago.

According to our indexes of meaning, amnesia is ignorance, and this state of pragmatic awareness is knowledge; but everything was incandescent when I had no memory of what things were. Unnamed, everything was knowable as never before.

Magpie to candlelight. Peacock feather to lava. A roomful of night.

I knew so much more then, during amnesia.

So it can begin to seem that this state of awareness is ignorance, and that that state of amnesia was knowledge.

It is useful to look at negative space, to ask what lives within us even when it goes unnamed, to ask what survives the book that self-combusts.

We fall into thinking that our inability to perceive something means it doesn't exist. Nothing is ever gone. Everything we think we have lost is still here, only as dust in the air we breathe. Our problem has always been that we cannot read dust.

I have thought too highly of language, our indexes, our power to name. I have mistaken myself for what is reflected in the mirror, mistaken the stuff I am and the stuff I am made from for the bits of it I am able to trap in language.

A year or so after I recovered my memory, and had become at home with who I was, I went to a party on a cliff overlooking the Golden Gate Bridge in San Francisco. I lived in a state of wonder, constantly overwhelmed with the richness of all my family stories, finally returned, learned anew. The belonging I felt was unprecedented. It made me tear up at a second's notice. And so, when a white woman drinking, for some reason, champagne asked what I did, I told her I was a writer. I told her that I wanted to write a memoir, that it was going to be about my grandfather who could move clouds.

I remember that the woman blinked at me, inclined her head to one side.

Oh, she said, in a small voice, and extended her champagne-flute-free hand to me. *Come, come.*

She wanted me to join her by the cliff.

I'm a park ranger, she explained when I hesitated, remaining firmly rooted where I was. *Come, let me explain to you how wind works.*

Which is the higher order? Is it to remember or to forget? Languaging or unlanguaging?

When I came back together, I remembered a lineage of memory. Not only of Nono and his forefathers, but of Nona and her fore-mothers. There were the stories passed from mother to daughter down the line to Mami and down the line to me—from abuela, bisabuela, tatarabuela, and further back in time, our tátara-tátara-tátara-tatarabuelas . . .

Back when we kept clothing in chests, one of us filled a chest with rocks to trick the family into thinking our clothes were still there, so we wouldn't be discovered when we ran away into the arms of a lover. One of us danced with Simón Bolívar, whom we considered ugly but magnetic: frankly, we were more entranced with our borrowed dress, which swept behind us like the tail of a bird. We survived massacres. Once, we hid behind a dead body. Once, we found a múcura, raw emeralds in a pot. We were forced to marry. We did not utter another word after being forced. We disappeared, no one knows where. We were a woman who appeared in two places at once. We fell down a well. We lost our memory. We waded into a lagoon, and looked into its reflection. We witnessed our memory—our story, map, and mirror—return.

· IV ·

ASH

~

We wake in the middle of a life, hungry.

—JANE WONG

24

GHOST

L et them take the body to burn, Mami says, as I am kneeling before my grandfather, who is blackened skull, shredded cloth, decomposing wishes that he did or did not fulfill.

The gravediggers are waiting for me to be done with whatever it is I am doing. I don't know what I am doing. I know something wordless has come to pass. My grandfather's femur is black-dusted with soil, and mine is still gleaming white.

Mami is a reflection of Nono, in the same way I am a reflection of her. I had believed that to look upon Nono's bones would be to look into the original mirror. But I don't have a singular experience of myself. Instead, I am refracted. Because to set a mirror before another is to create an endless labyrinth.

I'm out of sorts, and ask Mami, Do we want to see the burning? Sometimes I do this, speak to her as if we were the same person but only she has insight into how we feel. Mami shakes her head no.

Sensing that the moment with my grandfather has come to an end, the gravediggers slowly bend to pick up the corners of the tray. I remain kneeling as they straighten and tell us we can return for the ashes in two days. Over my shoulder, I observe them ferrying my grandfather down the hill—these strange men in gauzy hairnets and blue jumpsuits and yellow boots bearing my grandfather, the metal tray on which he rests blinking silver wherever it's hit by the sun, like it's all a strange moon landing.

There is a part of me that is my grandfather, perching inside, watching his own body travel down the hill among the gravestones and beyond what can be seen, to an unspecified location where it will be turned to ash. Even new land is recycled. The earth swallows up the ground we walk on and dissolves it, then throws it back up decades later, and we call it new. But it is old. We are always old.

Mami laughs all the way back to Bucaramanga: *Remember,* she says next to me in the back seat of Fabián's car, *how your tío Nil went to remove the body of his father, your great-tío Nil, from the crypt—and when he pulled the handle of the coffin to get it out from the recess in the wall, there was no coffin at all, just the body, which fell on him whole?* We don't remember—none of us lived it—but Mami is laughing hysterically about this. *The skeleton! Of his father! Dressed in a suit and everything? Just fell on him whole?* I don't want to laugh, but I end up laughing so hard I cry. Fabián has to pull over as we cackle in fits back and forth, until I am on the floor of the car, begging, *Stop laughing, stop, please, stop, it hurts.*

Fabián drops us off at our hotel. I have asked Mami to take me on a tour of her past while we are in Bucaramanga.

In a few minutes, she and I stand before one house I have never been to, but Mami says I have, since I visited it in my dream at the beginning of this whole undertaking. *Remember? Nono grabbed you by the hand and took you through the house and out the back? He pointed down to the river, telling you,* This is the scene? *This is that house. That river runs just behind it.*

We move to the sidewalk. Now, because the houses at the end of the block look similar, Mami is unable to decide exactly which one was theirs. An old man, all bony elbows and wrinkles, appears, suddenly standing next to us, asking what we want. I doubt he can help, but still I ask if he remembers whether a curandero lived on this block in the 1970s. *The witch doctor? That was Satanism!* He points to the house at the end of the block. *He lived over there. But he's long gone. Are you looking for him?*

Mami and I look at each other. *Yes.*

I knock on the door of the house he pointed out, but no one answers. Mami takes out her camera and begins photographing flowers, mutters to herself, then raises her voice to tell me she doesn't understand this desire I have to validate things. *You saw the house in a dream—what more do you want?* Mami comes up with a better idea—her childhood friend Valentina lives around the block, and we can just drop in and surprise her.

This is how I start to lose, bit by bit, my grip on reality.

Valentina hugs me first like she already knows me, and I'm the only one who doesn't remember. Her eyes rove up and down my face with attention; then she quickly hugs Mami. *Forgive me,* she says to me over Mami's shoulder. *It's just that you look exactly like your mother when we were young.*

Inside Valentina's house, we sit in the living room, and Valentina starts to tell me: *There was a boy who wouldn't leave your mother alone. Do you remember, Sojaila?* This last she says while looking at me, and I open my mouth as if I could answer.

Antón, I hear Mami say.

Antón! Yes. He was always insisting you drop by his house to say hello after school. Valentina lays a manicured hand on the bare wall. *There was a painting here. One day you said,* Watch, Valentina, *and you walked your fingers along the path in the painting. It was a little road that led to a little house.* I am going to Antón's house, *you said.* I am walking to his doorstep; here I am knocking on his door. *And you knocked on the painting? We spent all afternoon together, until the sun went down. But the next day, Antón walked up to you and said,* Sojaila, why'd you come to my house to stare at me? You left without saying a word! *Remember?*

Her conviction when she looks at me, like I absolutely must remember the story she's just told, makes space in me for my mother's ghost. Valentina covers her face. *Why am I talking to you like you're your mother? Sojaila, come sit between us, so I stop getting confused!*

Down the block is another of Mami's friends she thinks we can drop in on.

Mami and I throw rocks at a shuttered balcony. We don't know if he still lives there, but our ability to be charming together gives us confidence that we can get away with a lot. A man appears, grasping the rail, angry at first, then beaming. *Sojaila!* he says at me, then at my mother. *I am coming right down, don't move an inch!* He brings us hot chocolate on a tray. He asks if I'm as much trouble as my mother was, and before I can answer, he tells me that one teacher got so fed up with her he finally forced Mami to teach the class, so she could see what it was like. Mami sent everyone to the principal's office. He laughs for a moment, then turns to my mother. *Help me, Sojaila—is she the same, or very different?*

Different, Mami says, unsure, I think, of how to elaborate.

Same intensity, though, he says, looking into my eyes.

All day, I am my mother's ghost. We go to the other house in Bucaramanga where the family lived, the one that's not by the river, and there an old man walking under a tattered umbrella stops us. *You used to live here,* he says to me. *I remember you.*

Sex workers pose together at the end of the street, readjusting their cleavage so it's low, laughing. I feel the I that is my I dissolving, like during my days with amnesia. The edges that I am feel porous, barely there. I grow empty of myself.

At night, we meet one of Mami's old boyfriends. I am too much for him to take. It is night, but the street is bright from streetlamps. When he sees me, I can tell I have ripped something open in him. He's in pain. He tents his hands around his mouth. Mami and he kiss on the cheek, and then he and I do the same. When we brush skin, I can tell he is shaking. I try to put him at ease by asking if he dreamt anything the night before, but this makes it worse. He stares at me, breathless, wild-eyed. Mami laughs at him. *I used to ask him that every day.*

Mami's old boyfriend is kind-faced, and is still in love with my mother. I know by the way he watches me through the rearview mirror as we get into his car, startled and mystified. We are going to a restaurant thirty minutes away, in Lebrija. As he starts the car, pulls out onto the road, and accelerates, the air around me begins to feel like a foreign, pressurized space, filling up with a history I am a part of and yet don't remember. He eyes my mother and me like we are both shadows visiting from his past. And every time he looks into my eyes, I see his gaze tilting past me to a place he and I never shared, in love. His gaze is so urgent and sure, I begin to feel like I *could be* my mother at fifteen, in love with him. When he looks at my mother, he seems baffled and observes her for long seconds, before saying, *You haven't changed one bit.*

Mami is sitting in the front with him. *It's strange how much time has passed.*

It begins to rain and he says, *You want to know what your mother was like back then?* His eyes flash in the rearview mirror. *Exactly like you! To travel to the past, all I have to do is look in your direction.*

We turn around and drive down what I know from a street sign is Carrera 27. He wants to show me the stage where the love story he is about to tell me takes place. He is pointing to the dark silhouettes of buildings, left and right, telling me which areas were desolate hills, which streets were cobblestone. My window is covered in angled lines of water, and all I can make out is the dark mountain range of the Andes in the horizon. He tells me to come close, and I lean in between the front seats as he points to one dark silhouette. *That is where I met your mother—the glorious Colegio Santander.*

This is also where Papi went to school, so I know it's a high school notorious for graduating communists. I sit back and lower the window facing the building where they met. I let rain hit my face and cover the door handle and the seat. I blink in the night, roll up the window, and say, as casually as I can, *So you were a communist?*

He inhales sharply, blinking at me like he's suddenly realized I am nothing like my mother.

Mami says, *The girl is quick and likes politics; it's almost like I didn't raise her, but I did. I never showed her a newspaper, I don't know where I went wrong.*

I am still staring at him, expecting an answer.

Yes? He's surprised he's answered me in truth.

A radical one? I ask quickly. He laughs nervously, and even though he doesn't answer, I know that, yes, this means he's either a current or former guerrilla member, and I just have to find out to which group he once did or now belongs.

I haven't given you his name. He never meant to tell me the story about being a guerrilla member, only the story about being in love with my mother, but as he starts to tell the one, we find it is intrinsically tied to the other. This makes sense to me. Being in love, entering the space of war—which is the space of death— these are all hauntings. The moment we enter those spaces, reality is up for grabs.

He asked me to not use his name, because there are repercussions for speaking. Later, as Mami and I are traveling outside of Bogotá, I will use her phone to chat with him online. I want to know how he is, say hello. One night, I ask him about his taste in books, and he tells me he reads Ernesto Sábato in moments of depression. Ernesto. It's as good a name for him as any.

In the car, Ernesto, who dated my mother for two years, forty years ago, says: *My love for your mother was boundless. I remember everything, everything.* He laughs sweetly. *The thing was to go on day trips.*

I was never allowed to go—I had to sneak out, Mami says.

Not always. I asked your father for permission twice, and he said yes.

But you said we were studying.

Well, of course! The permission was for you to come over to my house because we were completing a special school assignment.

I always gave you my swimsuit the day before, remember, so no one would find it on me?

I took it home afterward and washed it for you, he says to me. *Returned it to you the next day clean and dry.*

I am quiet, listening. I am the audience, and also the ghost.

I was always afraid of your father. He transmitted an impossibly calm certainty, a potential for aggression. . . . He was mystifying. He looks to me, sitting in the back. *You asked if I was a radical communist. I was. The police wanted to kill me; I distanced myself from your mother to protect her. Other groups became violent.*

So—the M19, I say.

What? He looks to me, then to Mami.

You belonged to the M19.

Mami smirks at him. *I tried to warn you to be careful—she's quick.*

I know a lot about the M19. They were an intellectually rigorous armed group that militarized in the 1970s, after what was suspected to be a fraudulent election. They counted poets, professors, and even a priest among their ranks. Their military actions were sometimes abstract. In 1974, they stole, for example, Simón Bolívar's sword from a state museum. The performative action was a metaphor for taking power back. They were also behind the siege at the Palace of Justice in 1985, which ended in a fire that killed more than one hundred people and eleven Supreme Court justices. To this day, nobody is sure about what happened inside.

At the restaurant, Mami goes to ask for a table, and Ernesto holds my hand. *All the violence of that time—the memory of your mother kept me afloat.*

Nono married her to that abusive man, I say.

I know, I feel so guilty—I put distance between us to protect her; then I lost her.

I nod. I sense a well of grief in him. *You've so many hauntings.*

The apartment I was renting was filled with guns, floor to ceiling, he says.

Really?

Those guns were distributed, sent to the mountains. We were fighting for those who couldn't fight for themselves.

Mami is waving us forward; she's gotten us a table. *You still love her,* I say. He squeezes my hand tighter. *Don't tell her—I want to tell her.*

Over dinner, Ernesto doesn't tell my mother anything. When I ask him what it was like to be a man in Colombia, he begins to tell me about torture. He shares two techniques he was taught to endure it.

One is called the Brick.

You focus on a small point on the wall—in our case, a brick. You bring the small point of the brick closer and closer, until it becomes all you can see. They can hit you, do anything, and you remain outside of it; you are inside a brick.

The White Method is dangerous, because it can generate many anxieties. Essentially, you force yourself into an out-of-body experience. You watch yourself being tortured from above. You won't feel the pain then, but it comes back to haunt you later.

I nod, knowing exactly what he means. This is what happens to me during a panic attack, when I can't endure the suffering of it—the White Method. *Did they torture you in order to train you?* I ask.

Yes.

How?

The worst was when they strapped our testicles with electric-shock machines. After a moment's silence, he adds: *Colombia is very difficult. The grudge that armed groups hold is very old. Older than you or me.*

We are quiet for a moment, and then Ernesto begins to tell me about a boy named Hernando, who was sixteen and a friend of theirs from high school when they were in the tenth grade. I realize that all this time he's been working up the courage to tell this story, the reason why he put distance between himself and Mami. One day when school got out, snipers shot into the crowd of students. Ernesto heard the bullet crack by his ear, felt the wind of it, and when he turned, Hernando was dropping to his knees, and there was a smoking point at his forehead. The bullet was meant for Ernesto—that's what he was told later—and so he distanced himself from everybody, not wanting anybody else to get hurt.

It's the first time Mami is hearing this, though she was there when the shooting occurred. She says she knew it all back then— not the specific details, but that he had chosen revolution. *Some things are larger than love,* Mami says, and the unspoken between them grows. I excuse myself and go wash my hands in the bathroom.

When I return, Mami and Ernesto are laughing together. I don't know if Ernesto has told her that he loves her or not. The stories he told about politics and the violence of men were for me: he knows Mami is not interested in them. He's returned me to myself in this way. No longer feeling like Mami's ghost, I let them be. I go outside to get some air.

When we're back in our hotel, I ask Mami if she's sad that it didn't work out with him. She shakes her head no. *Nono told me to stay away from him, that the pain I would feel if we stayed together would be more than I could bear. Hearing him tonight, I can see why that would have been.*

I think about Mami and Ernesto, and how we have a hand in creating our own ghosts. We think we are done with a place, or a person, and wrest ourselves away. But when leaving happens in a wave of distress, when we leave what we still love, we conjure our own ghost walks into being.

Once, a black vulture sat on a tree. Nono said that through its staring, it confounded his senses, made him believe he was walking when he was only marching in place. Maybe there is a black vulture for all of us, something that peers from a branch, casting a spell. We believe we advance even when we are stuck, passing the same shrub again and again, thinning the ground.

There are many chulos in Bucaramanga, the black vultures that witches are said to turn into when they want to fly. As we wake the next day and wander around the streets near our hotel, Mami expressly asks me to not photograph them. *You can't just do what you want here!* She means Bucaramanga in particular, but also Colombia in general.

Can't I?

I kneel down with ceremony and press the shutter, then go through the process of developing the Polaroid—guessing the air temperature, calculating the appropriate time for which the picture has to remain mixing with the strip emulsified with chemicals. When it is ready, I peel it off and wait for the image to emerge. As the white film slowly blooms clouds of color—ocher, sienna, olive green—I list in my head all of the things that allow other realities in: chulos, amnesia, lagoons, waterfalls, violence, love.

When the image crystallizes, I stare.

Did it come out bewitched?

That is a middle-aged man speaking. He's been watching Mami and me from his rocking chair some paces away, smoking a cigar.

Yes, Mami says, stepping away from me. *It did.*

It's just a light leak. I haven't had leaks in any of my other shots in all of my stay in Colombia, but, technically, that's what it is, that's what I am looking at.

The middle-aged man stands, saunters over to verify the level of curse I captured in the photograph. I allow him to look. He widens his eyes at the photo as if to take in the whole thing in one go. Then he shudders and, taking a step back, tells me it is very bad. This isn't his first experience with witches either. Once, a chulo followed him around as he was walking down the street, glared down at him, dove, and slapped him in the face.

A chulo, a bird, slapped me in the face! I felt every feather of its wing like the fingers of a hand!

Mami and I are immediately on the side of the witch.

Who knows what you did to her, Mami says.

Must have been some grievance, I say.

The middle-aged man purses his lips to make them small. *Well, your photo. You can't carry around a haunted image. You must throw it away.*

You're telling me what to do? I stare at the middle-aged man, wildly hoping he continues to try to order me around. Mami drags me away. *You're going to get us in a fight—and I no longer have the fitness for it.*

Mami, I say, laughing, *you can take that man, can't you?*

Mami grins. *Yes, well, but what would the community think?*

I can tell Mami wants me to throw the image away, too, from the worried look she gives me as I tuck the Polaroid away into my bag, but she doesn't ask.

It's the middle of the day, but Mami and I head to a tavern where tío Ariel's eldest, my cousin Gabriel, performs with a mariachi band, just as tío Ariel used to do. It's like I'm a young girl again. We sit at a booth, and all of tío Ariel's family is there. Mami is across the table, next to Mariana; I sit between my cousins Gabriel and Omar. All around us are Mariana's children, charismatic and gentle, ranging from eighteen to thirty years old. I look at Gabriel and Omar in the reddish light. Gabriel is in full costume. There are silver tassels hanging from his shoulders, fine silver embroidery running along his arms. It's been many years since we've seen each other, maybe a decade. We are ordering beer when Gabriel gets up and saunters onto the platform where the band plays. There are three guitars, one violin, and two trumpets. To the swell of music, Gabriel retrieves the mic and glides back to us, singing to Mami and me, calling us, just like his father once did, divine. *Mujeres, mujeres tan divinas, no queda otro camino que adorarlas.* In a collapse of time, it is tío Ariel, kneeling before me.

When the song ends and Gabriel rejoins our table, and his group plays on without him, I tell him that I feel, when I see him, that I am before tío Ariel. Gabriel laughs into his beer, tells me I am like the Mami he remembers from when he was young.

We stare at each other, uncomfortably, until I say, *Did you know people are still leaving little papers at Nono's grave, asking for miracles?* I speak loudly so they can hear over the music. Across the table, Mami catches my eye and glares. I am not supposed to be calling attention to the grave, or what might no longer lie there.

Yes, I know many people who still go up there. Omar sips his beer, distracted. *People tell me all the time about miracles they asked for that came true, that he granted. My godmother goes up there all the time.*

He glances at me, then stops to read my face. *Why—are you interested?*

I nod, realizing my excitement must be palpable. *Do you know if your godmother's prayers were fulfilled?*

Yes! Omar sets his beer down. *Do you want to meet her and ask? We can go right now. She's only five minutes away.* As I gather my things, I remember that Omar was this way even when we were little—always willing to change our games based on my whims. We take our leave, promising to come back in an hour, and I hop behind Omar on his motorcycle.

The woman's name is Samira, and she's not officially Omar's godmother, but she took pains to care for him once his father passed. Omar was tío Ariel's most difficult son, and always in trouble. He was too smart for rules, and often broke them. Samira listened to him when no one would, guided him when he needed, and served him many home-cooked meals. When I tell Samira I'm related to Omar, she holds my hand and guides us both into her living room, like we're children she's not seen for some time. She tells me she remembers vividly when Omar was a boy. I remember too. The family used to call him *the terror*. He was always playing pranks, setting things on fire. He never played pranks on me, though. Omar tells his godmother that I've been thinking about my grandfather and that I have a question.

I am wondering if any of your prayers were fulfilled, I say. *As his granddaughter, I wonder what his influence has been, when it's been so many years since he left.*

The woman joins her hands in prayer, then sweeps them out to the sides, presenting to us everything in her house—the living room and spiral staircase (in whose direction I think I hear parrots), the shelves, the plants, the record player. *Everything you see I owe to your grandfather.*

Everything?

Everything.

The house?

Everything.

There is love and gratitude in Samira's voice. She has taken care of his grave, as people who ask for miracles tend to do. She lights candles and offers prayers in exchange for his help. It is a lovely thing, to be the granddaughter of someone so entrusted with people's small and big emergencies, especially since it's been almost three decades since his passing. I also know that it is not what he wanted. It won't be widely known for a time that we've moved Nono. The soil was placed back into the grave on the same day as the disinterment, but it will be obvious that the grave was recently disturbed. We hope nobody will ask questions, at least until we can set Nono free.

Samira has shown me with pride that my grandfather has taken care of her, and maybe he has, and maybe she deserves it, for looking after Omar. I don't even know if I believe that my grandfather can grant miracles. So I am quiet, and smile at her, and thank her for telling me. Omar and Samira catch up about other things, and she gives me recommendations for where to eat, and we leave.

In our hotel, I tell Mami about Samira, thinking she will be happy that I got to the bottom of the question of who was leaving requests and prayers at Nono's grave—or at least of *one person* who treated his grave as miraculous—but she snaps at me. *Nono devoted his whole life to healing. All his life, he took the hurt of other people and healed it in his body. He was very clear to me when he knew he was going to die—he wanted rest.*

I feel guilty about not saying anything close to that to Samira. When Mami is in the bathroom, getting ready for bed, I flip through the Polaroid photos I've taken, my growing collection of things that have been touched by what's spectral. There's one photo I particularly love. I took it at tía Nahía's house, in Cúcuta, when she showed me another of Nono's belongings that survived. It is a bronze sculpture of hands, palms cupped into a bowl. When I ask her what Nono kept in it, she looks at me confused. She blinks a few times. *Nothing. Of course.*

I thought then about how inheritance can look like that—our open hands, holding nothing—but it is not nothing that we hold, only what can't be seen. In a moment, Mami will come out of the bathroom and I will put all my photos away, but for a long moment, I pore over the Polaroid of the chulo I was told is a witch. The chulo sits in the middle of the composition, and at each side of it, there's a spill of gold. I think about how useless language can be. The golden gleam at the right of the photo looks to me like a window. It is ghost, light leak, metaphor.

Nono's hands full of nothing. Cúcuta, 2012

The black vulture. Bucaramanga, 2012

ASH

When you unearth haunted treasure, you're supposed to trace a circle on the ground; recite the sequence of creation in order and in reverse.

These were incomplete instructions Mami once overheard Nono give his nephew, who was going treasure hunting, for the first time, with the men.

Mami is fifty-six now, and Nono is white ash inside a plastic bag inside a blue velvet pouch that tía Perla carries inside a tote bag.

He is something we have unearthed.

We are walking in the forest in the Eastern Cordillera of the Andes, on part of the path Nono would have taken on his way out of Ocaña at the beginning of his annual journey to visit with curanderos and tribes and his other women.

In the world before me, here, where I am walking, Nono pulled on his burro saddled with divination supplies, and in Ocaña Nona hid from her children in their outhouse, crying until she was laughing, until her weeping looped back and she was crying again. A circle is a straight line haunted by something living at its middle—a ghost that causes it to bend and bend.

Sometimes when you speak two truths it means forgiveness, Mami always says, explaining to me why she has never been angry at Nono. *He was a bad man to my mother, and a good father to me.*

In the forest, we advance toward the murmur of the river. I am leading the way. At some good spot in the water, we will release the ashes of this man from whom we all came.

———————

When I look at a map, what I see is a painting, an abstract likeness I can understand on its own terms, separate from the erratic spinning of space set off when I turn right or left. I understand that in Colombia most of our water meets, and though it is the same water, we give it different names. Later, I will look for many hours at two maps, the one on my phone where I marked the location where we walked, and a map of all the water in Colombia, and I will note that the burble of water we are hearing but not yet seeing comes from far to the east. I will see that we are near the base of the Andes, and that the water is called Sogamoso—in Chibcha, *dwelling of the sun.* And farther east, in the place where it snakes over the Eastern Cordillera, it is called *silver thread in the mountain on a full moon's night,* but in Bucaramanga, where it flows behind the second house Mami lived in, it is Rionegro. And beyond Rionegro, where we do not go, the water gushes across the valley between cordilleras and joins a larger body of water, which runs south to north, into which many of our waters flow, and which unmouths into the Caribbean. The Magdalena. Its old name is Guaca-hayo, *river of tombs.* When I finally find the Salto de Tequendama, near Bogotá, the waterfall into which I once nearly fell, I see that it eventually joins the Magdalena too. Even I, before seeing any map, as I am tracing the same path my grandfather once did, would find the Magdalena if I just followed in the direction the water streams.

Once, Guaca-hayo carried the bodies that were offered to the water in funerary rites. Now it carries victims of war.

All things that meet can create a vortex. Every surface of water can be a mirror, a place full of sky.

I am thinking about the journey Nono will take when Fabián leans over me and says, *You're so quiet, I bet you're passing wind.* I snort and slap my hand across his chest, but Fabián cackles and cowers against a palm tree.

Dejen la guachafita, Mami yells, furrowing her brow; then she twirls and steps into a dance. *Can't you see we are carrying a dead person? Why can't anybody in this family be serious?*

The three of us observe her go feral into the path. Tía Perla whispers, *I wonder who the first deranged person in this family was.* Fabián whispers back to his mother, *You're as deranged as tía Sojaila—don't delude yourself.* Then he calls loudly to mine: *Don't let anybody sour your joy, Tía. Shake what God gave you, eso, sin miedo!* Fabián claps his hands to make music for Mami, and so do I. The tote bag, and therefore Nono inside a plastic bag inside a velvet pouch, hanging at tía Perla's shoulder, bounces as she shimmies. Soon we are all dancing to nothing. There's a trill of chirps falling from the tree canopy. I remember my job is to watch the ground and the tree limbs for snakes, and I return my attention to the task, humming the song I was dancing to in my head. Soon we are all singing it: *Rosa, qué linda eres, Rosa qué linda eres tú.*

The directions from the shared dream took us as far as the disinterment. My dream gave us the river. Now we are following our interpretations of our interpretations. We will release the ashes at a body of water that we know to listen and see. The roar of the river is growing.

Our dead are so numerous now, along the banks of the Magdalena, fishermen often find corpses entangled in their nets. Villages along the Magdalena observe the forensic procedures to identify the dead and send them to their loved ones, but they adopt the dead whose fingertips have been erased by the water. They give them names and burial, offer shivering candles and fresh flowers. In Puerto Berrío, a little south of where we are, the town cemetery includes a Pavilion of Forgotten Ones, where hundreds of anonymous tombs find rest in the recesses of an adobe columbarium, and where the living bring feathers and grains and fruits to the disappeared. Likely, they are victims of paramilitaries, drug cartels, or guerrillas.

In Colombia, anyone could, in a quick turn of events, disappear. To adopt the forgotten ones is to break a silence that protects executioners. It is to remember.

Rosa tú eres la diosa, Rosa qué linda eres tú.

There are known and unknown circles.

As we finally arrive at the riverbank and are taking off our shoes, dusting our feet, I see myself in a flash, starving and sinking in a lake in Virginia, not realizing the limits of the body, that there is no mercy, that we are things engineered to drown. Back then, I dropped, a tightening rock, and water sealed above me like a grave.

I wonder if I finally, truly, incontrovertibly believe now that dreams can be foresight.

We splash into the river, feeling the rush of the current nip at our knees, and slowly tread toward three rocks at the opposite bank where we can sit. I think about how, before I had any idea that we would disinter Nono and carry his ashes to the river, I saw him point to this same water that is now glittering over our legs, telling me here was where the scene was to take place.

Foresight is to be haunted by the future; ghost means to be haunted by the past.

Once each of us finds a seat, tía Perla produces plastic gloves from her bag. She brought them so that she can release the ashes into the water without touching them, she tells me, and then Mami gives us instructions for the things we are to repeat once we begin.

I am not listening.

I am staring at the white ash inside the plastic bag tía Perla has unknotted and set down for a moment by her feet as she folds the velvet pouch into her tote bag.

Before I can think about what I'm doing, I pinch some ash and put it in my mouth. Nobody has seen. I hold my head in my hands and swallow.

I am scared by what I have done. Call it grief. Call it derangement. I am woman-ghost and quicksand, dispossessed of everything but this moment. I hunger for what can speak to my bones.

My sister said: *What's interesting about your memory loss is that even while you had no memory you never stopped being you. The being excited about amnesia, keeping your suffering a secret—that is so you.* And Mami assented, rolling her eyes. *Who else suffers an accident and falls in love with the void?* She said it unironically, so I stared at her for five full seconds before reminding her: *You. You did that.*

Tía Perla lowers the bag into the river. She doesn't shake the ashes out, like I would have, but lets the current of the river fill the bag and take Nono away. Mote by mote, I watch my grandfather leave. Nono is ashes called back to the water, white swallowed up in blue. He looks exactly like a cloud, a gust casting itself across the current. I stand and let my gaze follow the path the ashes take—past rocks, toward the river bend.

At the bend, in the short distance, three white cows step out of the forest. They hoof their way to the river, then lower and lap at the white streak that is Nono. *Do you see them?* I ask, worried for a moment that I am seeing things. Mami nods. She is praying, and I am supposed to be repeating after her, as Fabián and tía Perla are doing, but instead I stand and watch the cows take their fill, wanting to prove to myself that they are really drinking up my grandfather. They stretch their necks, full of Nono, then saunter back into the forest. All of nature is hungry. I sit down on the rock, stunned, and then I repeat the words Mami wants us to say. We are saying a prayer Nono taught her, for seeing off the dead. We sit and repeat the words, staring at one another, staring at the ground, letting the words wash over us, wash over the rocks, wash over everything.

In our hotel, Mami washes our obsidian earrings in salt water to rid them of all that their mirrors have seen. When she is done, she lies down next to me. We are tired. I reach and pet her snake ring, the one she has worn on her left thumb since before I was born. Mami smiles and stretches over the bed, plucks up the little bottle of lotion she keeps at her nightstand and covers her thumb in it. She has to pull and twist the ring so it goes over the bone of her knuckle. I sit up, worried, speechless. I have never, in my whole life, seen her take the ring off. It's a protection and a connection to her lineage. She's not supposed to ever take it off.

What are you doing? Can it come off? What are you doing?

She inclines her head as she continues to pull, and finally she holds the golden circle in her hand. She reaches for my hands, first the right, then the left. She pushes the circle onto my thumb. I stare at the golden ring on my hand—and for a moment, with its slender brown fingers and red nails, it looks to me like my mother's hand. The snake head rests atop my lower knuckle like on a rock. *Friendly snake,* I say, petting it, looking into the glint of its emerald eyes, darker and deeper than I have ever noticed.

It's already at home on your hand, Mami says.

Why are you giving this to me?

It was time.

I cannot keep my eyes off the snake, cuddling against my thumb, the pretty diamond-shaped head with hammered texture, the little nostrils, the lips shut and long, not menacing, but poised with the power of an inherent strike, the gold that is brushed at the sides—so animate, this ring, its tail coiling around my thumb.

Nono once saw the ghost of a snake entering my nursery. He watched it slither into my crib, and when he lifted the veil it was asleep, sidled up to me. Snakes are made to withstand a journey between extremes: cold and hot, the desert at day and in the night. In our stories, they are fire-born too, they are the women of the lagoon.

During amnesia, when I knew myself to be a barren landscape, I didn't think it was possible to cuddle up to the edge of the world. Now I think it happens without our trying.

How do you feel? Mami asks.

I lift my eyes and meet my mother's. *Like I've been crowned.*

She holds my hand, her tan fingers over mine, the snake peeking in between.

———

I know what it's like to lose the past. Forgetting is a way of dying. Remembering, a type of resurrection. There's a turning to it. Every step taken in remembrance is a turn.

Going on a ghost walk involves tracing the bend of a circle, and arriving at the beginning over and over again.

It is late at night. Mami is completing the prayer we began at the river. She needs to see it to its conclusion for Nono's safe passage. I can't sleep either. While Mami prays, I open the book on the history of Ocaña I bought, in whose pages I have tucked the black-market photograph of Papá Luciano. Mami's voice is a murmur, a wind, words I barely catch. On the pages of the book, there's a report addressed to the Spanish Crown, written in 1578 by its envoys. The letter details land acquired, the number and culture of Indigenous people, and the progress of colonization. The men who wrote the report say that the original people of Ocaña had no rites or adorations, only a cult to the dead. "The naturals live in the mountains, huddled up against the cliffs, barbarously they live, not knowing or having ever known a Sir or Master. Their inclinations and way of life are living in drunkenness, unearthing and carrying their dead, whom they dance with and carry for long distances in revelry. They make a boisterous party out of the reburial of their dead."

Once, we buried things to offer them to the earth; now we bury things to keep them from the living.

I close the book. The truth of a thing lies elsewhere, not in what is written, but in its breathing and becoming.

When you unearth haunted treasure, you're supposed to trace a circle on the ground; recite the sequence of creation in order and in reverse.

Words in my mother's mouth were once alive in my grandfather's, and if I speak them now, on this page, this makes a circle.

Once, there was an empty well, a long throat of earth Mami fell into, through which she lost her memory. Like an inheritance, I lost my memory too. On my way to pick up a black dress, I sailed through the air and cracked my head against the ground. Mami lost consciousness deep inside a circle, but I sat, awake and amnesiac, on the floor of my apartment, rearranging the skirt of the black dress around me in an orbit. Nono was a man who could move clouds, then a cloud moving through water, and three white cows plodding into the forest.

The forest swallowed Nono and then the clouds. A circle skirted me in amnesia, and Mami sailed through a throat in the earth. The empty well brims now, again full of water, our first mirror.

When Nono was alive, he feared lagoon women who wanted his drowning.

Say I was once this woman. Say I hungered. My only craving has been for what lies untold in me, for what lies at the center.

After survival, there is the survival of the survival.

It is useful then to ask what lives on beyond the book that self-combusts.

The person who escapes.

The mind that forgets itself.

The culture that is thought to be erased.

The answer is everything.

Everything survives.

Dawn is breaking when Mami finishes her prayer, and I ask her for a story, even though we have been up all night.

She looks at me, then says, *No peace lasts.*

I think she will say more, but then she does not.

I stare at the ceiling.

It is the most perfect story that's ever been told.

Mami, Fabián, and tía Perla, getting ready to release the ashes. At a good spot of water, 2012

Nono. 2012

EPILOGUE

Back in Cúcuta, when Mami and I have only a day left, Fabián picks us up in his car. We drive down the Malecón, the avenue by the Pamplonita River, where groups of musicians gather looking to be hired. We want them to play music for us in tía Perla's backyard, which is not as expensive as you'd think. When we're deliberating whom we want to employ, I see tía Perla use the same strategies as when she's buying avocados from a street vendor.

She asks where the musicians are from, what repertoire they know; then she grows grumpy, casts into doubt whether what they're saying is true, and asks for a sample. We drive and stop every few meters, tía Perla going through the same lines, Mami and I giggling in the back.

At night, the six musicians we engaged play love songs. I bring them water and compliment their singing, and Mami asks after their love life. She is giving one of them advice when tía Nahía arrives with her husband and daughter, demanding to know if we've disinterred Nono behind her back. I look to Mami. Mami doesn't take her eyes off Nahía as she asks her what she means. *I slipped a piece of paper into Nono's casket the day of the funeral, asking for a miracle. He hasn't fulfilled my request. If he was disinterred, I need to know, because that's not good.* After a pause, she adds, *For me.*

Mami's face darkens in what I know to read as anger, and I glance at Fabián, who for a moment looks into my eyes, then, as if suddenly realizing his chair is too hot, jumps up and asks the musicians to play old cumbias—the *good* cumbias, he calls them, the ones he knows Mami and I love to dance to. I hear Mami begin to reprimand Nahía for making requests when Nono didn't want any, and Fabián is pulling me to my feet and asking me to dance. The bats are flying overhead, diving from time to time. It is dusk. On the patio, Fabián and I are circling each other, singing, and his cheekbone, crowned in sweat, is opalescent in the dim light, and then everyone is with us. It feels just like when we were young and we were learning that some of life is a sum, heaviness against lift, and one way to carry it was to dance, to offer it up. But we are older now. The musicians love Mami, as do we all. I watch her wind herself like a spiral, like a thing that contains all of time. She is the natural center of the music, and our dancing. When I go to sleep, I can still see her dance.

I think about her dancing on the airplane on my way back to my life. I see her stomp when the silver snake of the Chicamocha is beneath us, the eastern range of the Andes, the cerulean of the Pacific.

Then, in San Francisco, spent and alone, I lie in bed thinking I can hear in me my grandfather's voice. I fall asleep into a tunnel of time, then sit up into amnesia.

I am a flash of palpitations, a landscape of sweat.

I can't breathe.

Fear is an unlettered prayer.

I begin to count, begin at one, follow the numbers up like they're a labyrinth.

I get to fifty-six.

At fifty-six, I remember my mother.

ACKNOWLEDGMENTS

I'd like to thank my family, far and near, for the world they reared me in, and their care thereafter. To cousin Fabián and tía Perla, a special thank-you, for always welcoming us to their home as if it were our own.

I am so grateful to my brilliant agent, Kent D. Wolf, for helping me shape the story early in the process, and the biggest thank-you to my incredibly gifted editor, Margo Shickmanter, for being such a light in the complex process that was writing this book. To all my team at Doubleday—Ana Espinoza, Tricia Cave, Erin Merlo, Lorraine Hyland, Kathleen Fridella, Pei Loi Koay, Emily Mahon—thank you, from the bottom of my heart.

Thank you to everyone who shared about their lives in Ocaña. And to the historian Luis Eduardo Páez, who graciously gave me some of his time.

Nana Kwame Adjei-Brenyah, R. O. Kwon, and Lauren Markham were with me every step of the way as I was drafting this memoir in 2020, a hard year for us all, as were my beloved brujas, Tanya Rey, Nancy Jooyoun Kim, Yalitza Ferreras, Angie Chau, Amber Butts, and Meron Hadero. Thank you. Thank you to Rachel Khong, Anisse Gross, Esmé Weijun Wang, Colin Winnette, Andi Mudd, Caille Millner, and Margaret Wilkerson.

Thank you to the National Association of Latino Arts and Cultures, Hedgebrook, Djerassi Residency Artist Program, and the Camargo Foundation for their support in the writing of this book.

This book was hard to write. I am eternally grateful to Jeremiah, who not only shares the artist's life and understands what it requires, but who kept me whole through this process. Thank you, most of all, to my mother, who told me stories, and in telling me stories, taught me how to live.

A NOTE ABOUT THE AUTHOR

Ingrid Rojas Contreras was born and raised in Bogotá, Colombia. Her first novel, *Fruit of the Drunken Tree,* was the silver-medal winner in First Fiction from the California Book Awards, and a *New York Times* Editors' Choice. Her essays and short stories have appeared in *The New York Times Magazine, The Believer,* and *Zyzzyva,* among other publications. She lives in California.